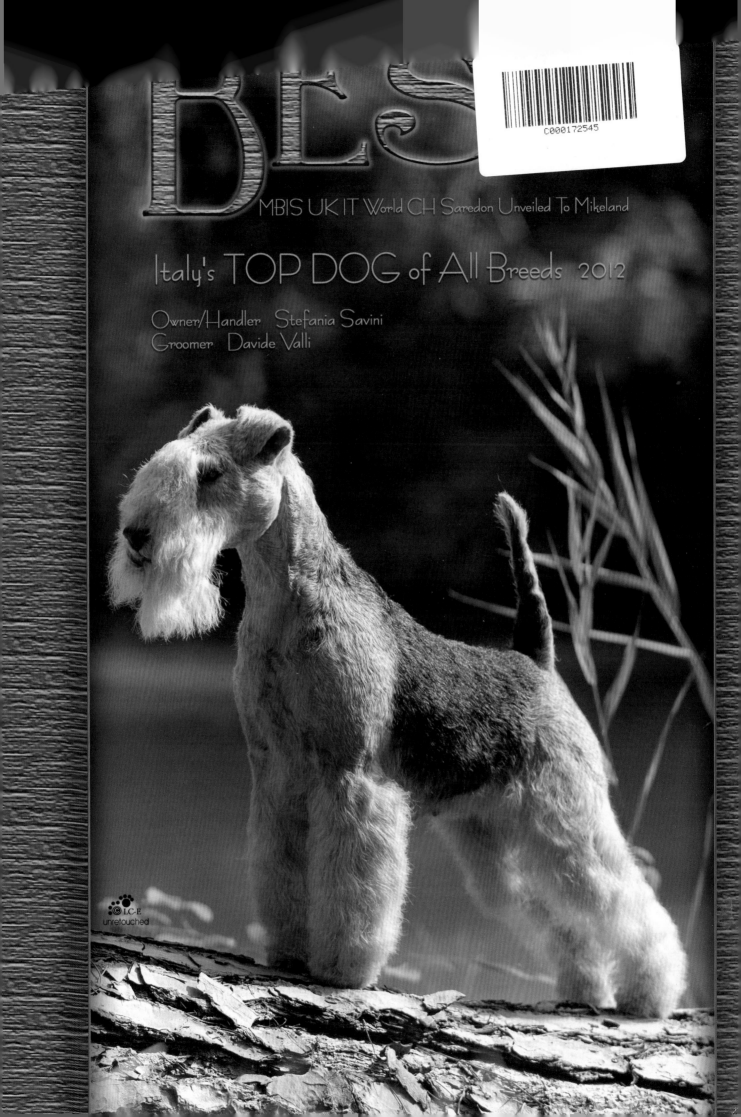

annual 2013

Derek Smith's winner of the Pro Plan/Dog World Pup of the Year 2011 final was Stuart Plane's Scottish Terrier Ch Stuane Florette. It was 25 years since Stuart last won the competition with another homebred Scottie, Ch Stuane Enchanted. Florette had by then won seven groups and a reserve BIS, and in 2012 she took two more group wins, reserve BIS at Leeds plus many more successes, her total currently standing at 22 CCs.
photo Walker

Contents

Jilly is Top Dog 2012

Unbeatable in the Top Dog 2012 table, run by Dog World and Arden Grange, is the Petit Basset Griffon Vendéen Ch Soletrader Peek A Boo, bred by Gavin and Sara Robertson (pictured above) and now co-owned by Sara with Wendy Doherty from Canada. She is handled usually by Gavin, sometimes by Sara – both were successful junior handlers, Sara topping the UK and international finals, and have campaigned previous BIS winners.

'Jilly' won her first CC as a puppy in 2010 and sprang to wider fame at Crufts 2011 when she was BOB as a junior with her second CC and went on to win the group and reserve BIS.

She took eight group wins in all during 2011, including the Houndshow, the latter just a few days after her first all-breeds BIS at Paignton. She was RBIS at East of England and City of Birmingham and ended the year as top hound. She also travelled to Amsterdam and topped the Winner Show there.

During 2012 she repeated her Houndshow BIS at the golden jubilee event, where she is pictured with judge Jill Peak, Roly Boughton of Dorwest Herbs and acting chairman Hector Heathcote. All-breed BIS wins numbered six, at Boston, Manchester, East of England, Welsh Kennel Club, Scottish KC and South Wales. She was reserve at the May SKC and Belfast and won no fewer than 18 groups including the other Houndshow in Scotland.

She is by Ch/Dutch Ch Cappuccino van Tum-Tums Vriendjes, bred in Holland from Soletrader parents, ex CC record holder Ch Soletrader My Aphrodisiac, and is the first PBGV to take the Top Dog award.

photos Dalrymple, Johnson

Production

Annual editor: Simon Parsons
Project leader: James Morrissey
Production: Colin Swaffer, John Clement
Editorial: Simon Parsons, Adrian Marett
Advertising: Fay Newman, Gary Doran, Sam Edworthy, Adrian Marett, Pam Blay, Marina Scott

Published and distributed by:
The DOG WORLD Ltd
Williamson House, Wotton Road
Ashford, Kent TN23 6LW
Telephone 01233 621877
Fax 01233 645669
Email annual@dogworld.co.uk
Website www.dogworld.co.uk
Subscriptions www.dogworld.co.uk/
subscribe-now

Also publishers of DOG WORLD,
Britain's top selling weekly
canine newspaper
Copyright The Dog World Ltd
Printed by:
Advent Print Group
19 East Portway Industrial Estate,
Andover, Hampshire, SP10 3LU
ISBN: 978-0-9567535-1-9

Front cover:

Featured on the front cover is the Wire Fox Terrier Ch Travella Star Craft, a multiple group winner and top Wire Fox Terrier 2012. She is owned by Franki Leung and Antonio Almeida, bred by Bill Browne-Cole and handled by Richard Allen. The photograph is by Alan Walker.

See also page 35

MIX
Paper from
responsible sources
FSC® C018353

photo Johnson

photo Johnson

Crufts 2012

Group winners on the move

©Johnson

photo Walker

Elizabeth
tops the most controversial Crufts ever

Review by Simon Parsons

'A GREAT show in every way but one' was the headline to our Crufts 2012 report and many felt it was a tragedy that an outstanding event was marred by the veterinary checking disaster, which is dealt with in detail in the following pages.

Virtually ever other aspect went brilliantly. The show has a new principal sponsor, food company Eukanuba having entered into a three-year partnership with the Kennel Club. In 2010 and '11 there was a title sponsor, furniture company dfs, but this ceased after Lord Kirkham sold the company. Major sponsors continue to be insurance company Agria and Samsung Electonics.

The entry was 21,029, just under 400 down on 2011 but still the world's largest show, and once again the overseas entry was up, to 1,388 dogs. Golden Retrievers remained top breed with 516 dogs. The number of visitors was increased to 145,176.

Although the mood among the showing community increasingly angry throughout the four days, the average visitor would probably not have noticed anything amiss, with the usual flawless organisation by Vanessa McAlpine and her team.

A new layout to the main ring with a 'star-spangled' backdrop added some sparkle, and, apart from the veterinary checks, incidents were rare, other than the sad and unexpected death of a Dogue de Bordeaux.

The line-ups for the groups were as cosmopolitan as we have come to expect, and a reminder of quality that has emerged in recent years from the Eastern European countries, including group winners from Slovakia and Hungary.

In addition to the usual Friends For Life, an attempt was made to please the crowd with the Crufts Factor, based on TV's *X Factor*. General view was that the idea needs more work. It will be attempted again in 2013.

For the third year the show was featured on television, on More4, with the coverage extended to two hours each night. As usual

©Johnson

Crufts

Best in show at Crufts was Margaret Anderson's Lhasa Apso Ch Zentarr Elizabeth, pictured with judge Frank Kane and Kennel Club chairman Professor Steve Dean. Although this was her first all-breed BIS win at seven years old, she has been a consistent top performer at group level throughout her career, and a few months earlier had been the UK's representative at the Eukanuba World Challenge in Florida, where she achieved third place among the world's top dogs. She retired from the ring after her Crufts win, previously achieved by only one other Lhasa, her multiple ancestor Ch Saxonsprings Hackensack. Later in the year another Lhasa bred by Margaret won another of the world's principal shows, when Zentarr Morgan, now living in Italy, topped the FCI European Winner Show in Romania.
photo Johnson

there was live streaming of the event too. The TV show was fronted by popular Clare Balding who made such an impression with her work at the Olympics and Paralympics later in the year, along with Jessica Holm and Peter Purves – Frank Kane missing this time as he judged BIS.

Although the controversial aspects of the show were mentioned, many felt that

all sides of the debate, which by then was raging on the social networks, could have been more strongly presented.

Ratings were highly satisfactory, more than 2.7 million viewers, and later came the good news that the BIS judging will be returning to mainstream TV, as Channel 4 is televising it in 2013. This means the BIS programme will start an hour earlier, and so will breed judging on the final day at 8am.

Imported register breeds are to compete at Crufts for the first time in 2013. Dogs may qualify at some overseas shows as well as in IR classes at UK events. On the debit side, car parking will increase to £10, including for the disabled. This will affect LKA 2012 as well.

Veterinary checks split
the world of dogs

WINDSOR CHAMPIONSHIP SHOW

BEST SHOW

©Johnson

Runner-up to Top Dog 2012 is likely to be the Toy Poodle Ch Vanitonia You'll See, owned by Lee Cox and Tom Isherwood who are profiled later in this *Annual*. He took three all-breeds BIS awards at three consecutive shows within two weeks during 2011 and followed it up with the top award at British Utility Breeds. During 2012 'Graham' has won five more BIS, at WELKS, Windsor, Leeds, Driffield and Belfast, and was reserve at Three Counties, August Scottish Kennel Club and Midland Counties. He and Lee are pictured at Windsor with chairman Oonagh Gore, Antony Bongiovanni of Royal Canin, patron, the Earl of Buchan, judge Michael Quinney and secretary Irene Terry.
photo Johnson

THERE WAS no question about what was the dominant news story in the world of show dogs in 2012.

In last year's ANNUAL we carried the story that the Kennel Club had decided that best of breed winners at general and group championship shows in the 15 'high profile breeds' would have to be inspected by the show veterinary surgeon before being allowed to compete in the group. Dogs of these breeds who won three CCs would also have had to pass a check before claiming a title.

These breeds were the Basset Hound, Bloodhound, Bulldog, Chow Chow, Clumber Spaniel, Dogue de Bordeaux, French Bulldog, German Shepherd Dog, Mastiff, Neapolitan Mastiff, Pekingese, Pug, Shar-Pei, St Bernard and Chinese Crested.

Professor Steve Dean, who was Crufts vet until he succeeded as KC chairman during 2011, said: "The guidance which we will issue to show vets will focus on clinical signs associated with pain or discomfort which will come under the main headings of external eye disease, lameness, skin disorder and breathing difficulty. The vet will be looking at signs

such as ectropion, entropion, corneal damage, dermatitis, breathing difficulty on moderate exercise, or lameness. In the Chinese Crested the principal issue will be the presence of skin damage arising from hair removal and thus signs of clipper rash or chemical insults to the skin will be looked for."

The idea wasn't totally new, as Crufts BOB winners in these breeds had already been looked at by the show vet for the last couple of years.

Warning bells

Whatever one's view on the idea, it was last December when warning bells really began to ring when it emerged that at Crufts 2012, the KC would not be using its own teams of vets to do the inspections, but was seeking 'to ensure absolute independence' by asking the British Veterinary Association (BVA) to supply vets for that purpose.

This idea rather backfired as instead of appointing vets to do the job, the BVA asked for volunteers. It was stressed that they would be representing neither the BVA or KC; however their selection would

be done jointly by the two organisations.

The closing date for application was February 17, just over two weeks before the show. At the time details of what to look for in each breed were given, and it was specifically stated that 'the assessments are not intended to require any diagnostic aids'.

In the event the number of vets who applied was 'very low'; the exact number was never revealed but some thought it may have been as low as three.

All too soon Crufts was upon us and as breeds began to finish judging on the first day it quickly became apparent that all was not well. First the young Pekingese bitch failed her check, then the Bulldog bitch, a tremendous winner in her breed. 'Dogdom's darkest day', Andrew Brace called it.

Friday saw the Clumber Spaniel bitch from Croatia fail, a big winner at group level all over Europe under experts including the Crufts group and BIS judges. Two breeds failed on Saturday, a previous Crufts BOB winning Mastiff bitch and a Neapolitan Mastiff from Belgium. The heartbreak continued into Sunday when the Basset Hound, a

© Will Harris

The Dog World in 2012

Since arriving in the UK from the US in early 2011, the Irish Water Spaniel Sh Ch/Am Ch Whistle Stop's Elements Of Magic CD, RN has made a big impact on UK show rings. Owned by Judith Carruthers with his co-breeder Colleen McDaniel, he won three all-breed BIS in 2011, plus a gundog group show, and was leading gundog, a position he will occupy again in 2012, taking BIS at Paignton plus all three gundog group championship shows, plus reserve at Driffield, as well as the group at Crufts. Seen with 'Merlin' and Judith are Gundog Society of Wales vice-chairman John Prosser and BIS judge Stephen Hollings.
photo Harris

multiple CC winning male, failed.

Owners, of course, were devastated, indeed the Basset's owners, leading breeders Derek and Heather Storton, have not shown since. The judges who sent them through were in general not much happier, these including top all-rounders such as Zena Thorn Andrews and Ferelith Somerfield who have always done their best to put up only healthy-seeming dogs, and senior specialists like Bert Easdon.

Several of the dogs had been looked at by other vets and found not to have any problems, including the Bulldog who had been examined as successfully in a pilot for the checks last year, and the Basset who was immediately checked by the owner of the other CC winner, himself a vet. Nevertheless there is no right of appeal.

The vets concerned, Will Jeffels, who is show vet for UK Toy and did the checks on the first two days, and Alison Skipper, a former exhibitor, initially declined to comment, though Mrs Skipper later wrote a comprehensive article explaining her reasoning. She said she understood breeders' reactions but that even though some aspects could be improved, both she and Mr Jeffels thought the initiative was worthwhile.

Clearly the reasons in individual cases had to remain confidential between vet, owner and KC, unless the owner wished otherwise, but it soon became evident

that in most cases the deciding factor had been eye conformation, blemishes from old injuries in the case of the Peke and Bulldog. This led many to wonder whether one was supposed to keep one's show dogs restricted, rather than let them have a normal life where there is always the risk of a minor injury.

The question of 'haw' also emerged. Although breeders in breeds such as Bulldogs and Clumbers have tried to breed away from excess haw, progress is inevitably slow and in any case how far do you want to go without losing the breed's characteristic expression? Many who saw the Clumber expressed the view that other BOBs had much more obvious haw but were not looked at because their breeds were not considered 'high profile'.

Logical?

An already tense situation was further exacerbated when initially it was announced in the group ring that the breeds who were missing from the line-up had not been 'confirmed'. Later this was changed and the breeds concerned weren't even mentioned, as if they didn't exist. Press releases were also issued which many felt suggested the KC was gloating over the failures.

The logic of the situation was also questioned. How could a dog be deemed unworthy of going in the group or

receiving a best of breed card, yet still keep its CC which says it's worthy of the title of champion?

Others felt that Crufts, in the full glare of publicity, was not the most sensible show at which to introduce the new regime.

One of the vets had used a pen torch to look at the eyes, in spite of the promise that no diagnostic aids would be used. This was blamed on poor lighting in the areas provided for the examinations but few were convinced and the KC later reiterated the 'no implements' rule. Much later in the season, that did not stop one vet using a stethoscope in his examination, and another a pen torch!

All through this the official KC line was that the checks were necessary and were a success. Professor Dean said: "I am aware some exhibitors were disappointed about those breeds that did not pass but this should not detract from the very real progress several of these breeds have made in improving breed health."

The following week he answered questions about the checks and said that if breeders, exhibitors and judges play a full part, the checks 'should be a simple confirmatory procedure which could be dispensed with in a decade'. Harvey Locke, past president of the BVA, was one to praise the KC initiative.

The following week the two vets concerned said that "we should be proud to assist Steve Dean and the other KC members who have been courageous enough to take this step."

Among those to speak out against the checks was the German Kennel Club which made the point that checking just one winner would have only a minimal effect on breeding stock; that it is not possible at a show to do a thorough veterinary examination, and that it is 'degrading and insensitive' for the exhibitors. The American KC officials also made it known that it would not follow in the KC's path.

KC annual meeting backs the checks

THE SPRING show season got under way three weeks after Crufts and after the events there everyone wondered with much trepidation what the year would bring. The first testing ground was UK Toy, with the same vet, Will Jeffels, who had failed the Peke and Bulldog at Crufts. In the event he passed the Peke BOB – Ch Yakee Ooh Aah Cantona who went on to become one of the year's top winners and who has been checked at least 16 times – another Peke who needed her champion title confirmed and the Chinese Crested. But what of the Pugs? The two CC winners made the decision, to ringside applause, not to compete for best of breed.

The summer all-breeds show began with WELKS and here the Basset and Bulldog CC winners refused to challenge for BOB. A Shar-Pei who needed her title confirmed failed the check, apparently due to what the vet considered a skin problem, and at the National a Neapolitan Mastiff failed.

For some reason no veterinary surgeon was provided to do the checks at the German Breeds show in Dortmund with CCs on offer. One of the BOB winners there was the same Clumber from Croatia who had been denied her Crufts BOB. This was her third CC but as she hadn't passed the check she still can't add a UK title to her countless others. To add insult to injury, the KC later sent her owner a show champion certificate in error.

Next stop was the KC's annual meeting. With two discussion items and a proposal regarding the veterinary checks on the agenda, many wondered whether there would be another members' revolution, as had happened with coat testing the previous year.

'Strong message'

In the event, though the discussion was impassioned, when it came to it Glynn Payne's proposal to review the process was lost by 56 votes to 92. The chairman felt that this 'sent out a strong message about the KC's commitment to ensuring that winning show dogs are healthy examples of the breed'. Nevertheless there would be a wider consultation to see how the checks would evolve.

Perhaps the deciding factor in the vote was the warnings about how a decision to stop the checks would be perceived by those outside the dog world, even though the motion simply called for them to be made 'fair and equitable'.

Also, the item was moved to the end of the meeting, which like the previous year broke for a lunch break, and attendance

The most frequently health-tested dog of any of the high profile breeds must surely be the Pekingese Ch Yakee Ooh Aah Cantona, owned by Philip Martin (left) and handled by co-breeder Bert Easdon. The kennel's fourth all-breeds BIS winner, he won at City of Birmingham and at Three Counties, where he is seen with judge Ferelith Somerfield, dog show chairman Maureen Micklethwaite and agricultural society president John Inge, the Bishop of Worcester.
photo Walker

was thereby significantly reduced.

Subsequently General Committee member and field trial man Alan Rountree caused some astonishment by a letter which was scathing about how the show world is perceived, saying that some of those who spoke at the AGM seemed intent on 'turning shows into beauty pageants'.

At Crufts six out of 15 breeds failed their tests; would that pattern be replicated at later shows? It soon became obvious that the answer was no, as the show vets tended to pass almost all the dogs who came before them. This took some of the heat out of the situation and fewer and fewer breeds took a stand by refusing to challenge. At the May Scottish KC, the Shar-Pei CC winners did so, and at Southern Counties only one of the Basset CC winners challenged, but in general things returned almost to normal.

Nevertheless the experience remains unnerving for those whose dogs have to go through the checks, especially as the vets seem to vary considerably in the

thoroughness of the examination. Some went over them more or less as a judge would, some looked in far more detail and moved the dogs a great deal.

As eye conditions were the main reason for the Crufts failures, trying to bridge the gaps between what vets and judges or breeders were looking for became a priority, and the KC addressed this by hosting two seminars on eye conformation, presented by Professor Sheila Crispin who is a distinguished ophthalmologist along with her other roles. Priority was given to those judging the relevant breeds in the near future.

Both were well attended with plenty of at times lively discussion. Steve Dean reiterated that the KC did not regret what had happened at Crufts, feeling that the checks are the best way to demonstrate that it's not the show dogs who are the problem. Nevertheless even he had to agree that the checks tell you absolutely nothing about the overall health of a breed.

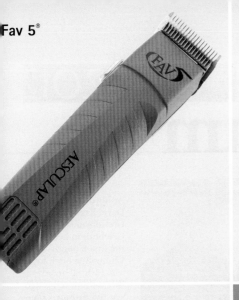
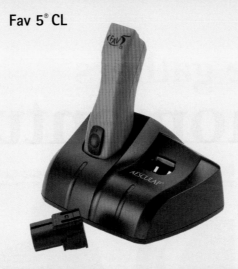
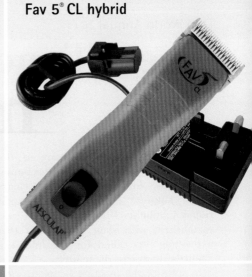

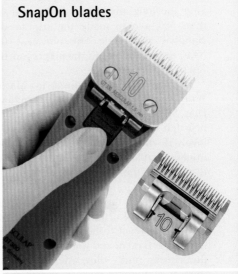

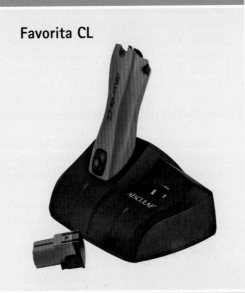
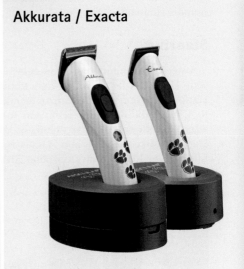
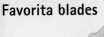

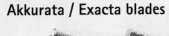

The Alliance gathers momentum

AS CRUFTS progressed many in the dog showing community were becoming increasingly angry about the veterinary check failures. A Facebook campaign called Exhibitors Choice and Voice was established, with such momentum that a meeting was called for the following Thursday to discuss the matter.

In spite of the meeting being so soon after the long and tiring show, no fewer than 320 people made the trip to the National Motorcycle Museum near the NEC, among then 61 KC members and 108 Assured Breeders.

The meeting was chaired by Martin Wyles, who is chairman of Birmingham Dog Show Society, and after extensive heartfelt discussion of the issues involved, those present voted to start an organisation known as the Canine Alliance to represent the views of breeders, judges and exhibitors.

They invited the KC to suspend the veterinary checks; to agree that, on the available evidence from Crufts, the existing system was flawed; and not to re-introduce the checks until 'they are transparent, there is clarity and fairness and they are non-discriminatory'.

Steering

A steering committee of 14 was elected, with Mr Wyles as chairman and Robert Harlow as secretary. Their first meeting took place the following week, and soon after that three Alliance members, Mr Harlow, Mike Gadsby and Lisa Croft-Elliott, met KC secretary Caroline Kisko

and canine activities executive Kathryn Symns. The KC did not agree to suspend the checks but asked the Alliance to send in specific proposals.

Various representatives of the high-profile breeds also had meetings with the KC at which ways forward were discussed.

One idea which appealed to many of the Alliance members was not that there should be fewer veterinary checks, but more – perhaps an arrangement whereby all dogs who compete in the show ring or who are bred from have a clean bill of health. Members were asked to comment on a proposal that all such dogs have two health checks, one before it is a year old and the second before it is bred from.

The Alliance also feels that KC membership should be more representative of the average breeder and competitor.

Although it had met senior KC staff members, the Alliance was disappointed that the club's chairman Steve Dean did

not agree to a meeting in spite of specific invitations; indeed the organisation has scarcely been acknowledged in KC publications or announcements.

Throughout the year the Alliance has continued to comment on the significant issues, suggesting that the KC should do everything in it power to ensure that 'KC registered' actually means something.

In Novemeber the Alliance's first general meeting of members took place, attended by around 85 people. Earlier in the day the committee had met representatives of the high profile breeds.

There had been comments that the Alliance had not come up with a viable alternative to the veterinary checks, so at this meeting a suggested way forward was proposed: that judges of every breed, not just the 'highly persecuted' 14, fill in a form similar to the one those who judge the high profile breeds are currently issued with, giving their opinions of the current state of the breed – this would be similar to what happens in Scandinavia.

Stuart Mallard also suggested that all dogs are graded, in a similar manner to what happens in FCI countries, but with special emphasis on health issues. Only those graded excellent would be placed.

Members supported this idea which it was felt would be a meaningful alternative to veterinary checks and would also show the outside world that dog people were serious about health issues.

Others suggestions included that a dog should require a basic health certificate before it qualified for Crufts or the Stud Book, and that the Alliance should attempt to be represented at the Dog Advisory Council and the Associate Parliamentary Group for Animal Welfare.

At that point membership of the Alliance stood at 1,656 including 155 from overseas – a larger total than the KC membership!

At Border Union David Reese's Ch Copymear Celebration became the first Smooth Chihuahua bitch to win a UK all-breed BIS at this level. Judge was Bill Browne-Cole and also pictured is chairman Douglas McKay.
photo Dalrymple

BIS at both the National at Birmingham and the National Working and Pastoral Breeds was Suzanne Blake's Newfoundland Sandbears Stride'n Style, who became a champion at the former. He is Suzanne's second BIS winner; they share the same dam Kjalarnes Glamour Baer at Sandbears, and are by different sires both of whom Suzanne borrowed from Europe. He is seen with Birmingham chairman Martin Wyles, judge Robin Searle, Suzanne and her husband Andrew.
photo Johnson

©Johnson

The future:
random checks on all breeds?

BY MIDSUMMER we were becoming complacent. Apart from the Crufts disaster, only two dogs had failed their veterinary checks since then. Was it all going to go away quietly?

Indeed for one of the 15 high profile breeds there was cause for celebration in July when the Kennel Club removed the Chinese Crested from the list. It had always been an anomaly as the reason for its inclusion had not been conformational exaggerations, but the fear that exhibitors were shaving or clipping excess hair or using hair removal products. The General Committee said it was satisfied that issue was no longer of sufficient concern for the breed to stay on the list. Needless to say, the breed clubs were delighted.

But at Welsh Kennel Club we had a rude awakening. Two best of breed winners failed, a Neapolitan Mastiff and a Chow, both of whom had passed previous checks. The Nea had in fact earlier scored a rare group placement for the breed. In his case the grounds for failure were 'eye conformation which means tears drain laterally' plus scarring and hair loss of jowl, while the Chow had 'slight conjunctivitis'.

The evening before, in his address to the WKC dinner, Professor Dean had praised the concept of the checks and the fact that failures were so few. "The simple fact is that the dogs winning BOB in the high-profile breeds are passing because they are free from signs of ill health related to exaggerated conformation.

"In some sectors outside our world this has come as a surprise, but we should all be delighted that the hard work put into reducing harmful exaggeration in these breeds has demonstrably borne fruit so rapidly."

Since then a Mastiff, a French Bulldog and a Bulldog have failed due to various eye issues, plus a Pekingese and a Dogue de Bordeaux, the latter due to a slightly inflamed ear.

Perhaps the KC has taken some notice of the protests for a working party which includes two vets and three breeders, one of them from a high profile breed, has been set up and will report at next year's KC AGM. Until then the checks will continue in their present format; who will do them at Crufts 2013 is not yet known.

One possibility for change, it seems, might be random checks on BOB winners in all breeds.

Bath was a good show for the high profile breeds who have been through so much this year, as no fewer than four of them won groups, and BIS was the St Bernard Chandlimore Sparks Will Fly over Samhaven, believed to be the first bitch of the breed to win a group, let alone BIS, at this level in the UK. She is pictured with judge Clare Coxall, co-owner Tan Nagrecha whose third BIS winner she is, president Chris Laurence and co-owner Alison Grainger. She gained her title later in the year.
photo Walker

CO-ORDINATOR FOR THE 14 BREEDS
The first 'High profile breed co-ordinator' has been appointed by the Kennel Club. She is Charlotte McNamara, who with her mother owns the Lynbank kennel in one of the 14 breeds, the Pekingese, and is a graduate of Manchester University. Her job is 'to provide proactive support the clubs and health co-ordinators of these breeds, liaising with them, judges and exhibitors to work towards improving in every way the welfare, health and general well-being of all dogs and the high-profile breeds in particular'.

At Richmond Ch Ragus Merry Gentleman became the fifth Norwich Terrier to win BIS at a general championship show, all of them handled by Lesley Crawley. He won the group at Crufts while still a junior, and is leading the terriers in the Top Dog table. With them are co-owner Matthew Oddie, chairman Nick Bryce-Smith and judge Ronnie Irving. He went on to take RBIS at Darlington the following week, and later at South Wales.
photo Johnson

K.G. PRODUCTS

Est. over 65 years
243-251 City Road, Fenton,
Stoke on Trent, Staffs ST4 2PX
Tel: 01782 844866 Fax: 01782 744162
www.kgproducts.co.uk
Email: mail@kgproducts.co.uk

Proud to be the UK main distributors
and service centre for AESCULAP.
Manufacturers of EASY CLIP and EXTRA HANDS.
Stockists of Aesculap, Oster, Moser and
Wahl Clippers and Blades.
Wide range of grooming equipment.

AESCULAP
THE NAME YOU CAN TRUST FOR QUALITY AND EFFICIENCY

FAVORITA 11
Powerful and robust, the Favorita 11 clipper is designed for daily, continuous use and has proved to be a 'must have' in any grooming business due to its speed and reliability.

FAV5
Same body as the Favourita 11 but takes detachable blades which are available in various sizes in Aesculap's famous high quality german steel. Also takes Oster, Andis, Thrive and Moser.

NEW FAVORITA CL CORDLESS
It's here, THE cordless clipper to replace all others. Fast, robust with 60 mins running time from the 50 min charge. Complete with 2 batteries for continous clipping. Takes Favourita 11 cutterheads so quality of cutting guaranteed!

AKKURATA
50 mins operating time from 120 mins charge time. 1/2mm-2 1/2mm cutting heights. 4 comb attachments included.

EXACTA
40 mins operating time from 240 mins charge time. 1.5mm cutterhead height. 1 comb attachment included.

SERVICE CENTRE

A SERVICE FOR THE EXPERTS BY THE EXPERTS

With over 50 years of experience, we are Aesculap's authorised service centre in the UK.

We service all types of professional clippers - both horse/cattle and dog.

Our blade sharpening is done by hand on Aesculap's grinding wheel which is still by far the best way, giving better results & extending the life of your blade.

We sharpen all types of blades & scissors and work to a 48 hour turn around.

SUPAJET
Professional dryer. 2500w element, 3 temperature settings.

TORNADO 98
Both a dryer & a blaster. Complete with flexible hose.

POWERJET
High velocity blaster with wall bracket, hose and attachment.

EASY CLIP
Spray oil/cool lube. Essential to keep blades in top condition.

EXTRA HANDS CONTROL STAND

360 degree rotating arm. Adjustable height. Complete with straps.

Rubber top, ribbed grooming tables in 3 sizes. Flat folding.

PDE 2 falls flat

The May Scottish Kennel Club BIS winner was Heather Blackburn-Bennett's Pointer Sh Ch Kiswahili Martin at Kanix, handled by her mother Joanne. He is the family's first BIS winner after more than 60 champions in Miniature Dachshunds and Pointers. In the line-up are convener Irene McManus, chief steward Frank Whyte, Alison Morton of Royal Canin and judge Robin Newhouse.
photo Johnson

KC PRODUCES ITS OWN FILMS

The Kennel Club has released a half-hour film entitled *Dogs – A Healthy Future*, which focuses on the efforts which have already been made to address health and welfare issues, and what is being done to ensure progress is maintained.

It is narrated by Clare Balding and among those interviewed are KC chairman Professor Steve Dean and Dog Advisory Council chairman Professor Sheila Crispin, Bulldog breeder Norman Davis, geneticist Dr Sarah Blott, Julie Evans who imported the Dalmatian with a Pointer ancestor, KC committee member Graham Hill and health and breeder services manager Bill Lambert. Much of it was filmed at Richmond show in 2011.

Shortly afterwards a second film was produced warning people not to buy from puppy farms, and later three YouTube films were produced with the aim of helping puppy buyers.

Meanwhile *Around the Dog World*, a television programme produced by dogworld.tv, has continued to be featured regularly on Horse and Country TV. Among other things viewers have been able to see group judging from an number of the major championship shows, plus interviews with judges, owners and expert commentators.

THE DOG breeding community's heart sank when we heard that a sequel to *Pedigree Dogs Exposed* was planned. Although the first programme in 2008, produced by Jemima Harrison's Passionate Productions, had been an arguably necessary wake-up call to all dog people to put the dogs' health first when making breeding decisions, many thought various aspects of it were unfair, some of these concerns subsequently being backed up by Ofcom.

Should the Kennel Club take part in the second documentary? Requests were made to interview KC representatives but the club decided to turn them down, because of the way it was treated in the first programme.

In the event the sequel, broadcast the week before Crufts, was a bit of a damp squib, covering relative little new ground and going over some of the ground featured in 2008, including the issue of syringomyelia in Cavaliers. It was claimed that there had been 'some progress but not enough', and Ms Harrison felt that a new regulatory body was needed owing to the KC's 'inextricable link' to breed clubs.

The tone, with some exceptions, was slightly more measured than in the first programme, and even DOG WORLD agreed wholeheartedly with one of Ms Harrison's contentions which was that it is pointless looking at any one aspect of the situation of dogs in Britain in isolation; a 'joined up' approach is needed.

After many group wins, the Bouvier des Flandres Ch I'm Special Inessence Movado at Kanix took his first BIS award at Darlington under Liz Cartledge (left). He is owned by Fiona Lambert (right), Janet Hughes and his American breeder Pat Murray and handled by Dave Killilea. Richard Compton, owner of the venue Newby Hall, chairman Sarah Allsopp and secretary David Guy complete the line-up. Movado was also RBIS at the Scottish Working and Pastoral Breeds. The Kanix affix was therefore borne by two BIS winners during the year; the Pointer was at one time owned by Sigurd Wilberg who imported his sire from New Zealand, while Fiona now runs the Bouvier side of the kennel – Movado is the third Kanix Bouvier BIS winner, and currently heads the working group rankings.
photo Dalrymple

Hardest part for us to take was a segment on juvenile kidney disorder in Boxers. While not wishing to minimise the issue, we disliked the way two kennels were pilloried and felt that there must also have been differing and perhaps equally valid points of view.

Unlike last time, there was very little reaction to the programme, though the British Veterinary Association (BVA) president Carl Padgett shortly afterwards called on the Government to take action on regulations for breeders, and the BVA called for a further review of the Standards.

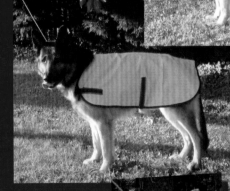

A standard for breeders

THE DOG Advisory Council (DAC), chaired by Professor Sheila Crispin and consisting of experts in a number of fields, though only one person from the breeding/showing world, has made various pronouncements during the year. In March it said that a long-term strategy for outcrossing and back-crossing could be the only way of seeing improvement in certain breeds.

Later it produced a document about the eight problems it has prioritised: ocular problems linked to head conformation; breathing difficulty linked to head conformation; syringomyelia and chiari-like malformation; idiopathic epilepsy; heart disease with a known or suspected inherited basis; breed-related and inherited skin conditions; limb defects including hip dysplasia and elbow dysplasia; and separation-related behaviour.

The Kennel Club felt more emphasis should be given to conditions where puppies are bred and sold.

Potentially more significant was its standard for breeding dogs, which was submitted to ministers in September. This is a 12-page document of 'minimum standards which must be met to provide good health and welfare for all dogs involved in breeding'. The council hopes that buyers will take the standard on board and refuse to buy from anyone who cannot or will not meet it.

Much of it is common sense, similar to what would be required of an Assured Breeder, but other aspects, such as temperatures within accommodation, seemed unnecessarily prescriptive, and yet others would make breeders' lives very difficult. For example not only bitches but also stud dogs would not be able to be used before two years old, and inbreeding coefficients must be lower than 12.5 per cent, thus barring half-sibling matings and effectively stopping serious line-breeding programmes. Bitches would be able to have only one caesarean, and breeding stock must be trained to come when called, sit and stay!

Steve Dean, writing as DOG WORLD's veterinary correspondent, felt it lacked common sense, was unnecessarily dictatorial and would punish the innocent, while Assured Breeder Scheme manager Bill Lambert felt it contained 'aspirational or vague ideals' to which no one is going to subscribe.

Professor Crispin said that the DAC

Jacky and Dave Mitchell's Swedish-bred English Springer Spaniel Sh Ch/Nord Ch Barecho Hold Your Horses at Peasblossom was BIS at Southern Counties. In the line-up are vice-president Joyce Baker and her grandson James Barker, group judge Rainer Vuorinen, secretary Angela Cavill, judge Zena Thorn Andrews and chief steward Bill Bunce.
photo Johnson

Two English Springers have taken the top spot in 2012. At Midland Counties it was the eight-year-old bitch Sh Ch Trimere Tigra, handled by Ann Corbett for her daughter Sarah. She had previously topped the Welsh Kennel Club in 2009. Judge was Ann Ingram from Ireland, seen with chairman Robert Greaves and vice-president June Tonge.
photo Walker

would continue to work with the KC and 'other key stakeholders' on a breeding standard which will apply to all types of dog and is 'practical, proportionate, inspectable and enforceable'.

What was not clear is why, if it is still a work in progress, ministers had already been issued with a version which in many dog people's eyes is none of those things.

Anyway, the KC and DAC are now in consultation in the hope of sorting out the difference between the DAC standard and the ABS requirements.

PUPPY PACK NOT UNIVERSALLY WELCOMED

A PUPPY contract and information pack was launched by the British Veterinary Association, Animal Welfare Foundation and RSPCA. It ran into criticism from the Kennel Club which felt it concentrated too much on what not to do. The KC also regretted that its Assured Breeder Scheme was not mentioned.

Among the pack's suggestions was that puppies with an inbreeding coefficient of more than 12.5 per cent 'should be avoided'. The Dog Advisory Council did welcome the pack, and the organisations which produced it said the KC could have had input had it wished.

Blackpool
falls victim to the weather, again

WEATHER-WISE, much of the summer was disappointing, and waterlogged ground forced a number of shows, including WELKS, Three Counties, National Working/Pastoral and both Scottish Kennel Clubs to go totally indoors or to change their layout. Border Union was pretty muddy but much worse was to come a week later.

Many will recall Blackpool show in 2008 when exceptional gales caused the show to be abandoned halfway through the final day. Surely that was sufficient bad luck for one society? But no, and in 2012 only the first day's judging took place at the society's own ground at Marton. Almost a month's worth of rain fell throughout the day in the region. The rings turned to a sea of mud and water. Somehow everyone got through the day's judging of the toy, terrier and utility breeds but many cars found it almost impossible to leave the car park.

By the end of the day it was obvious the show could not continue and at 6.15pm secretary Steve Hall and the committee made the decision to abandon the next two day's judging. Health and safety considerations were paramount, and it did not help that attempts to find an alternative to the by now impassable show car park proved fruitless.

The news was immediately broadcast on the social networks and just three exhibitors turned up on Saturday and five on Sunday, along with a number of local people who had read about the show. Exhibitors spent much of Saturday helping tow out their fellows from the caravan park.

The society quickly announced that as its own bills still had to be paid, exhibitors would not receive a refund, news that was not universally welcomed. Sympathy was felt for the society on its second disaster within a few years, but others felt more progress could have been made on improving the show site. Later Blackpool announced that entry fees would be reduced in 2013 for the four groups that were not judged this time.

Windsor the following weekend was a complete contrast and in the heat the society again took a zero tolerance approach to 'dogs in cars' and judging in several rings was suspended until dogs of those breeds had been dealt with.

But East of England was not so fortunate and another torrent of rain forced the society to move all the judging inside. It wasn't easy; by the second day the benching had been removed from the main building and even judges' reception was used for rings. Thank goodness for the modern atrium on the showground – and everyone pulled together

Bournemouth show has for some years been hoping to move from its long standing venue at the New Forest Showground, which although pretty had its disadvantages, notably traffic congestion. After many tribulations the association finally bought its own land at Pikes Farm, Organford, just off the A35 to the west of Poole. This involved a slightly longer journey for many exhibitors but without the same potential for jams. The extensive green field site was blessed with good weather for its debut and most agreed the site has great potential.

Moving up from RBIS in 2011 was Sue Ellis' Alaskan Malamute Ch Chayo All Eyes On Me, only the second of the breed to achieve this in the UK. The first was his uncle also owned and bred by Sue, one of whose wins was at Bournemouth. In the meantime his brother has also won a group there! Also pictured are chairman Mick Howes, judge Jean Lanning, president Julia Iles-Hebbert and show manager Jasper Courtney. Sadly secretary Denise Courtney, who had not enjoyed the best of health recently, died later in the year.

photo Harris

to make the best of things.

This was the first time for ten years the dog show had been combined with the agricultural show which suffered worse than the dog section. Throughout the wet summer many rural events were cancelled including, sadly, the Game Fair planned for Belvoir Castle. Exhibitors may grumble but consider how much worse the situation is for the traders who depend on such events for their livelihood.

The Kennel Club's big International Agility Festival was another casualty when its venue at Kelmarsh Hall was declared unusable at the last minute. To everyone's credit a new venue was found at nearby Rockingham Castle and the festival, with nearly 2,200 entrants from as far afield as Japan, went ahead successfully.

Consultations are all the rage, and Britain's oldest show society, Birmingham, has done an online survey to see what exhibitors want from the National show.

LKA 2011 showed an increase of more than 600 entries on the previous year, and

Boston 2012 drew a record entry, but after that the trend was downwards. Of the all-breed shows in the first half of the year only WELKS drew a marginally increased entry, and Bath and the May SKC had the biggest drops.

Later, though, things began to look up – perhaps a sign that confidence in the economy is tentatively beginning to return. Leeds, City of Birmingham, Richmond, Darlington and Belfast all drew better entries than in 2011, though Driffield saw a substantial drop.

The long standing clash between the Houndshow and National Gundog will at last be resolved in 2013 when the former is on the first Saturday in August and the latter on the Sunday. In recent years Paignton has followed on immediately but this society would like to start on the same weekend. The dates had not been confirmed by the KC at the time we went to press but needless to say this has caused some protest, not least from National Gundog and trade stand holders.

Are you a breeder?

Baby Milk Pro Biotic
- Puppy milk for motherless rearing from day one
- Low lactose content (max. 25 %)
- With special probiotic cultures to stabilise the gut
- Especially suitable for the rearing of sensitive puppies

Mini Baby+Junior 29
- 29% protein - adapted to the specific needs of small breeds up to a maximum of 10 kg at the age of 1 - 12 months

Medium Baby
- For puppies of mid-sized breeds from 11 - 25 kg
- From 4 weeks up to and including 5 months
- Perfect for the first phase of life until second dentition

Medium Junior
- For young dogs of mid-sized breeds from 11 - 25 kg
- From 6 months (after second dentition) up to 15 months
- With reduced protein content (25 %)

Maxi Baby
- For puppies of large breeds over 26 kg
- From the 4th week up to and including the 5th month
- Perfect for the first phase of life until second dentition

Maxi Junior
- For young dogs of large breeds over 26 kg
- From 6 months (after second dentition) up to 18 months
- With reduced protein content (23 %)

A breeder scheme by experts for experts:

- **High quality tailored nutrition for all breeds with Happy Dog's Unique LifePlus concept**

- **Feeding from gestation to maturity with Happy Dog Baby & Junior 2-Phase concept**

- **Extensive support through our veterinary centre**

- **Unbeatable breeder discount & puppy packs***

The Happy Dog Baby & Junior Products 2-Phase Concept

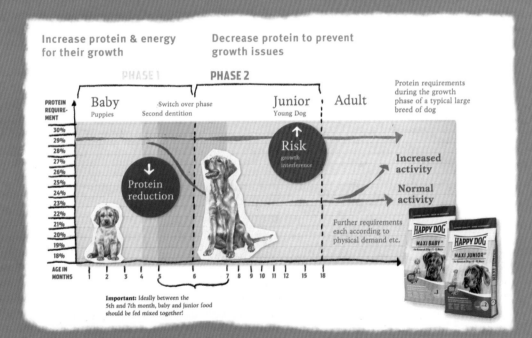

Request a free Breeder Information Brochure for an in-depth insight on our philosophy and products

A FAMILY RUN BUSINESS SINCE 1765
I guarantee the best **quality.**
GEORG MÜLLER, WEHRINGEN/BAY.

HAPPY DOG®
Trusted Feeding
Since 1968.

Is there a case for two-tier registration?

BREEDERS who register five or more litters a year are being asked by the Kennel Club to produce a copy of their breeder's licence. So far two thirds of those involved have done so and the KC has stopped registering puppies from the remainder.

Some who study the records supplements in detail were surprised when the chairman said later in the year that the KC would never knowingly register puppies bred by puppy farmers. We suppose it depends upon how you define a puppy farmer. At least having to provide the licence is a start.

At the KC's annual meeting, Judith Robin-Smith raised the possibility of a two-tier registration system; she would also like to see an official pedigree issued with all registrations.

The establishment view is that the Assured Breeder Scheme already effectively provides a second tier, but there was much support for the proposal and the KC agreed to examine the possibilities.

Subsequently it introduced a wide-ranging consultation on what was the way forward for its registration system. Senior committee and staff members attended question times and public meetings around the country to discuss this and other issues.

Evidence

That a review of the system might be necessary was reinforced when chairman Professor Steve Dean appeared as a witness before the House of Commons' Environment, Food and Rural Affairs Committee (EFRA) which is scrutinising the Government's dog control and welfare policies. This is also considering the measures on tackling irresponsible dog ownership, and the response to Professor Sir Patrick Bateson's enquiry into dog breeding.

The committee is receiving evidence on a wide variety of dog-related topics, from whether controls are required on breeders, compulsory microchipping, licensing, the Dangerous Dogs Act (DDA) and the role of the police, welfare organisations and local authorities.

The KC submitted a written response, highlighting the positive work which has been done and calling for amendments to the DDA.

Later Professor Dean and Dachshund breed council chairman Ian Seath appeared before the committee as witnesses, and committee chairman Anne McIntosh MP and

Associate Parliamentary Group for Animal Welfare chairman Neil Parish, as well as some leading vets, raised the question of why, if the KC is so keen on health testing, it continues to register puppies from parents which have not been tested.

The KC's line has always been that it is a 'Somerset House for dogs', merely recording parentage, and that it is at least better if the less responsible breeders' activities are recorded for all to see. Whether this attitude will be able to continue remains to be seen.

Many other aspects including education, close breeding, the recording of health data, breed Standards and so on, were raised at the hearing.

The presidents of the British Veterinary Association and the British Small Animals Veterinary Association told the committee that the Dog Advisory Council should be made a regulatory body, and that legislation on breeding should be updated 'to ensure the future health and welfare of dogs and puppies'.

The government, though, seems to be unconvinced of the need for further legislation, judging by the comments of Parliamentary Under-Secretary at DEFRA Lord de Mauley, who felt that the DAC should remain an advisory body and that problems would be best tackled from within the 'industry', supported by the KC and the charities which have done some 'quite impressive' work, he said.

Meanwhile, the Kennel Club and Dogs Trust had launched the 'Puppy Plan', a guide to socialisation produced by dog behaviourist Carolyn Menteith aiming to give puppies the best start in life.

Many welcomed the idea, recognising that lack of socialisation is the cause of all too many problems in a dog's later life, but some of the detail raised eyebrows among experienced breeders.

As usual there were some modification to the detailed breed-specific requirements for members of the Kennel Club Assured Breeder Scheme. A more general change was that those who do not breed but who own a stud dog may join. The scheme itself is still aiming towards accreditation and it is understood that big changes are planned for 2013.

Yvonne Miller's Boxer Ch Roamaro First Issue by Walkon won her second all-breeds BIS at LKA 2011. Judge was Albert Wight and vice-chairman Anne Bliss presented the magnificent trophy.
photo Walker

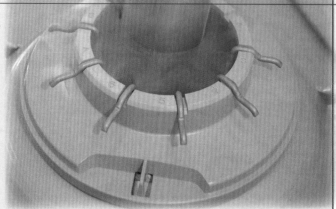

Registrations
take a dive

REGISTRATION figures for 2011 were 243,841 compared with 257,062 in 2010. This was the lowest figure since 2002 though in general the figures have not varied dramatically over the past 20 years.

As usual Labradors were top breed with 39,964 dogs, though more than 4,000 down on 2010, followed by Cockers, English Springers and German Shepherds. The English Setter, with just 234 registrations, joined the list of 'vulnerable' native breeds.

Research is being carried out at the KC's Genetics Centre, showing the dangerously low effective population sizes in some of the numerically small breeds. It is hoped that strategies can be developed to increase genetic diversity, possibly including outcrosses to another breed.

A further decline was shown in the figures for the first three quarters of 2012, 174,936 as against 187,185 for January to September 2011. One breed which bucked the trend, to the consternation of its supporters, was the French Bulldog which is also being imported from Eastern Europe at an astonishing rate. For example, no fewer than 89 were imported in the second quarter of the year, the vast majority from that region.

Heading the pastoral group in the Top Dogs table at the time of going to press was the Australian Shepherd Ch Allmark Fifth Avenue, owned by Neil Allan and Robert Harlow and handled by Neil's wife Angie.

She was conceived when her dam was sent to be mated to a dog in the US and was top Aussie 2011 while still a puppy. Among her 2012 successes was BIS at Working and Pastoral Breeds Association of Scotland, where she is pictured with chairman Irene McManus, and RBIS at Welsh Kennel Club.
photo Dalrymple

CCs REMAIN IN SPITE OF LOWER ENTRIES

The NUMBER of challenge certificate sets of offer in 2014 has increased by 17; 27 have been added and ten withdrawn. This means the Kennel Club has added extra CCs into the mix in spite of entries generally falling; had the usual formula been followed there would have been a net decline of 73 sets.

The unpopular single CC for best of breed will finally be phased out in 2015. Once again the KC has been generous with the allocation for that year, not making any reductions even when entries have declined, so instead of a reduction of 41 sets, an extra 34 sets are available, and 13 breeds have benefited from the removal of single CCs.

Breed and general clubs have been asked to give their views on how CCs should be allocated in future, and a working party has been set up to discuss the issue. Whether this will just concern itself with details, or whether it will take a wider view and examine questions like 'should every breed have CCs at every show', is not clear.

CCs in Dortmund, CACs at the National

LAST YEAR we reported the Kennel Club's plan to have challenge certificates on offer to the 'British breeds' – including those, like Salukis and Afghans, developed in the UK, as well as those which originate here – at the German Kennel Club (VDH)'s national show at Dortmund in May. Each would have a British judge and both British and German CCs would be on offer.

A week later, the German breeds were to have German judges at Birmingham's National Dog Show, and after some confusion it was established that they would have German CACs on offer as well as the British certificates.

This was only the second time CCs were offered outside the UK; the first was for the Irish breeds when the Irish Kennel Club hosted the European Show.

The plan was that the German show would not clash with any British all-breeds show. Unfortunately a spanner was thrown into the works when the VDH had to move its event to the same weekend as the Birmingham show. A few breeds therefore had two sets of CCs on the same day; in many others it would have been impossible for exhibitors to attend both shows and in the event very few UK exhibitors showed in Germany and vice versa.

Nevertheless both events saw an overall increase in the entries in the relevant breeds. All went well, though there was some difficulty in finding out who the winners were in Germany and in a few cases the judge awarded a CAC but not a CC!

On each of the three days of the British Breeds events in Germany, the BOB winners, as well as appearing in the group, was able to try for a separate 'best British breed' award. Only two of the three were there on the final day to compete for overall best British breed, which Albert Wight awarded to Britta Ludsteck's Border Collie Int Sh Ch/Ger Ch Simaro Bruce Darnell, from Germany.
photo Roberto

Clarges Street
move falls through

AS LAST year's *Annual* went to press, we reported that a special general meeting of the Kennel Club members voted overwhelmingly to approve a move of the club's London premises a short way down Clarges Street as part of a development plan of the whole Clarges Estate.

The incentive would have been the sum of £12 million plus all expenses paid, with the new offices in a fully refurbished building which would be slightly larger and considerably better equipped than the present one.

At the time it all felt almost too good to be true and sadly that proved to be the case.

In May came news that Chelsfield, the company which had wished to buy the property, had withdrawn. Exactly why was not revealed, but it is understood that the problems were nothing to do with the KC.

Later another company, British Land, entered into an agreement to buy the Clarges Estate but as yet there is no news as to what extent this will affect the KC.

The November meeting also voted, unanimously, to approve a plan to convert the KC into a company limited by guarantee. This would have various advantages, bringing the club into line with many similar 'not for profit' organisations and limiting the liability of the trustees and General Committee.

A draft constitution was produced and members invited to a meeting in February to iron out the details. The main areas of concern were that proxy voting will be allowed but not postal voting, and that the quorum for a special meeting will move from 30 members to five per cent (currently 65). These were explained at the annual meeting where the proposals were agreed.

The third item discussed in November was a proposal to grant the Animal Health Trust an interest-free loan of one and a half million pounds to develop its cancer centre. This was also passed, but with greater opposition – by 115 votes to 86.

Ferelith Somerfield gave BIS at National Terrier to the American-bred Irish Terrier Ch/Am Ch Fleet St Fenway Fan, owned by Tony Barker (second right) with Victor Malzoni from Brazil who in an unusual double also owned the Montgomery County BIS in the US. Handler was John Averis whose mother Judy bred the RBIS-winning Lakeland. Also pictured are chairman Max King and Shannon Thomas of Royal Canin. An all-breed BIS winner and top terrier in 2011, Fenway Fan has now handed over to his half-sister Ch Fleet St Fire And Ice, who has been a multiple group winner and is seen at the National, winning the group under Stuart Plane, where she went on to RBIS. She is owned by John, Tony and his wife Jean.
photos Walker/Johnson

After nine group 2 awards Sarah and Rosemarie Jackson's Maltese finally took top spot at the UK Toydog Society's fortieth anniversary show., judged by Alan Bendelow (right). The Jacksons had also taken this award with his sire Ch Benatone Gold Ring and grandsire Ch/Am Ch Hi-Lites Risque Gold Fever. On the left is secretary Tom Mather.
photo Walker

DOCKING GOES AT LAST IN NORTHERN IRELAND

THE WELSH Government undertook a second consultation about new draft regulations for breeders, to reflect the needs of breeders who were already acting responsibly. The plan was for a licence to be required for those with three breeding bitches on the premises and who breed three of more litters within 12 months. Another such consultation took place in Northern Ireland.

In April Northern Ireland became the first part of the UK to introduce compulsory microchipping. Puppies must be chipped at 12 weeks, to be reduced to eight weeks from 2013. The Welsh Government has done a consultation on a similar proposal. The NI regulations also say that breeders who produce three or more litters a year must be licensed.

The only part of the UK without a docking ban is Northern Ireland, though one was scheduled to come into effect in April 2012. It will now start on January 1, 2013 with maximum penalties of two years' jail and an unlimited fine. Exemptions, as in the rest of the UK, may be made for some working dogs and in emergencies, though these dogs may not be exhibited at any show which charges either an entry fee or an admission fee.

'Danger' dog stalemate

ONCE AGAIN little if any progress has been made in reforming the dangerous dogs legislation. The cost of kennelling and caring for seized dogs was claimed to have spiralled out of control, increasing by 63 per cent in a year in the case of the Metropolitan Police. The major welfare organisations, veterinary profession and trade unions organised a petition calling for new legislation but nothing has happened.

Meanwhile the rescue situation continued to cause concern, particularly of Staffordshire Bull Terriers, and Battersea launched a campaign to 'reconnect people with the gentle nature of this misunderstood and increasingly shunned' breed.

Around Christmas several of the welfare organisations said they were stretched to the limit as owners were forced to give up pets due to the continuing economic downturn.

It was revealed that in 2011 2,493 'dangerous' dogs or those of a banned breed or type were being held by the 29 police forces in England and Wales which kept records, at a cost of at least £3.7 million.

Instead of scrapping the Dangerous Dogs Act (DDA), DEFRA Minister of State Jim Paice announced yet another consultation in April, seeking views on whether it should be extended to cover all private property. He also sought views on whether microchipping should be compulsory for all dogs. Many campaigned felt this was a missed opportunity to revise the DDA. At the EFRA committee hearings later in the

year, Lord de Mauley reiterated that, on police advice, the government was unlikely to remove the breed-specific elements of the Act.

One area in which progress was made was in new guidelines from the Sentencing Council, which allows judges and magistrates to give out tougher, more consistent sentences under the DDA, including 18 months' custody for allowing a dog to be dangerously out of control and injuring someone.

Meanwhile the destruction of Lennox, said to be a Labrador/American Bulldog cross, in Northern Ireland caused widespread protest. He had been seized by Belfast dog wardens in 2010 and later assessed to be a danger to the public, even

Best in show at Scottish Breeds was Trevor and Birgit Hayward's Smooth Collie Foxearth French Eclipse. Sold as a pet as a puppy, she was returned to her breeders in 2011 and won her title in five shows at the age of seven!
photo Dalrymple

COAT TESTING LIMBO

Coat testing was the big news story of 2011, starting with the controversial tests at Crufts, where two Miniature Poodles and two West Highland Whites failed. This led to a virtual revolution at the Kennel Club's annual meeting, the suspension of the tests and the reinstatement of those dogs' awards. The Kennel Club instituted a consultation and a meeting with people from the breeds most often affected.

Amazingly, almost nothing has been heard on the topic during 2012. The KC has met members of the Poodle fraternity and others, but as yet no new proposed regulations have emerged. At the KC AGM, members were told that 'good progress' was being made in the review of the practice. It is understood that we will have to wait until the 2013 AGM to see what changes are suggested.

though he had served as a therapy dog and was described as the 'soulmate' of his owner's disabled daughter.

A visitor from Ireland, bred in Sweden from Spanish parents, was Dave Cavill's choice as BIS at Working and Pastoral Breeds Association of Wales. This was Jimmy Duggan's Siberian Husky Ir Ch Bedarra Cold Paws Warm Heart for Leorient, handled by his wife Anita Foley-Duggan. On the left is show manager Tegwyn Jones.
photo Harris

Consistently successful in the group rings, including RBIS at WELKS where group judge was Di Arrowsmith, was the Labrador Sh Ch/Am/Can Ch Salty Dog of Tampa Bay. A big winner in his native US and now a veteran, he has been handled during his stay in the UK by Anthony Allen for owner Linda Hess.
photo Walker

Winner of the Eukanuba champion stakes final, and so entitled to represent the UK at the Eukanuba World Challenge in Florida in December, was Nigel and Trudy Blythin's Bichon Frisé Ch Arthlorn's Ready To Rumble, handled by Tamara Dawson. Judges were Harry O'Donoghue and Meg Purnell-Carpenter, and on the left is Julie Nottage from the sponsor.
photo Walker

Many regret that the 2011 Petplan junior stakes final, held just before Manchester 2012, will be the last such event after nearly 20 years. This event was always unusually exciting as it was judged on a points basis. Winner of the 'final final', judged by Rafael Malo Alcrudo from Spain, Patsy Hollings and Rodney Oldham, was Charlotte Roskell and Michaella Dunhill-Hall's Shiba Inu Ch Vormund John Paul Gaultier. The sponsored stakes classes have continued in 2012 but the winners no longer go forward to a final.

Dog World/Royal Canin Top Stud Dog 2011 was Eve Ciechonska's Irish Setter Sh Ch Caskeys Concept at Aoibheanne, and DW/Yumega Top Brood Bitch was Trish Hallam, Dee Hardy, Sue Kite and Jeff Gillespie's Basenji Ch/Am Ch Klassics Million Dollar Baby at Tokaji, a BIS winner and breed CC record holder. They also led the 2012 rankings at time of going to press.
photo Dalrymple

Once again the finalists in the Kennel Club breeders competition made a spectacular sight as they paraded in Crufts' main ring. The Lireva Pomeranians bred by Averil Cawthera-Purdy (left) were the winners.
photo Walker

Was this the first time three puppies from the same litter had qualified for Pup of the Year? An older sister had also previously done so. The Basenjis Tokaji Texas Ranger, Kentucky Blue and California Dreaming are pictured with Danny Cullen, Trish Hallam and Dee Hardy. All are now champions and Texas Ranger was RBIS at LKA 2011. Their dam is Million Dollar Baby.
photo Walker

The final of the Kennel Gazette Junior Warrant Winner of the Year competition was judged at Crufts and the victor was Sue Smith and Val Freer's Samoyed Ch Nikara Diamond Dancer.
photo Johnson

Kennel Club of Jersey 125th Anniversary Canine Festival

Saturday 15th & Sunday 16th June 2013

The President and Committee are delighted to invite you to join with them in celebrating 125 years of the Kennel Club of Jersey.

We are hosting a two-day event on 15th and 16th June 2013 to be held at the Royal Jersey Showground to include a Crufts qualifying breed championship show on the first day with top UK judges Mrs E Cartledge and Mr F Kane.

Junior and Senior Handling classes judged by Sue Whitehead will be held on Saturday.

An agility and obedience show will take place on both days.

A companion show will be held on the Sunday, along with a handling master class day.

In addition with the aim of promoting responsible dog ownership there will be good citizens testing and demonstrations, dancing with dogs performances, parade of breeds, talks, displays and stalls with all things canine.

There will be a social event on Saturday evening at the Showground and all are invited.

Caring for the welfare of Jersey dogs for 125 years

Design : Joseph Lee-Brown | jwlb.net   Image courtesy of Jersey Evening Press

For more details **kennelclub.org.je**

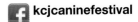 **kcjcaninefestival**

Email **press@kennelclub.org.je**

Sponsored by

Winner of the Welsh Kennel Club's Top Dog competition for 2011 was Cliff and Helen Howell's Beagle Dialynne All Spice for Emorlen.
photo Johnson

Peta As Therapy Show Dog of the Year was Rita and Paul Bartlett's Greyhound Ch/Ir Ch Jet's Its Been A Hard Day's Night at Ransley, seen with Peter Parkinson of Hi Life, judge Tom Mather and Muriel Iles.
photo Harris

Astrid Ogilvie chose Julie Carruthers' Italian Spinone Bannobrig Al Fresco to win the Scottish Kennel Club Open Show Dog of the Year competition.
photo Dalrymple

Lisa Gudgin and Marina Scott chose Hollie Kavanagh handling a Dobermann as Coventry Ladies' Kennel Society Adult Handler of the Year. They are pictured with CLKS secretary Anne Defaye.
photo Showphoto

The Dog World in 2012

Winner of the Northesk Trophy for best in the gamekeepers classes at Crufts was Jo and Mark Izard's German Shorthaired Pointer Jennaline Ello Jibble, pctured with judge Linda Partridge and Ben Chudley of Chudleys Dog Food.
photo Walker

The Scottish Kennel Club's Show Dog of the Year 2011 competition was won by the Irish Wolfhound Graystone Farunah from Gartlove owned by James and Ann (left) Macaulay. Also pictured are Alison Morton of Royal Canin and judges Bert Easdon, Maggie Mulholland and Keith Nathan.
photo Dalrymple

Channel Island Dog of the Year under Albert Wight was Marie-Claire Hannigan's Afghan Hound Jsy Ch Jangels Just A Gigolo at Jahera. On the right is president Steven Edwards.

News in Brief

It is hard to keep up with the various organisations which are compiling reports on the dog world.

The Associate Parliamentary Group for Animal Welfare (APGAW) was not to be outdone by the others and its latest report calls for breeders of three (rather than five) or more litters a year to be licensed, the Assured Breeder Scheme to be independent with unannounced regular spot checks, health checks for all show dogs, compulsory microchipping, the Dog Advisory Council to become an independent state-funded regulatory body and the Kennel Club to endorse the British Veterinary Association/RSPCA puppy contract when next it is reviewed.

Last December, the KC had opted not to attend an APGAW meeting as Jemima Harrison's Passionate Productions was being allowed to film the meeting. At the meeting there was much focus on breed Standards, questioning whether the KC's revisions to them had been robust enough.

The Dog World in 2012

The Bichon Frisé Ch Pamplona Bring Me Sunshine, owned by Michael Coad (right) and handled by him or partner Geoff Corish (left), not only became Top Dog 2011 but at the last show of the year broke the breed CC record formerly held by his grandsire. He is Michael's fourth Bichon record holder; three of them were Top Dog and the other was runner-up.
photo Walker

Carol and Roger Almond's Ch Malia Valentine at Changtse has taken the Tibetan Spaniel CC record.
photo Walker

Rae Ganna's Ch Keepcot Connoisseur took the Otterhound CC record from his grandsire.
photo Johnson

Diane Mottram's Ch Mybeards Dream took the Polish Lowland Sheepdog CC record from a half-brother also bred by Diane.
photo Johnson

Adi and Jan Chambers' Mittel, Ch Nosregor Bewitched for Musique, is now the CC record holder both both varieties of German Spitz.
photo Garbutt

Rachael Reddin and Ruth Bussell's Portuguese Water Dog Ch Rarjo She's The One now holds the breed's CC record.
photo Johnson

News in Brief

For the first time, the spring 2012 *Breed Records Supplement* included details of whether litters were born by caesarean section, and if so whether they were elective or emergency. Such details are meant to be provided by the breeder when they register the litter. The Kennel Club later reminded vets that they were supposed to report any caesareans or operations altering the natural conformation of a dog.

The Kennel Club's long-standing campaign to ban electric collars suffered a blow when a review by the Companion Animal Welfare Council suggested that, although these can be abused, the issue is more complex than sometimes suggested and that some who use them are genuinely looking for a solution to a potentially serious problem.

Shortly before Crufts the Kennel Club ruled that a dog's exhibit number must be displayed at all times on its cage or crate while at a show. It was felt important to be able to identify the owner if a dog is found to be in distress or blocking a gangway. Another concern was the possibility of dogs maneouvring soft crates off their benches if not properly secured. Whether this has subsequently been enforced is not known. Judges are now supposed to report to the show secretary dogs withdrawn from competition at their suggestion or request.

Kennel Club disciplinary hearings have once again been rare. A Podengo breeder was warned, censured and fined £1,000 for producing false paperwork related to four dogs. A Rough Collie breeder was banned for two years for being 'verbally aggressive and abusive' at a show. Two agility competitors were fined after a scuffle at a show. The committee also imposed penalties on a number of people who had been convicted by courts.

CH TRAVELLA STAR CRAFT

Owners
F LEUNG and A ALMEIDA

Breeder **BILL BROWNE-COLE**
Handler **RICHARD ALLEN**

Alan W Walker

Three of the Fox Terrier breed clubs co-operated to run a Fox Terrier Expo, with CCs for both breeds two days running. It attracted a number of overseas competitors. A 'supreme' award was offered for the overall winner who was, appropriately, the Wire Blackdale Supreme, who had won his UK title in nine days. The judges who helped him take top spot, Paolo Dondina, Frank Kane and Ruth Barbour, are seen with Andrew Goodsell handling and owner Harry O'Donoghue from Ireland.
photo Croft-Elliott

The first UK Bullmastiff of the Year competition was won by Julie Lindley's Ch Hyerdunscars As Gud As It Gets. Judges were Sigurd Wilberg, Linda Wade and Billy Warren.
photo Lewis

At the Beagle Association's fiftieth anniversary championship show, Diana Brown and Sally Kimber awarded BIS to Brian Foster and Jen Davies' Australian import Ch/Aus Gr Ch Orobay Graceful Triumph.
photo Kyprianou

Among the many victories for Lee Cox and Tom Isherwood's Toy Poodle Ch Vanitonia You'll See was the first Poodle of the Year contest, judged by Melva Nathan, John Gillespie and Penny Jones.
photo Brace

The Northern Samoyed Society celebrated its fiftieth anniversary by hosting the breed's third world meeting. At the society's championship show Denise Edmondson from South Africa gave BIS to Lisa Bobrowski's Ch Vandreem Imperial Hermioni by Berezniki, a big winner over several years and RBIS at Richmond 2012.

News in Brief

The Akita Ch Ruthdales Next Top Model was stripped by the Kennel Club of all her awards including the utility group at Crufts 2010, a group and RBIS at Blackpool and 12 CCs, under the rule which states that no act of operation which alters the natural conformation of a dog or any part thereof may be performed.

Among new DNA testing schemes developed are those for copper toxicosis, for Greyhound neuropathy, for prcd-progressive retinal atrophy and primary lens luxation in the Chinese Crested, for neonatal cerebellar cortical degeneration in Beagles, for exercise-induced collapse in Labradors, for polyneuropathy in Leonbergers and for PRA in Golden Retrievers. A control scheme will tackle congenital stationary night blindness in the Briard. All breeding stock must be hereditarily clear or have a DNA test and carriers may be mated only to clears.

The British Veterinary Association/Kennel Club scheme to tackle syringomyelia and chiari-like malformation in Cavaliers, Griffons and other breeds, involving grading of an MRI scan, was launched early in 2012. It is hoped that estimated breeding values can be calculated in an aim to reduce the problem down the generations. The scheme has not been universally welcomed in Cavaliers, at least.

The European Council and European Parliament agreed that controls should be maintained to keep the UK free from the tapeworm echinococcus multilocularis. In other respects the pet travels rules were simplified on January 1, 2012 to harmonise with the rest of Europe, making it significantly easier for dogs to travel into the UK. Animals from the EU and from listed counties such as the US and Australia no longer need to be blood tested and can travel just 21 days after their rabies inoculation.

A number of individuals and organisations, including Dogs Trust, have expressed concern, saying it will be a case of 'when' rather than 'if' the UK gets rabies.

Such fears were exacerbated when someone bought a Malamute, who had allegedly come in from Bulgaria with his littermates, and found that the papers were fake and he was not microchipped. It was also reported that the checking points at Dover were unmanned for much of the time.

The British Veterinary Association has also expressed concern about reports that a significant number of animals coming into the UK are not being checked, especially as the number of dogs travelling has almost doubled in a year. It has asked DEFRA to provide a contact number vets can call if they believe an animal has entered the country without complying with the regulations.

dogworld
we know dogs

subscribe to Britain's favourite canine newspaper and save money

premier subscription: £116

full access: Dog World and the Dog World Annual delivered to your door, the Dog World digital edition plus full access to the Dog World website including breed notes and show reports • pay by direct debit only
All these extras for 3p per week

print subscription: £100

Dog World newspaper delivered direct to your door • pay direct debit only
Pay only £1.93 per issue

digital-only subscription: £60

get Dog World online and save pounds! – this subscription includes digital access to Dog World, the Dog World Annual and full use of the Dog World website including breed notes and show reports • pay by cash/card only
Dog World for only £1.16 a week

Subscription hotline: **01795 592854**

or subscribe online at
www.dogworld.co.uk/Subscribe-now

DIRECT Debit

Bill Glover judged the Agility Championships at Crufts and his winners were: large, Will Rogers and Nedlo Black Magic; medium, Natasha Wise and Ag Ch Raeanne's Flipping Heck; small, Bernadette Bay and Ob Ch Obay Itz Got Pizazz.
photo Walker

The Kennel Club Championship for English Springer Spaniels was won by Andy Whitehouse's FT Ch Doncaster Star.
photo Rawlings

International Gundog League Retriever Champion 2011 was Keith Broomfield's Labrador Kaliture Black Spruce.
photo Rawlings

Ben Randall's FT Ch Heolybwlch Fatty won the Kennel Club Cocker Spaniel Championship for the second year running.
photo Rawlings

Natasha Wise and Ag Ch Raeanne's Flipping Heck have now won the FCI International Agility Championships three times, most recently in the Czech Republic.

News in Brief

Sadly, dog thefts continue to be reported. A high-profile case involved six Tibetan Spaniels from Heather Simper and Liz Scoates' Clydum kennel, including the breed's 2011 top dog. Thankfully all were recovered after an extensive publicity campaign. Even at shows exhibitors need to take care – at Border Union a Cairn Terrier was removed from its bench, eventually being found in another cage, and at Bournemouth a Chihuahua disappeared. It was later recovered in Southampton. A debate ensued on whether exhibitors' passes serve any purpose.

In January the Kennel Club met representatives of the Fédération Cynologique Internationale to discuss the mutual recognition of judges. In 2011 the arrangement whereby the top 16 UK judges could award CACIBs in all breeds which have CCs in Britain came to an end. It is hoped a way forward can be found.

No year would be complete without the RSPCA slamming breeders. At the end of 2011 the charity announced that puppies are suffering because they are bred for their looks rather than health, welfare and temperament. The Kennel Club immediately fought back.

The RSPCA is aiming to end the euthanasia of rehomable animals by 2017.

It has a new chief executive, Gavin Grant, returning to the charity after 21 years. In 1989 he had caused a stir with the infamous 'mountain of dead dogs' display at Crufts which brought him into strong conflict with the KC officials of the time. He appears to have mellowed somewhat and now hopes the two organisations can find some common ground.

Young Kennel Club membership starts at six years old. Children younger than that are now catered for by the Rufus Club, aimed to be 'the perfect place to introduce young members of the family to the wonderful world of dogs'.

The Kennel Club has decided the Kooikerhondje, Lagotto Romagnolo and Spanish Water Dog from the gundog to the working group in 2014. The issue arose because of the possibility the breeds might one day get CC status, in which case there would need to be breed-specific working events which judges could attend and where dogs could qualify for a champion title. The breed clubs had suggested formats for such events but the KC felt that the type of work suggested was 'not that which might be expected of a gundog'.

Inevitably this caused considerable consternation among breed people who are by now used to being in the gundog group. Previous communications from the KC had not led them to believe such a change was contemplated. The KC was expecting this reaction and said it would listen to appeals; each breed has now appealed and these are being considered by the KC as we go to press.

The Club Français du Bullmastiff et du Mastiff,
invites to its major 2013 events.

The Championnat de France on Saturday 1st of June
in Marseille

The Nationale Championship show on September 21 & 22
In 2012, 103 Mastiffs and 92 Bullmastiffs
were entered at the Club Show

Metz International Meeting on November 1st, 2nd & 3rd
Seminar and 2 specialties

Information on the Club website http://www.mastiff-bullmastiff.com
to subscribe to the Club and receive
the Club magazine: Amclass@aol.com

CF
BM

**Club Français
du Bullmastiff et du Mastiff**

Welcome in France!

The French silent film *The Artist* took the Oscars by storm, winning best picture among many other awards. Much of its charm derived from the delightful canine star played by Uggie the Jack Russell, seen with the show's leading lady Bérenice Bejo. The nine-year-old former rescue dog paid a flying visit to London where he attended a charity screening of the film in aid of Dogs Trust. He is pictured (right) with the trust's chief executive Clarissa Baldwin along with Freddie, another Jack Russell who was rehomed through the trust and now lives with Clarissa's son.

Paula Scott's Pointer Barley, who regularly visits a care home's patients with dementia, is HiLife Pets As Therapy Dog of the Year.

Kathy Ingham, who has four times been runner-up, won the Obedience Championship for Bitches with Ob Ch Ruskath Portent Image. Lyn Tozer was the judge. Kathy last won a Crufts Championship 31 years ago. Jen Jessup, next year's judge, and manager of the Welsh team who won the inter-regional competition, presented the trophy.
photo Harris

At Crufts the Obedience Championship for Dogs was won by Christine Roberts' Ob Ch Bheinn It's Cuddly He's Dudley, pictured here with trophy presenter Dennis Ashley and judge Lyn Tozer.
photo Harris

Winners of the Kennel Club Working Trials Championships were Andy Baker's WT Ch Sid The Lemons Squeezer (TD) (above right) and Les Payne's WT Ch Little Rough Rhinestone (PD).
photos Beasley

Popular winner of Crufts' Friends For Life competition was Buster, an English Sprtinger owned by RAF Police Sgt Michael Barrow. He is an explosives sniffer dog, now retired, who did several tours of duty in Afghanistan. Actress and comedian Jennifer Saunders made the presentation.

News in Brief

Breed clubs will be allowed to hold a class for champions at their shows, separate from the main judging and with a separate judge, in which case being beaten in the champions class would not preclude a dog being regarded as unbeaten if it did well in the main show. Several clubs already hold special classes together with the club show, giving another judge the chance to build up a CV.

The Kennel Club Charitable Trust has launched awards to provide funding for individuals carrying out innovative research to improve dog health. The Lifetime Achievement Award carries a £10,000 prize fund, the International Prize in Canine Health £40,000 and the Student Inspiration Award £10,000. The awards are underwritten by Shirley and Vernon Hill; he is the founder of Metro Bank.

The Kennel Club is to refuse to register the progeny of matings in any breed in which both parents are merle or dapple. Already in some breeds, where merle does not naturally occur, the KC will not register puppies of that colour; French Bulldogs have been added to this list. Bearded Collies appear to be an exception, and people within the breed protested strongly about a plan to allow registration of merles.

Many regretted that the dog world did not do more to celebrate the fact that 2012 was Olympic Year for London. Here footballer Michael Owen carries the Olympic flame through Battersea Dogs and Cats Home, accompanied by Rory, a Staffordshire Bull Terrier seeking a home, while Sally Hyder and her Canine Partner Harmony carried the flame along Edinburgh's Royal Mile. At the games themselves, former Kennel Club employee Crista Cullen was a member of the British women's hockey team which took a bronze medal.

2012 was of course the diamond jubilee year for the Queen. She is pictured meeting Hounds for Heroes' Allen Parton and his assistance dog EJ at a meeting at the Houses of Parliament. Later, at a charity golf match she chatted, about Corgis no doubt, with the US' Peter Green and Beth Sweigart.
photo Menaker

John Tovey's Labrador Dez has been declared Guide Dog of the Year.

English Springer Theo, a working dog with the Royal Army Veterinary Corps who died within hours of his handler Lance Corporal Liam Tasker being killed in Afghanistan, has been awarded a posthumous Dickin Medal by the PDSA.

Celia Bourne, the exceptionally caring dog warden for South Gloucestershire Council, won the Kerry Williamson Memorial Award for an 'unsung hero' of the world of dogs. Kerry's husband Adrian Willson made the presentation.
photo Walker

News in Brief

The topic of benching is a perennial one with a large proportion unoccupied at all the shows. This was especially evident at Belfast where the benching has to be imported at considerable expense yet is little used; shows run under Irish KC rules do not have benching and seem to cope!

The Kennel Club is to try a two-year experiment of allowing certain championship shows to do away with benching. However this will not start until 2014 and will apply only to shows with fewer than 1,200 entries, which currently applies only to Scottish Breeds and Hound Association of Scotland.

The number of dog bite victims admitted to hospital rose by a third in four years, NHS statistics revealed. Under tens were the most likely group to suffer severe injuries, and the Kennel Club called for greater awareness of child safety around dogs.

A fire at a kennel in Ireland killed 14 show dogs of various breeds. They were in the care of handling team Justin and Dorothea Carroll. Among them was the German Shepherd who has taken three Top Dog all breeds awards in Norway, Zanta av Quantos, and well known dogs in Afghans, Sealyhams, Pembroke Corgis and Spanish Water Dogs, among other breeds.

The Kennel Club and National Dog Warden Association are launching the UK's first qualification for dog wardens, recognised by City & Guilds.

The Dog World Award of Excellence went to Trevor and Birgit Hayward, tremendously successful breeders of the Foxearth Smooth Collies and Miniature Wire Dachshunds. Their helpfulness to other breeders and brave fight back after a car accident made them extra worthy winners. Simon Parsons (centre) presented the trophy.
photo Walker

TOP DOG PRODUCTS **100%** guaranteed for your complete satisfaction.

Perfect Health & Condition
For all dogs, from Pet to Show Champion.

SUPPLEX - Mobility

From the hundreds of joint care products, which do you choose? SUPPLEX plus HA offers your dog the very best veterinary spec joint mobility formula at an affordable price.

Each 755mg capsule contains:

- **250mg - Glucosamine HCl**
- **300mg - MSM pure**
- **200mg - Marine Chondroitin**
- **5mg - Hyaluronic Acid (HA)**

The 120 capsules pack offers 2 months maintenance for a 25kg dog.

Available as capsules or powder.

NATURAL CALM - Calmer

For stressful periods including shows, fireworks, training and travel. Suitable for long or short term use without side effects.

PREBIOTICS - Digestion

Effective in assisting with digestive problems (persistent loose/jelly motions) and recovery after illness.

MOBILEAZE - Mobility

100% natural - maintains mobility and optimum joint function.

Rich in silica which helps protect cartilage and lubricate joints.

The 250ml pack should last a 10kg (22lb) dog over 6 months*!!!

MONTMORILLONITE

Far more effective than kaolin.

VITALCOAT - Skin & Coat

Palatable combination of fish and vegetable oils, essential fatty acids, vitamins and starflower oil (highest GLA), in a convenient pump pack.

BENEFITS - show winning glossy coat, healthy skin and maintains mobility in older dogs.

PREVENTS - greasy coat, scaly or itchy skin and excessive moulting.

The 250ml pack should last 20kg (22lb) dog over 8 months!!!.

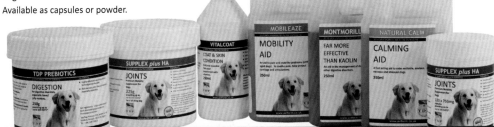

BUY 2 GET THE 3RD **FREE** Cheapest Item Free

Order Hotline: 01508 530813. Secure online ordering: www.aviform.co.uk

TDP, Aviform Ltd, FREEPOST NATE 944, Long Stratton, NORWICH, NR15 2BR. (no stamp req'd)   E&OE

The Dog World in 2012

Dr Ruth Barbour stepped down after 23 years on the Kennel Club General Committee, and from the Dog Health Group and the Finance and General Purposes Sub-Committee. She made an enormous contribution to the club's work, especially in the field of training, education and breed Standards. Valerie Foss has retired from the General Committee under the 75-year rule. She too has made a big impact on the club's activities in many areas, not least with the library and gallery and through the Young KC.

One of the dog world's best loved personalities, Marion Spavin, announced her retirement from judging, and later in the year friends helped her celebrate her ninetieth birthday with a big party. She is pictured with Kay Baillie, Marina Scott, Simon Parsons, Adrian Marett and Stuart Baillie of DOG WORLD.

Four new members were elected to the Kennel Club General Committee: David Guy of the Donzeata Griffons, secretary of Darlington and now, since the retirement of Ellis Hulme, chairman of UK Toy, Mark Cocozza of the Freecloud Afghans and other breeds, Paul Harding of the Pringham Bulldogs and French Bulldogs and Manchester secretary, and Jan Wood of the Ardencote Whippets, Greyhounds, English Springers and Parson Russells.

Miriam and Norman Butcher (seated) celebrated an astonishing 50 years as joint secretaries/treasurers of the Poodle Club. Norman is still a committee member and Miriam remains as treasurer.
photo Dove

Dog World columnist Dr Mike Tempest of the Mikudi Tibetan Terriers in Ireland has been made an Associate of the Royal Agricultural Societies'(Royal of England, Royal Welsh, Royal Highland and Royal Ulster), in recognition of distinguished achievement in the agricultural industry.

Maureen Hennis has retired as chief executive of Pets As Therapy. She has been involved with the concept since its foundation nearly 30 years ago.

Leta Ogwen-Jones, patron and former president of the Midland and Northern Counties French Bulldog Club, celebrated her hundredth birthday.

Patron Aileen Speding was the first recipient of the British Collie Club's lifetime achievement award. Secretary Duna Jones made the presentation.

Jim Nixon has retired after 18 years as Paignton's chairman. David Creech has succeeded him.

Former Belfast secretary Jackie Stubbs has returned to the post after a gap of several years.
photo Crawford-Manton

News in Brief

The Kennel Club has agreed to accept registrations of imported Irish Red and White Setters which have been crossed with Irish Setters. In effect it had no choice, as the Irish KC had already agreed to the crossbreeding programme, but UK breed clubs were not happy.

The topic of people judging and their partners exhibiting at the same show was discussed even more than usual during the year, coming to prominence on several occasions, such as at Crufts when someone judged a group and his partner competed in the group immediately following; at a show when a leading dog normally handled by the day's group judge still competed in the breed; and when a dog won the group but was withdrawn the next day from BIS as the exhibitor's husband was judging another of the groups.

The Kennel Club has taken over the governance of the sport of rally from the Association of Pet Dog Trainers. Very popular in the US, its resembles a cross between obedience and agility, with competitors following a signed course involving up to 50 different exercises.

Britain has a new Kennel Club-recognised breed, the Turkish Kangal Dog. In reality this means splitting the Anatolian Shepherd Dog breed into two types; owners have until April 1 to apply to have their ASD reclassified as a TKD.

Boxer enthusiast Kian Pellow won the Young Kennel Club's Shaun McAlpine Award, from the six-11 years class. He was presented with the trophy by Shaun's parents, Ed and Cindy.
photo Siddle

Young Kennel Club Agility Dog of the Year was Chloe Marchon with Cloudtenn Fuel For Life.
photo Walker.

Winners of the Good Citizen Dog Scheme Pre-Beginner Obedience Stakes final at Crufts were Rachel Spencer and Littlethorn Colt at Tobermoray.
photo Walker

Winner of the Inter-Regional Obedience competition at Crufts, judged by Anita Neal, was the Southern team by just one point. Team manager was Fred Burns and members were Sharan Wicks with Lupitoonz Boo Boo Ballistic, Nicola Linbourne with Morillo Supa Star D J, Lorraine Gardner with Kiyonari Look No Further, Sue Howard with Cleynehage J U Box, Lesley Holmes with Campresse Weymouth Wonder, Fran Godfrey with Kings Farm Carbon Copy at Sunridge, Sheila Rodger with Pepsanner Tazmania, and reserve, Jean Ennis with Wienbridge Elsa. Vince Hogan represented *Our Dogs*.
photo Harris

Winners of the flyball final at Crufts were the Broxburn Flyers Dog Training Club. This team also won in 2009 and three of that team are still members.
photo Walker

Winners of the the international heelwork to music competition at Crufts were Thierry Thomas from France and Ubac du Mas de la Rabeyrine; freestyle, Sue Betteridge and Glenapline Katie; and heelwork to music, Heather Smith with Moonlight Magic Dancer.
photo Walker

The Dog World in 2012

Ch Belroyd Pemcader Cymro, owned by Kevin Dover(handling), Allan Taylor and Idris Jones, is the first Cardigan Corgi to take RBIS at a UK general championship show which he did at Manchester under Ann Arch. With them are show manager Eric Broadhurst and chairman Bob Gregory. Sadly Idris died later in the year.
photo Johnson

The first Large Munsterlander to win a UK championship show group is Robert and Tracey Hargreaves' Sh Ch Ghyllbeck Rapax who won at the National under Andrew Brace.
photo Johnson

First black and tan Griffon to win a group is Barbara Murray's smooth Ch Beauview Brave As A Blizzard. Judge here is Jill Peak.
photo Johnson

Princess Michael of Kent attended a ball held to raise funds for Battersea Dogs' and Cats' home in its 150th year.

The first DOG WORLD Rescue Symposium was hailed as a great success. Pictured are managing director Stuart Baillie, rescue correspondent Geraldine Cove-Print, Natasha Cooper of Lincs, Essex and Trent Boxer Welfare and dog law expert Trevor Cooper.

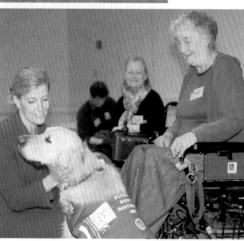

Best in show winner at Premier Groom was Linda Barker.

Alison Rogers won the British Dog Grooming Championships, having topped two of the classes.

The Earl and Countess of Wessex visited the Canine Partners charity as part of the royal jubilee celebrations. The Countess is pictured with Sue Sherlock and Lancelot.

Jitka Krizova was best in show at Mastergroom, after winning two of the six categories.
photo Beck

Young Kennel Club National Show Handler of the Year was Ella Armstrong. Judge of the Crufts final was Leila Tarabad and on the left is Marina Scott representing sponsor DOG WORLD.
photo Siddle

Gary Gray judged the Junior Handler of the Year final at Discover Dogs and chose Abbie Stoutt handling the Siberian Husky whom she had made a champion during the year. Stuart Baillie (left) represented sponsor DOG WORLD.
photo Waddell

KYC member Amelia Siddle, featured in last year's *Annual*, was commissioned to paint the 2012 Crufts BIS winner. During the year Amelia won two groups handling her mother's Pointer Sh Ch Wilchrimane Ice Maiden, who also topped the Young Kennel Club stakes final at Crufts under Valerie Foss.
photo Walker

Winner of the first Welsh Junior Handler of the Year competition was Catrin Roberts, seen with judge Sue Whitehead and organiser Dr Philippa Pearson.
photo Harris

Crufts chairman Gerald King presents the YCK's John McDougall award to Tom Stannage. Mr King has now become chairman of the YKC, succeeding Valerie Foss who becomes president.
photo Dog World

Scottish Junior Handler of the Year 2011 was Ashley Place judged by ex-junior handler Seonaid Macandrew. With them is vice-convener Chris Holmes.
photo Dalrymple

Espen Engh from Norway judged the International Junior Handler of the Year final at Crufts and selected Raquel Colaço from Portugal.
photo Walker

Juniors expand their horizons

Marina Scott talks to three younger exhibitors who have interests beyond the UK show scene

Fran McWade

– scanning bags at the Olympics

Fran the Olympic volunteer.

Young Kennel Club member and Papillon exhibitor Fran McWade, 19, from Crowthorne in Berkshire, tells me why showing dogs helped her spend the 2012 summer as a volunteer for the London Olympics.

After a very long and stressful process I was finally deployed to the Lee Valley White Water Rafting Centre to become part of the London 2012 Olympic Games!

Before I was employed by G4S I had to pass my SIA door supervision course that would give me a licence which would enable me to become part of a security team. After my success at passing with 85/91 I was given physical and theory training in PSA (pedestrian search area), body search, bag search and patrolling.

I was also chosen to become an x-ray scanner so I was given further training, with many assessments in which you had to gain high pass marks to proceed to the next set of training and assessments.

After all my training was completed and I had successfully passed I was able to control and identify images from a Rapiscan x-ray machine. I found this extremely interesting and exciting, especially as it has now given me another future career option in HM Customs.

My first day was really nerve-racking. I was put on to the screening area where all the officials came through, so I met the press, athletes, referees, coaches, trainers, physiotherapists and any other important people!

After a couple of hours, I felt really comfortable and I loved scanning the bags, ensuring no one was brining in any prohibited items, and when I was on bag search I had to search the bags that had suspicious items in or were too cluttered to see clearly on the x-ray screen. I had to search the bags of one of the athletes from Slovenia; while I was doing so he asked for my number!

On one of my shifts on x-ray I came across a rubber duck in someone's bag which was very amusing!

On another occasion a blind man with his guide dog had to pass through the body metal detector. I was on body search at

Abigail Goree

6-11 years
Bracco Italiano
Bonario
Berlesque

Abi and Sienna have had a very successful year with a win at Crufts in the BASC young handler class and many placings in handling and breed classes throughout 2012.

Alice Potter

6-11 Years
Cocker Spaniel
Chancegate Blue Lancer

©Johnson

Congratulations Alice, achieving **3rd at Richmond, 2nd at Crufts YKC Handling, Winning YKC Handling at West Country, National Gundog, Driffield**, and many others wins and placings in Gundog Handling this year!

51

The White Water Rafting Centre where Fran worked during the Olympics.

Emily Adams

Dobermann
Ourouse Miss MoneyPenni JW
'Missy'

Congratulations Emily and Missy on your 2nd place achievement, at your first 12-16 Working Group JHA Semi-Final at Richmond

We are so very proud of you both

the time and his dog set off the machine! I was secretly glad because that meant I was able to search the dog. It was lucky I was on body search as I'm sure other people may not have known how to search the dog or where to start. I searched the dog as if I was a judge.

My knowledge of being a dog handler also helped me keep the situation under control, I knew guide dogs were working dogs so you are not supposed to distract them while working so I ensured I stayed professional and got the job done as quickly and as thoroughly as possible.

Many young people at dog shows have exceptional communication skills with adults and officials; when I first started handling and I first met Marina Scott I was so nervous because I had read her book and she was like a celebrity to me!

MIN WITHEYMAN

JHA 1st at LKA, Bournemouth, WKC, YKC 1st at National Terrier, Bournemouth, WKC and Crufts
Thanks to all judges and everyone who has helped Min
RCC at Three Counties under judge Robert Ross

©Johnson

HOLLY LAMBERT

16 years old with Pomeranian
BENLEASE ACE OF SPADES AT POMSTAR ShCM

Well done Holly on your 3rd place at Richmond. All our love Mum and Dad

After some time of meeting top breeders and handlers, I became very confident at speaking to important people in the dog world and because of this I felt that I was able to stay polite and professional in front of the athletes and officials. I was able to speak to them clearly and I didn't get nervous.

I have always seen and heard junior handlers being polite, thoughtful, helpful and knowledgeable. I really do think the skills we learn while handling, such as patience, pride, looking presentable, winning, losing, animal behaviour, welfare and geography, give us exceptional skills when it comes to our futures. For example, at job interviews I always have the brightest suits!

Driving, we know where all the main roads are so travelling becomes much easier and less stressful. Knowing how to lose is a very valuable lesson; we learn to not feel too disappointed and we can learn from our mistakes or improve our performance for next time!

Lucy Hankey
– success in disciplines galore

Ever tried to train in more than one canine discipline? Lucy Hankey, 16, from Twickenham, explains how she finds time to compete in heelwork to music to handling and grooming to Cani-X.

I live with four dogs – Beagles Bertie, eight, and Missy, four, a rescue Lurcher called Willow who is 13, and Sam the Border Collie who is one year old. My friends think the dog sports are cool but a bit mad too! I'm taking my GCSEs now and particularly enjoy textiles.

My life involving competitive dog sports started when I was

Fran handling at Crufts.

Lucy and her team.

five, initially trying junior handling and breed classes with my grandma's two Chihuahuas. This keen interest inspired me to get my own dog to train and eventually show, so I saved my money for two years until I got my Beagle Bertie (Simeldaka Mosta Lad).

Training with Felicity Freer at Rushmoor Ringcraft, we entered many junior handling competitions and stakes classes and managed to make it to Crufts every year in either discipline. In 2006, we won our JHA class at Richmond and were placed fifth at the UK Junior Handler of the Year final.

At this stage my canine interests started to broaden, and I started attending agility classes with Bert and nine-year-old Poppy, who both absolutely loved it. In typical fashion, Poppy showed the Collies how it was done!

After seeing Mary Ray and Richard Curtis (both of whom I really

Practising their heelwork to music moves.

Melissa Phillips

– on the Irish Circuit

Melissa Phillips, 15, from Pontypridd, Mid Glamorgan explains what it was like spending the summer in the Emerald Isle for the famous Irish Circuit with her Kooikerhondje, Buddie.

On August 16, Buddie and I travelled down to Port Talbot to meet friends who I was going to be travelling and staying with during the Munster Circuit. The ferry took four and a half hours and unfortunately I didn't get a wink of sleep due to somebody snoring extremely loudly.

A green star win for Buddie and Melissa.

look up to) on the TV, I was keen on getting my Beagle to 'dance' like the professionals, which, as you'd imagine, is quite hard with a stubborn scenthound!

Since then I have done many charity demonstrations at shows and fairs. As my passion for heelwork to music increased I craved competing and couldn't manage that with Bert, so I borrowed my trainer's dog at the BMC academy, Jake a Border Collie, and we succeeded at many competitions including winning at Crufts two years running.

Now I have Sam (Moshanta Midnight Whisper), my own Border Collie whom I train in various disciplines: HTM, freestyle, Cani-X and a little obedience. He's won every HTM competition we've entered to date!

I also train and take part in Cani-X, with our other Beagle Missy (Simeldaka Wardija Lady) and take her along to our local park to run every Saturday, where's she's quite a hit with the other runners!

This year I was nominated for and won my age category in the Shaun McAlpine award, which was an honour. I also tried a few grooming competitions and achieved fourth at Crufts this year, where two weeks' work experience at a dog groomers came in handy!

At Clonmel, Buddie was graded excellent and was awarded his first green star and best of breed under Pascual Asensi Peinado. I was in shock as I stepped out of the ring as this was my first green star that I had ever had!

While I was in the handling classes it started to drizzle slightly so I had my first taste of showing in the rain but unfortunately we weren't placed. My first day of Irish showing went successfully although our gazebo broke!

The second show was Killarney where again Buddie and I had a successful day gaining another excellent, green star and best of breed, this time under Chris Laverty. I also handled two Tibetan Spaniels for Lorna and Brian Locke whom I was staying with. Buster gained a second in open dog and Fanwy gained a third in junior bitch. In the handling Buddie and I gained a fifth.

Melissa also handled a brace of Tibetan Spaniels.

On August 23, we travelled to Limerick where Buddie was graded 'very good' due to backing away from the judge but was placed first in his class. I handled the Tibetan Spaniels again but this time Buster had first in open dog and Fanwy third under Ann Rode.

The last show, Tralee, was very successful with Buddie taking his third green star and best of breed under Catherine Collins and he was also shortlisted to the last six in the group! I handled Buster to third in the handling and went in the brace stakes with the Tibetan Spaniels and gained a respectable second.

Ireland's shows are extremely different from those in the UK, all shows being outside with no undercover shelter/rings – if it rained you got wet! The grading system was extremely good and should be introduced into the UK. Lastly, Irish people are very welcoming and friendly.

Note to anyone going to Ireland remember your wellies and gazebo! Hopefully I'll be going over to finish off Buddie's Irish champion title next year.

Ireland is beautiful and an experience I won't be forgetting soon. Make sure you go to Blarney Castle to kiss the Blarney Stone for luck!

TALITHA MASSEY

BOYNHAMS UTTER NUTTER RAGEMMA JW

RINGLANDS RAINBOWS TO CHASE

Judge Shannon Roberts

In 2012 Talitha Massey has again reached the final line-up in her Group in both the JHA Semi-finals and the Crufts YKC finals

Former Papillon Junior Handler of the Year, Talitha was last year the Overall Winner of her Group at South Coast Handler of the Year

ELISE O'CONNOR

6-11 Years Utility

Tibetan Terrier
Khados Dancing Bear

Congratulations

2nd Place JHA Semi-Finals

Panda has been exclusively trained and handled by Elise to numerous wins in JHA and YKC Handling classes this year

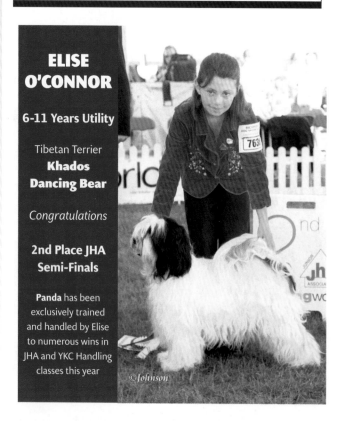

©Johnson

JAMES WINKLEY-BALMER
11 years

Whippet
Ch Crosscop Brilliant That's Me

James has never been placed at Richmond before as this is his first time. He got Dave his Whippet at the end of March and started handling soon after. His first big show was SKC in May where he managed a 2nd in YKC handling, then Border Union where he was placed 1st in JHA class, then onto Leeds where he was 1st in his YKC class thus qualifying him for Crufts. James has also won handling classes at some of our more local open shows and breed classes.

A study in line-breeding
The Lythwood Shetland Sheepdogs

ONE OF Britain's most exceptional dog-breeding achievements must surely be to produce eight homebred champion males in direct line.

We know of only two kennels to have achieved this, Osman Sameja's Ozmilion Yorkshire Terriers – indeed their line stretched for even more generations – and the Lythwood Shetland Sheepdogs bred and owned by Derek and Phyllis Rigby.

Their first was Ch Lythwood Brandy Snap born in 1971, and the line continues down to the current males Chs Scooby Doo and Starlight Express, both made up in the last two years.

Derek has been fascinated by livestock breeding and showing since he was a child, starting with mice, guinea pigs and rabbits, producing a best in show winner at Bradford, the 'Crufts of rabbits', while still a schoolboy. Today he is showing a Holstein calf who represented Shropshire at the All England Championships.

Through his friend Cyril Stanley he was introduced to the dog world. His first interest was Collies but realising you could take two Shelties where you could take one Collie, he opted for the smaller breed and started with a Moldeva bitch 53 years ago. His first efforts didn't get him where he wanted, so he obtained another Moldeva from different lines, mated her into the famous Riverhill strain, and so began the Lythwoods.

This led down to Brandy Snap, a double grandson of the great sire Ch Jefsfire Freelancer and from several generations of Lythwood bitches.

A little later he used the famous Ch Sandpiper of Sharval and produced Ch Lythwood Sky Master. Ever since, combining the Brandy Snap and Sky Master descendants has proved an infallible recipe for success for the kennel, meaning that for each of their champion males, they have had a bitch of suitable breeding to complement him and carry on the line.

Very seldom has there been any need to buy in, or to use outside studs, but in recent times the Lythwoods have co-operated with several other kennels to mutual benefit.

In total the Lythwoods have now produced 33 UK champions, a number of whom have had a significant impact on the breed. Although groups have been won, the champions are seldom campaigned much beyond

compiled by Simon Parsons, with help from Aud Jorun Lie

The Mid Western Shetland Sheepdog Club honoured Phyllis and Derek Rigby for their achievement in producing eight generations of champion males.

their title. "A champion is only as good as what it reproduces," says Derek.

Priorities in their breeding plan are to maintain the classic British type, elegant, agile and not heavy, with the ability to twist and turn as a working sheepdog would need to do, 'a racehorse not a carthorse', along with the true head and expression. A strict eye is kept on size, and all the dogs are measured.

It helps that the kennel has the space to run on puppies for several months – the breed is notorious for being hard to pick as babies!

Although the dogs are in Derek's name – he compounded the affix for life when it cost seven shillings and sixpence – Phyllis plays just as significant a part in the story and both have judged round the world.

Their advice to breeders of the future: "You've got to have an eye for the overall picture you are aiming for, and don't run to the latest winner – look at what a dog is producing before you use him."

Featured on these pages are eight consecutive male champions, plus Sky Master – who was tied with his ancestor Freelancer as the breed's leading sire of champions for many years until this was recently topped by his great-grandson Shelridge Socrates – and Ch Lythwood Stage Wispa of Tegwel, the only Sheltie bitch to produce five UK champions, from three litters by Ch Lythwood Steptoe.

CH LYTHWOOD SKY MASTER, born May 1, 1981		
Ch Sandpiper of Sharval	Ch Sharval The Delinquent	Carousel of Melvaig
		Sharval Cilla Black
	Chamwood Gay Girl	Ch Rodhill Burnt Sugar
		Lingsacre Mandarin
Lythwood Snaffey	Ch Lythwood Snaffels	Ch Mistmere Marching Orders
		Drannoc Silhouette of Lythwood
	Lythwood Spree	Heathlow Harvest Time at Lythwood
		Lythwood Sundorne

CH LYTHWOOD STAGE WISPA AT TEGWEL, born April 11, 1993		
Tegwel Gold Sovereign of Sherringwood	Tegwel Gold Delegate at Allanvail	Lythwood Sandbagger of Tegwel
		Allanvail Gold Pearl at Tegwel
	Tegwel Seed Pearl	Ch Lythwood Sky Master
		Allanvail Gold Pearl at Tegwel
Lythwood Some Girl	Ch Lythwood Scrabble	Ch Lythwood Spruce
		Ch Lythwood Seanymph
	Lythwood Sky Train	Ch Lythwood Sky Master
		Ch Lythwood Seanymph

Eight generations of champion male Shetland Sheepdogs bred at Lythwood

CH LYTHWOOD BRANDY SNAP, born June 27, 1971

Jefsfire Allanvail Gold Spark	Ch Jefsfire Freelancer	Glenmist Golden Falcon
		Ch Heathlow Luciana
	Benvaila Crystal	Heathlow Sumburgh Marcus
		Heylens Christie
Lythwood Bonnie	Ch Jefsfire Freelancer	Glenmist Golden Falcon
		Ch Heathlow Luciana
	Lythwood Signorina	Choirboy of Heranmine
		Lythwood Sandpiper

CH LYTHWOOD SPRUCE, born August 10, 1977

Ch Lythwood Saga	Ch Lythwood Brandy Snap	Jefsfire Allanvail Gold Spark
		Lythwood Bonnie
	Lythwood Sayonaries	Heathlow Harvest Time at Lythwood
		Lythwood Solidus (by Salvador)
Lythwood Spree	Heathlow Harvest Time at Lythwood	Riverhill Right Time
		Upperslaughter Amanda
	Lythwood Sundorne	Lythwood Salvador (by Brandy Snap)
		Lythwood Sugar (by Brandy Snap)

CH LYTHWOOD SAGA, born September 16, 1976

Ch Lythwood Brandy Snap	Jefsfire Allanvail Gold Spark	Ch Jefsfire Freelancer
		Benvaila Crystal
	Lythwood Bonnie	Ch Jefsfire Freelancer
		Lythwood Signorina
Lythwood Sayonaries	Heathlow Harvest Time at Lythwood	Riverhill Right Time
		Upperslaughter Amanda
	Lythwood Solidus	Lythwood Salvador (by Brandy Snap)
		Lythwood Heida (by Brandy Snap)

CH LYTHWOOD SCRABBLE, born May 4, 1984

Ch Lythwood Spruce	Ch Lythwood Saga	Ch Lythwood Brandy Snap
		Lythwood Sayonaries (by Harvest Time)
	Lythwood Spree	Heathlow Harvest Time at Lythwood
		Lythwood Sundorne (by Salvador)
Ch Lythwood Sea Nymph	Heathlow Harvest Time at Lythwood	Riverhill Right Time
		Upperslaughter Amanda
	Lythwood Tar Baby	Ch Riverhill Ringmaster
		Lythwood Twiggy

CH LYTHWOOD STEPTOE, born July 18, 1988

Ch Lythwood Scrabble	Ch Lythwood Spruce	Ch Lythwood Saga	
		Lythwood Spree (by Harvest Time)	
	Ch Lythwood Sea Nymph	Heathlow Harvest Time at Lythwood	
		Lythwood Tar Baby	
Lythwood Sea Urchin	Ch Lythwood Sky Master	Ch Sandpiper of Sharval	
		Lythwood Snaffey (ex Spree)	
	Ch Lythwood Sea Nymph	Heathlow Harvest Time at Lythwood	
		Lythwood Tar Baby	

CH LYTHWOOD SACHA, born June 16, 2004

Ch Lythwood Shalako	Ch Lythwood Steptoe	Ch Lythwood Scrabble	
		Lythwood Sea Urchin	
	Ch Lythwood Stage Wispa at Tegwel	Tegwel Gold Soverign of Sherringwood	
		Lythwood Some Girl	
Lythwood Scarlet Ribbon	Moonlight Black Magic	Follyfox Firecracker	
		Morestyle Fleur De Noel of Terriwood	
	Lythwood Spritzer at Terriwood	Brilyn Hellraiser at Tegwel	
		Lythwood She's So Lucky	

CH LYTHWOOD SHALAKO, born February 9, 2000
One of five champions bred the same way

Ch Lythwood Steptoe	Ch Lythwood Scrabble	Ch Lythwood Spruce	
		Ch Lythwood Sea Nymph (by Harvest Time)	
	Lythwood Sea Urchin	Ch Lythwood Sky Master	
		Ch Lythwood Sea Nymph (by Harvest Time)	
Ch Lythwood Stage Wispa at Tegwel	Tegwel Gold Sovereign of Sherringwood	Tegwel Gold Delgate of Allanvail	
		Tegwel Seed Pearl (by Sky Master)	
	Lythwood Some Girl	Ch Lythwood Scrabble	
		Lythwood Sky Train (Sky Master ex Sea Nymph)	

CH LYTHWOOD STARLIGHT EXPRESS, born July 26, 2007

Ch Lythwood Sacha	Ch Lythwood Shalako	Ch Lythwood Steptoe	
		Ch Lythwood Stage Wispa at Tegwel	
	Lythwood Scarlet Ribbon	Moonlight Black Magic	
		Lythwood Spritzer at Terriwood	
Lythwood Shakira	Ch Burnmist Midnight Dancer at Lysebourne	Duchesnay Raindancer	
		Burnmist Darling Daisy	
	Lythwood Special K	Ch Lythwood Steptoe	
		Ch Lythwood Stage Wispa at Tegwel	

by Kennel Club
chairman Steve Dean

Reasons for optimism

Given the dreadful weather during 2012, the introduction of veterinary checks on the bests of breed from 'high profile' breeds and the downward trend in show entries, are there any reasons to be cheerful about the pedigree dog scene?

If you allow the newspapers and the doomsayers to help form your opinion the answer might well be no. However when taking a wider look at what is going on in the community and by speaking to grass roots people, a different view emerges.

The British character

During August the British showed how they can get behind an initiative and make it work. The example is of course the Olympics and Paralympics which were unrivalled successes.

Before the events the media were predicting doom and gloom and even now are still looking for a downside. One significant success factor was the enthusiasm of the large team of volunteers who helped make the games run smoothly and, of course, Team GB who rose to the challenge so superbly.

There are some similarities with the dog fancy here. Our circuit of events is run very successfully by dedicated volunteers and generally dog events run very smoothly. This year the weather certainly stretched resources and patience to the maximum at many of our shows but this did not stop them being enjoyable and successful.

Despite heavy rain and flooding, event organisers rose the challenge and in most cases overcame adversity. We may not have always enjoyed every day to the full but clearly dog people were determined to make the most of what was available.

Some very big national outdoor events were cancelled in 2012 but we lost only part of one major general championship show because of bad weather. Attending Blackpool on the first day, I thought it was amazing how those there made the best of it and completed the first day. Cancellation of the remainder of the show was inevitable for, historically, only Noah has demonstrated the foresight and strategy to survive violent tempest and flood and he had advice from on high.

The same attitude was demonstrated by the organisers of the International Agility

Manchester University Museum hosted an exhibition entitled The British and their Dogs, including items lent by Manchester Dog Show Society, the Kennel Club and the Natural History Museum. A number of show dogs attended the opening: pictured here are Paul Harding, Tom Mather, Chris Amoo, Steve Dean, Lindsay Pemberton, Valerie Foss and Andrew Dawson.

Festival dealt with a venue crisis and, in the space of a day, found a new site and went on to set up an international event successfully, receiving much praise in the process. Being there to witness the first day I saw just how fortunate we are to have skilful, willing volunteers who can face adversity so cheerfully and win through.

High profile breeds

The high profile breeds were dealt a significant setback when six of their bests of breed failed the veterinary check at Crufts. The emotional outburst was predictable and plenty of comment has been written throughout the year about personal emotions.

Some predict the end of dog showing as we know it; however the breeds affected have acted very positively and re-energised their efforts to demonstrate how seriously they have taken up the challenge of improving health.

On a personal level there have been several vigorous and constructive exchanges but the vast majority of those involved have been positive about finding solutions.

Crufts revealed a key issue centred predominantly around the conformation of eyelids and the associated clinical signs that tend to accompany a defective ability to blink. A series of seminars with the breeds, judges and the veterinary profession has already facilitated good progress and this is quite evident in the show ring.

By focusing on the few failures there is a danger of missing how, overall this year, the pass rate has been outstandingly good. This has demonstrated to the world at large that these breeds are not overwhelmed with poor health as some have claimed, at least at the level of the show community.

This has all been very helpful in seeking to move attention to the important source of poor health in purebred dogs. The core of any breed is unlikely to be deliberately producing unhealthy dogs yet they are the target of nearly all criticism. However, the largely unregulated breeders, who do not register their dogs with the Kennel Club, are the greater risk for producing dogs with poor health and using low standards for breeding and rearing puppies.

Falling show entries

The weather has not helped the attendance at dog shows but it is more likely that the economic climate is having the most effect on entries. The cost of fuel makes travel ever more expensive and therefore several shows have seen reduced entries although some have managed to keep the decline to modest levels.

The debate arising from this fall off in entries has pointed towards the selection of judges being the most critical factor when exhibitors decide whether or not to enter any given show. A welcoming atmosphere at a show was a secondary factor.

A wider allocation of challenge certificates (CCs) has been called for as

Pictured in Clarges Street are the winners of the Kennel Club Good Citizen Dog Training Scheme and KC Dog awards. First places went to: registered training club, Solihull DTC; listed status club, Warbstow Agility Club; breed club, Southern Finnish Lapphund Society; most effective council campaign, East Riding of Yorkshire; KC dog campaigner, Dog Walkers Action Group; local authority, City of London Corporation; Parliamentary, Welsh Assembly member Darren Millar; recognition, Dr Richard Prince.

a quick solution and this is now part of a review by a working group looking into CC allocation. However, several of the smaller breeds do not have extensive judging lists and could not cope with more CCs and there is little appetite among the show secretaries for a widespread increase in CCs.

Another oft-mentioned request is for champion classes to remove established champion dogs from the competition for CCs. This has the potential to change the show scene radically and cannot be considered without taking account of how this might affect the way we exhibit dogs in the UK in the longer term, not to mention the effect on the perceived value of the CC.

Looking forward

What about 2013? What should the average dog-exhibitor take note of? Can we anticipate what might affect our world of dogs during the next 12 months?

From the KC perspective key internal issues will be: the recommendations from the coat testing review; the outputs from the registration working party; the veterinary health check review group's suggestions for change; and the start of considerations about how we might allocate CCs in a fair and equitable manner.

Politically, expect the microchipping debate to progress further. Wales and Scotland are both set to introduce compulsory identification of dogs but the Westminster Parliament is lagging behind in both enthusiasm for introducing something similar.

We can anticipate quite a heated discussion about puppy contracts and the setting of breeding standards for both are being championed by external groups, with little realisation of what it really takes to breed good dogs.

Like so many initiatives, if they should be officially accepted there will be a significant impact on registered pedigree dog breeding and almost none on the puppy farmers and occasional breeders who do not register. That is unless we have a clear direction on effective controls on dog breeding across all sectors including crossbreeds and mongrels.

We need to work together to resist external 'ideas' and political opinions that make no practical sense and support those that do. In my opinion the pedigree world of dogs must put its own house in order and demonstrate we have done so. Therefore, the work being done on dog health, registration and coat testing are all vital to preserve the reputation of the registered pedigree dog.

Returning to the high profile breeds as an example, they are high profile because the external world (in this case the Council of Europe) regarded these breeds (and about 20 others) as having exaggerated conformation causing health issues.

The progress made since the launch of the high profile list in the UK in 2002 is outstanding. This will go a long way to demonstrating how the show ring can be a force for good. Yet the unregistered purebred pet dogs will still remain and continue to appear in veterinary clinics in poor health. These dogs contribute to the tarnished image some associate with the registered breeds unless we make it readily apparent these are not sourced from the registered dog community. How we do this is the debate that we will need to take forward next year.

As a closing comment I would return to the economic downturn. Until the economy picks up the number of dogs in need of a home will continue to increase. Breed club rescue groups do some wonderful work but the recession has placed significant financial strain on them.

Do not lose sight of the plight of the rescue dog and continue to support those who devote much of their lives to helping older dogs find a home. Not much is said about this form of insurance protecting the future of the dogs we breed and sell. We will need them even more in the near future and no doubt well beyond that too.

Light at the end of the tunnel

Can we be hopeful for the pedigree dog scene? I still enjoy showing dogs and I meet many of you who seem to share that view. Since becoming chairman I have had the opportunity to experience many types of canine activity and everywhere people and their dogs have been enjoying their day.

OK, so Blackpool's first day in 2012 stretched enthusiasm to the limit and beyond, but that did not stop those who were there meeting friends and exchanging views. Getting home afterwards felt really good too!

Even if we all have to tighten our belts to survive, we can be confident that the future will hold much for dog people to enjoy, simply because we are all enthusiastic volunteers with a passion for the dog as a companion and friend.

Star, a Norfolk Terrier owned by Dover and Deal MP Charlie Elphicke, won the Kennel Club/Dogs Trust Westminster Dog of the Year competition. She takes part in his campaign to stamp out puppy farming in Europe. Runner-up was Labrador Cholmeley, owned by Enfield MP David Burrowes, and third Gordon, a Rottweiler owned by Lindsay Hoyle, MP for Chorley. Wonder how he got his name?

Canine statues in the capital

The dog in art – Nick Waters

One of the dogs featured as part of the Burdetts Coutts memorial in St Pancras Gardens.

The two dogs and two lions are guarding this obelisk.

STANDING at Brook Gate on Park Lane, the Animals in War monument is one of the best-known of all London memorials. It is a powerful and moving tribute to the horrors of war and the debt we all owe to all the animals who served, suffered and died alongside the British, Commonwealth and Allied forces in the wars and conflicts of the 20th century.

From elephants to glow worms, cats to camels, so many species played a part and the numbers are staggering; eight million horses and over 300,000 pigeons alone.

The inspiration for the £2 million monument came from Jilly Cooper's book of the same name. It was designed by leading English sculptor David Backhouse and unveiled by the Princess Royal in November 2004, the 90th anniversary of the start of the first world war.

The curved Portland stone wall, the symbolic arena of war, is emblazoned with images of various struggling animals, including a German Shepherd Dog, and in the foreground are two heavily laden bronze mules progressing up the stairs through the wall, following a bronze horse and a bronze dog looking back for his companions, all weary from the trauma of war.

Dogs feature on a number of London monuments, some hidden away and others long forgotten. The most forgotten is Richard Claude Belt's imposing bronze statue of a thoughtful Lord Byron, his beloved Newfoundland Boatswain beside him looking lovingly up at his master. It was inspired by a line from *Childe Harold's Pilgrimage*: "To sit on rocks and muse o'er flood and fell."

It was erected by public subscription in 1881 and stands on a pedestal of pink and white marble donated by the Greek government, which is now pitted and discoloured by pollution. It stands beneath some trees on an island further down Park Lane from the Animals of War and the tunnel to it has long since been closed, so anyone wishing to see it has to take their life in their hands and cross Park Lane.

Jonathan Wylder's sculpture commemorating the first Marquis of Westminster, in Wilton Crescent.

The Animals in War monument, designed by David Backhouse, includes a German Shepherd Dog, as well as a bronze dog looking back at his mule companions.

Diana the Huntress with her hound, in Green Park, by Estcourt James Clack.

Elizabeth Frink's bronze *Blind Beggar and His Dog* fountain in the Cranbrook Estate.

A bag lady and her dog, from Paul Day's *The Meeting Place*, in St Pancras Station.

The earliest monument that features a dog is the high Victoriana Grade II listed Burdett-Coutts Gothic style Memorial Obelisk and Sundial in St. Pancras Gardens. It was designed by George Highton and constructed of Portland stone, marble, granite and red Mansfield stone, with extensive mosaic enrichment depicting flowers and the seasons.

It was unveiled in 1879 by Baroness Burdett-Coutts, one of the richest women in Britain of the mid 19th century, and is a memorial to the important people who had been buried near the church and whose graves had been disturbed by the encroachment of the Midland Railway.

On pedestals, one at each corner, are two lions for strength and power, and two dogs, for loyalty and devotion, which were modelled on Baroness Burdett-Coutts' own Collie.

Down the road, inside St Pancras station, is the newest London monument that features a dog. Paul Day's nine metre tall bronze, *The Meeting Place*, was unveiled in October 2007 and is modelled on an embrace between Paul and his French wife Catherine. It stands as a metaphor for St. Pancras' role as a terminus of the rail link between England and France.

At the base of *The Meeting Place* is a high-relief bronze frieze featuring images from the history of the tube and train; people queuing on platforms, soldiers departing for war, travellers drinking in the bar. Among these is a bag lady descending the stairs for the night with her faithful dog. Over the years the dog's head has been polished by countless hands stroking it as they have passed by to destinations unknown.

Moving to the east of London, two imposing molosser type dogs guard the Bonner Gate into Victoria Park. The ones that stood there from 1912 until 2009 were copies from the 5th century BC statue by Myron of Eleutherae and were presented to the park by Lady Regnart who devoted a substantial part of her life to charitable causes. It is thought they commemorate the heroic rescue of a child from a nearby lake by a dog. Vandalism led to their being removed and restored and replaced by replica dogs.

Nearby in a small garden at the corner of Mace Street and Roman Road on the Cranbrook Estate is Elizabeth Frink's bronze *Blind Beggar and His Dog* fountain. It was her first London commission and cost Bethnal Green council £1,000. Sculpted in 1959, it was originally sited in Bethnal Green Market but was also subject to vandalism and was moved to its present site in 1963.

The inspiration for the work was taken from the legend of the Blind Beggar of Bethnal Green. The most popular version is that Henry de Montfort was wounded and lost his sight in the Battle of Evesham in 1265 and was nursed back to health by a baroness. Together they had a child named Besse who became the Blind

Beggar of Bethnal Green and used to beg at the crossroads.

In west London, on the corner of Turnham Green Terrace and Chiswick High Road, near where he lived, is the bronze statue of William Hogarth and his Pug Trump. Commissioned by the local community, it was sculpted by Jim Mathieson and unveiled by Ian Hislop and David Hockney in October 2001. It was a late decision of the steering committee to add Trump to the statue and his maquette appeared at fundraising events for the work.

Nearby, just north of the River Thames and sandwiched between the A4 and the A315, is St. Peter's Square, an oasis of

These hounds guard the Bonner Gate into Victoria Park.

paired villas in classical style arranged around a central park which were completed in the 1830s. Some retain their original eagles, lions and dogs that were added as ornamentation.

It was at this time that Sir Edwin Landseer introduced the world to what rapidly became the most iconic of all Victorian dog portraits, *A Distinguished Member of the Humane Society*. Helped no doubt by this, the Newfoundland has become the breed that features the most on public statuary, particularly in America. Two large stone Newfoundlands, very much in the style of the *Distinguished Member*, look imperiously across St Peter's Square from the front of one of the grand properties.

Just inside the Palace Gate entrance to Kensington Gardens is a drinking fountain designed for dogs, although more frequently used by the park pigeons, which was erected in 1961. On the top is a playful bronze puppy sculpted by Silvia Gilley. It is a memorial to Esmé Saville Percy, actor, manager and producer with close ties to both Sarah Bernhardt and George Bernard Shaw but who is now all but forgotten.

On Wilton Crescent near Belgrave Square is a rather imposing five metre high bronze in the high Victorian taste, although it was sculpted as recently as 1998 by Jonathan Wylder. It was commissioned by the Duke of Westminster, one of the richest men in Britain, to commemorate Sir Robert Grosvenor, first Marquis of Westminster.

Robert Grosvenor was the developer of Belgravia and the model shows him studying his plans, his two faithful dogs at his side and his left foot resting on a milestone indicating that Chester, the location of the family country seat, Eaton Hall, is 197 miles.

On the plinth, as well as the family coat of arms in bronze featuring Talbot Hounds, is a quote from Ruskin: "What we build let us think that we build it forever."

Visitors to the Kennel Club who inadvertently leave Green Park tube station on the south side will be greeted by the newly restored and relocated fountain and statue of Diana the

BOW HERITAGE TRAIL

BOW
neighbourhood

THE DOGS OF ALCIBIADES

PRESENTED TO THE PARK IN 1912
BY LADY REGNART

One of a pair of Newfoundlands which can be found in St Peter's Square.

A bronze statue of William Hogarth and his Pug Trump in west London, by Jim Mathieson.

Huntress, also known as Diana of the Treetops as she is depicted rising from the uppermost branches of a tree. It was sculpted by Estcourt James Clack who in 1951 won a competition to design a statue and fountain for Green Park which was commissioned by the Constance Fund set up by the widow of artist Sigismund Goetz.

Sophie Ryder creates mystical creatures, animals and hybrid beings from a myriad of materials but she is best known for her larger than life Lady Hares. She also has a passion for dogs, in particular Lurchers; Sophie and the dogs run, work and sleep together. Just round the corner from the Kennel Club in Berkeley Square, she brings the two together like no other artist would in her sculpture, *Pink Lady Hare Dancing with Big Brown Dog*.

Undoubtedly the most poignant of all the statues in London that features a dog is the *Little Brown Dog* bronze statue hidden away in a quiet shady wood in Battersea Park. Those who know and love him adorn him with bows and flowers, something the little dog he stands as a memorial to would never have known.

It was sculpted by Nicola Hicks and unveiled in 1985. It replaced a much earlier monument to the little brown dog. Hicks' sculpture was funded by the British Union for the Abolition of Vivisection and erected by the National Anti-Vivisection Society to commemorate the suffering of millions of laboratory animals worldwide, but also to ensure that the suffering of one dog is never forgotten.

The suffering of the little brown dog began in December 1902 when Professor Starling performed his first operation depriving him of the use of his pancreas. During the following two months the dog lived in a cage, pitifully howling and whining. In February 1903 Starling opened up the dog's abdomen to inspect the result of his first operation. He then clamped the wound with forceps and handed the terrified animal to Dr Bayliss who made a completely new wound in the neck for the purpose of a lecture demonstration to students. After another half-hour, the animal, apparently suffering greatly, he was given to a Mr Dale, an unlicensed research student, who killed him either by chloroform or by surgical means.

On a traffic island in Park Lane: Richard Claude Belt's bronze of Lord Byron and Boatswain.

Sophie Ryder's *Pink Lady Hare Dancing with Big Brown Dog* in Berkeley Square.

A drinking fountain in Kensington Gardens in memory of Esmé Saville Percy, featuring a bronze puppy sculpted by Silvia Gilley.

The poignant memorial in Battersea Park to the Little Brown Dog, commemorating the victims of vivisection, is often bedecked with flowers.

A hard year for the ordinary exhibitor

by Sheila Atter

2012: a year to remember – or one to forget?

For most of us the season proper starts and ends with Crufts, and this year Crufts was a show that many will never forget. For successful Basset Hound exhibitors Derek and Heather Storton, it should have been a day to remember as their Ch Buzz Lightyear at Dereheath was awarded the dog CC and then selected for best of breed by one of the UK's top all-rounder and hound specialist judges, Zena Thorn-Andrews.

For Derek and Heather, the prospect of the newly introduced veterinary health checks for 'high profile' breeds was nothing to worry about. They were, after all, members of the Kennel Club's Assured Breeder Scheme, and had been committed to improving the health of their breed for many years. Indeed Derek was a former chairman of the Basset Hound Club health sub-committee.

The announcement that Buzz had failed the health check, his BOB would not be awarded and that he was therefore barred from participating in the group came like a hammer blow. There were similar decisions in other breeds too, and a shock wave ran round the NEC.

The atmosphere among exhibitors was one of disbelief, quickly followed by a surge of anger.

Another high profile failure came in the gundog group where the same thing happened to the much-travelled Clumber Spaniel from Croatia, Am/Dan/Hung/B&H/Slo/Aust/Lux Ch Chervood Snowsun. Here was another dog whose owner had continually put health at the top of her list of priorities and had travelled to the UK in the hopes of a major win – the group and BIS judges had both placed the bitch highly on the Continent. Again, the judge was one of the UK's most experienced and respected all-rounders, Ferelith Somerfield.

That there would be veterinary checks on the BOBs from the designated high profile breeds, those where conformational exaggerations were perceived sometimes to cause a problem, was no secret.

Indeed judges had been well briefed on what they should be looking for, so

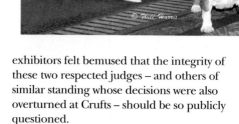

© Will Harris

exhibitors felt bemused that the integrity of these two respected judges – and others of similar standing whose decisions were also overturned at Crufts – should be so publicly questioned.

Despite the negative reaction from the show world, the general public and those who criticise pedigree dogs on a regular basis were soon sending congratulatory messages to the KC on its hardline stance and the move was portrayed as a slap in the face for greedy uncaring breeders, who put show ring success way ahead of the health and welfare of their dogs.

The negative publicity surrounding the Crufts failures was just too much for some. Derek and Heather Storton were so devastated that they immediately

For one of the dogs of a high-profile breed whose Crufts best of breed win was not confirmed, there was a much happier event a few weeks later. Mark Lee's Bulldog Ch Mellowmood One In A Million, handled by breeder Denise Lees, was declared the winner of the Canine Supporter Charity Contest of Champions. The judges were Dr Annukka Paloheimo from Finland, Tomio Fujihata from Japan, and Ricky Lochs-Romans and Dick Rutten from Holland. She had been top Bulldog in 2010.
photo Harris

Midland Counties CS and Dog World have run several competitions over the years for the best breed club year books. Coming up to date, they decided to reward websites this time, with four judges representing not only the show dog world but also the pet owner seeking advice on a breed, as well as acknowledging attractive design. Over 50 clubs entered and the winner was the English Springer Spaniel Club. Yvonne Billows and Sue Aston accepted the cheque, on behalf of webmaster Jane Eyeington, from Bonnie Scougall representing Dog World, and Rod Price, secretary of Midland Counties.
photo Walker

©Johnson

The Shar-Pei Club of Great Britain held an 'extravaganza' to mark the breed's thirtieth year in the UK, including a health seminar, sweepstakes and parade of champions. At the club championship show Jennie Baker (right) gave BIS to Tim Ball, Joy Bradley, Kristen Marshall and Lisa Myers' veteran Ch/Am Ch Asias Red Marsh Whip It Good whose daughter was RBIS. With them is American vet and geneticist Dr Linda Tintle.
photo Johnson

withdrew from all future judging appointments and have never been to a dog show since that fateful day at Crufts.

To those outside the world of pedigree show dogs, that might seem a somewhat extreme reaction, but anyone who has spent decades creating and nurturing a successful strain will understand completely the humiliation and devastation that they felt.

All through the year the debate about veterinary checks has rumbled on. The KC's reaction has always been to put a positive spin on the whole affair, and to deny that the examinations were over-zealous, although it has been very noticeable that at most of the subsequent championship shows vets have been far less rigorous in their inspection of the high profile BOBs and there have been few subsequent failures.

Many felt that introduction of the scheme at Crufts was a PR disaster, doomed to failure from the start, and the KC's much criticised public image took a further dent when an 'administrative error' saw the Croatian Clumber Spaniel sent her show champion certificate when she won her third CC at the British breeds show in Dortmund, despite still not having passed the requisite veterinary check as these were not available at that show.

The very idea of having CCs on offer at a German show for British breeds, and CACs being awarded to German breeds at a British show (the National, in May) was innovative, but in the view of many a fairly pointless exercise. However exhibitors in both countries did relish the idea of having their dogs judged by breed experts from the country of origin, and the experiment turned out to be quite a success. Whether it will be followed up in future remains to be seen, but the precedent has been set.

What might have been a somewhat unanticipated result that could in future be of slight concern to the KC was the realisation in some quarters that it wouldn't necessarily be too difficult for a show society to enlist the support of an overseas kennel club and run a show entirely under FCI rules, offering CACs and eventually even CACIBs here in the UK, bypassing the need for approval from the KC at all.

If social networking as a vehicle for passing information and views around the dog world had come to the fore in 2011 when, in the wake of the coat testing debacle that marred Crufts that year, Facebook became the means whereby those with strong views could be quickly united and rallied to action, in 2012 it became an essential part of the exhibitor's life.

Having a say

In the wake of Crufts it became very apparent that many ordinary exhibitors felt that they should have a say in the way our hobby is conducted and almost overnight the Canine Alliance was born. Huge support via Facebook and a fairly high profile steering committee meant that even the KC could not ignore the Alliance, although as the year has progressed it has become very noticeable that the two words 'canine' and 'alliance' are never uttered in sequence by anyone connected with the KC.

Doubtless some supporters have been disappointed that there was no instant capitulation over the high profile veterinary checks, but realistically that was never going to happen, and it is equally noticeable that the word 'sorry' is not in the Clarges Street vocabulary either.

It is inevitable that changes will take place very slowly and it remains to be seen just how much real impact the Canine Alliance will have in the long term – but there seems to be no doubt that for the first time the ordinary exhibitor has an organisation that can speak on their behalf.

It's easy to be introverted and forget that there is a wider world outside the show ring, and 2012 hasn't been exactly the most positive for pedigree dogs and their breeders.

Pedigree Dogs Exposed 2 brought more of the same, in fact much of it was simply a re-running of footage from the original programme, but even though we might not have been quite as badly criticised as some thought would be the case, it was once again an encouragement to the general public to look to the non-show breeders for their puppies, and a condemnation of the show world in general.

Dog breeding continues to be in the spotlight, and while token mention is made of those who are outside the KC's remit, the emphasis in all the various reports and recommendations on the breeding of dogs is placed on the perceived inadequacies and outdated practices of the show fraternity.

Many feel that the KC hasn't fought our corner as well as it might have done. The fact that many respected and highly ethical breeders are still resistant to the suggestion of joining the ABS has not helped, and stressing the idea that only puppies bred by members of the ABS can be guaranteed to be healthy has simply alienated these folk – not encouraged them to join.

Another PR gaffe was the distribution of a Puppy Plan that all breeders were encouraged to follow. Excellent in theory, the suggestions such as teach your puppy to eat from a frying pan were sometimes rather eccentric, and the tone in which the whole booklet was written was regarded by many to be more than a little patronising.

Do those who have responsibility for the running of the KC realise just how damaging these various episodes are to their image as far as the ordinary exhibitor is concerned? I suspect not.

While the chairman is exhorting us all to get involved with 'our' KC, to many the institution is as divisive now as it ever has been, if not more so. Efforts have been made to try to involve the ordinary exhibitor, but the scheduling of meetings hasn't been the most convenient for many and when the response is low the temptation is to stop trying.

One very positive move, however, was an online survey of opinions about the registration scheme. The outcome of this survey is, at the time of writing, still unknown, but it seems there was a good response.

If the KC publishes the statistics and takes note of the recommendations made by respondents at some point in the not too distant future, that will be a great day for the ordinary dog folk – but I'm not holding my breath too hard!

Ashleigh Butler and Pudsey pictured at Crufts.
phot Kennel Club Picture Library

Kirsty dressed for her routine to the *Frog Song* with her red Collie Roo.

by Richard Curtis

Could your dog be the next PUDSEY?

Over the past few years there have been various canine acts on the television show *Britain's Got Talent*. This year it was the turn of Ashleigh Butler and Pudsey, a team who have previously competed in agility and freestyle.

It looked as if this team had everything that the TV show would want in an act as Ashleigh is young and Pudsey is cute. They got through to the final and the tension built as they reached the final two acts where they were revealed as the winners of *Britain's Got Talent 2012*.

This duo performed to different types of music on the programme but they always used their strongest moves. Within a freestyle routine you always look to your dog's strengths in order to create your routine. There are no moves which have to be put in a routine so it is up to the handler to be as creative as they can. You always try to find moves that your dog is good at – in Pudsey's final routine they used some agility equipment which obviously, with him being an agility champion, suited him well.

Ashleigh says that Pudsey loves also to walk on his hind legs; in fact she says it's sometimes hard to keep him on four feet. You always want the dog to look as if he is enjoying the performance.

One important factor in training a good performance dog is to find out what reward the dog enjoys. Ashleigh says that Pudsey is very self-motivated but he has a special red tuggy which he loves. As well as his tuggy a lot of different treats are used to keep him motivated in training.

Most dogs will desire high category

rewards such as chicken, sausage and liver. Using these can help to get the dog's focus and encourage him to give a little more energy in a performance. Too much of one of these rewards is not good for the dog, not only for his health but also because if he has the reward too much, then he will not have such a high desire for it.

The aim is to use lower category foods in environments which are familiar to the dog or, when he is performing, something he has been doing for a while. When you are perhaps at a competition or at a new venue the dog hasn't been to, that is the time to bring out the very tasty rewards.

Where to start

With all the television coverage of Pudsey you would think that the sport of heelwork to music and freestyle would see an increase in the number of people wanting to take part. The only problem is that unlike other dog sports where there are classes in most areas, heelwork to music classes are much rarer so new handlers may not have somewhere local to attend.

A class does give new handlers a focus to their training and allow them to learn by watching others. Luckily there is a range of training books and DVDs on the sport which allows handlers who do not have access to classes still to get started in the sport.

When you are starting a young dog you shouldn't be eager to have the puppy doing lots of tricks. It is better to create a bond with the dog through play and time spent with him as this will stand you

in good stead later on in the dog's life. Ashleigh didn't start training Pudsey for freestyle until he was three which shows you that there is plenty of time to get started in the sport.

Teaching the individual moves/tricks can be quite easy but of course in a routine you need to put many moves together. When you start putting moves together it can be in a random order but when it comes to formulating a routine the order needs to be a little more structured. A good routine should flow from one move to the next without those awkward moments where nothing seems to be happening.

Finding the right music is always a real headache as there are so many factors that need to be considered. Firstly the music should suit the size and speed of the dog. If the music is too fast it could mean that the dog looks slow, and too slow might mean the dog looks as if he is being held back.

Secondly, the handler needs to feel comfortable moving with the music.

After considering these two factors you then have to think whether or not the audience might recognise the music. If they do then they can often get behind the routine a little more. In the final of *Britain's Got Talent* Pudsey performed to *Mission Impossible* which is a well known track.

It takes many hours to put the routine together as you need to listen to the music multiple times. When you start listening to the music there will be certain sections which lend themselves well to specific moves or sequences. If there are accents in the music these must be used, as the

Jill and River capturing the song *Happy Feet* well with their movements.

Corrine and her Parson Russell taking on a Spanish theme for their routine.

For once even dog people had to admit that Britain has indeed got talent, when Ashleigh and Pudsey won the programme's final.
photo courtesy Kennel Club Picture Library

Ann and Ccinno stepping out in style in their heelwork to music routine.

Richard and Pogo in a comedy snooker routine set to the *Pot Black* theme tune.

interpretation of the music is something that you will be marked on. Repeating a move too many times can be detrimental to the routine so the aim is always to present a routine with a varied number of moves.

When you have a rough idea of the routine, then it is time to see if some of the sections work with the dog. When planning the routine you should have taken into consideration the speed of the dog while it is performing certain moves but sometimes when the dog is actually performing a sequence it takes longer than you have estimated. So after this practice it might be necessary that you go back to the drawing board and re-choreograph various parts of the routine.

When you feel that the routine is finished then it's time to practise it without the dog until it becomes second nature. Some handlers find it hard to listen to the music, remember the routine and tell the dog what to do so if the routine is firmly in your mind this is one last thing to worry about.

All the practice takes a long time but eventually you will feel like entering a competition. Nerves can always affect a competition performance so getting used to performing in front of family members is a good start. Ashleigh says she tries not to show her nerves to Pudsey and acts confident but she also admits that a bit of nerves is needed for you to give a good performance.

You must always remember that no routine ever goes completely to plan no matter what level you are competing at. Above all it is essential that you and the dog enjoy your time in the ring so always keep smiling and having fun with the dog when in the ring.

The versatile Vanitonias

by Simon Parsons and Frank Kane

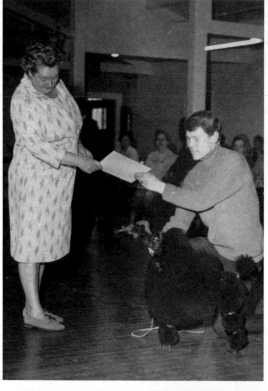

Roger Stone and the kennel's first Miniature Poodle Vanitonia Pelsinora In Style, winning under Catherine Sutton.
photo Young

Within the past three years, one kennel has won SIXTEEN best in show awards at general championship shows, this achieved by two homebred dogs of different breeds.

Such a feat is of course unprecedented in British dog show history, as is the fact that one of these dogs scored her eight wins within a single show season, winning the Pup of the Year, champion stakes and Top Dog titles during the same period.

As if this were not enough, the same era has produced homebred group winners in two other breeds, as well as further champions.

The young couple who have made such a mark on DOG WORLD's front covers is of course Lee Cox and Tom Isherwood of the Vanitonia Poodles, Chinese Cresteds and Clumber Spaniels. Their dramatic success in the all-breed rings is merely the icing on a substantial cake of solid breeding achievement in each of their breeds. In this they have skilfully built on a legacy left by the late founders of the kennel, Roger Stone and Graham Thompson.

To tell the first half of the story, let's go to an interview conducted by Frank Kane for DOG WORLD in the early 1990s, shortly before Lee joined the Vanitonia team.

The Vanitonia affix is now a household word in Poodles, not only in Britain but worldwide, yet Roger Stone and Graham Thompson never really intended to get involved in the showing world and their rise to fame illustrates a fascinating canine rags to canine riches story.

Roger was originally destined for a stage career as a dancer, training and appearing at the Bristol Old Vic and appearing in several shows in the West End. However, rheumatoid arthritis ended that career and Roger invested his savings in a pet shop in Bristol in 1962.

Struggling to get the business off the ground, Roger accepted a Poodle for trimming – he'd never trimmed before – and was horrified when the owner collected her to hear that she was going to be destroyed, the owner having wanted her tidied up before taking her to the vet's! Roger adopted the bitch, a cream Miniature called Honey, and so entered the world of Poodles.

He was joined by Graham in 1965 and together they bought a companion for Honey, an oversized brown Toy called Choccie, and, registered as Titania and Oberon, the two produced the first litter, whelped in the laundry basket, and containing two black dogs, Peter and Paul.

Really enjoying their Poodle family, Graham and Roger bought two Miniatures from Judith and Suzette Lovegrove (Silvlandia), and acquired more knowledge of the breed from them, but still there was no intention of showing until 1966 when they turned on the television to watch the Crufts programme, and there, strutting out with real Poodle style, was the apricot Toy bitch **Oakington Puckshill Amber Sunblush**, *taking BIS for Clare Perry (now Coxall).*

An apricot Toy was a must for the boys and with this in mind went to the Puckshill kennel of Bunty Dobson and acquired two! While at Puckshill they met Vivian Brown, the kennelmaid, and bought from her the silver Miniature **Brioletta Silver Cyrene**, *for sale because of Vivian's impending move to Bournemouth. She persuaded them to visit her at Bournemouth ch show, their first ever dog show, and they loved it.*

Vivian was working for the Pelsinora Poodles and there Roger and Graham saw a litter by **Ch Tophill Orsino** *and they admired a black dog puppy who went home with them. He was to become* **Vanitonia Pelsinora In Style** *after the registration of their affix – an interesting story in itself.*

Having had all their original choices of affix turned down Graham and Roger were discussing new names in a department store when a furniture van parked

A rare photo of Graham Thompson and and even rarer one of him showing a dog! He and Roger are exhibiting two of their early Poodles at a West Country open show.

Roger with the Miniature Vanitonia Meliora Make Out.

Winner of eight all-breed best in show awards during 2011 and '12, the Toy Poodle Ch Vanitonia You'll See, 'Graham'.
photo Croft-Elliott

Winner of eight all-breed best in show awards during 2010, Pup of the Year, Top Dog and champion stakes winner, the Chinese Crested Ch Vanitonia Unwrapped, 'Nora'.
photo Croft-Elliott

outside, advertising Vantona bedding. Their friend in the store suggested adding 'i's to it to suit the vanity of the Poodles – and so was born the Vanitonia affix.

Silver Cyrene and In Style were the two Poodles who lured the partnership to the show ring at Bristol limited show. Cyrene won the novice Poodle class, In Style won open and BOB and the bug had bitten! The following week under Catherine Sutton, In Style went RBIS at Stroud.

In Style was responsible for some nice winning at open shows and eventually it was this dog which brought the kennel its first red card at a championship

show at Leicester in 1969 under a judge awarding CCs for the first time – Olga Bullock, who today is president of Leeds show.

The next addition to the family was a white Toy dog and he came through a fortuitous introduction to Kathleen Rees of Conersk fame, and she was to be a mentor for the partnership, despite their going against her first advice when looking at the litter of white puppies. Kathleen had chosen the pick of litter for the boys but Graham's eye was taken by another in the litter and it was this one who went home to Vanitonia and he was to be their first prolific winner in the Toy ring.

He was **Vanitonia Snowboots from Conersk**, who went to his first championship show under Peter Kaye at Paignton and won five classes. He went on to be a most consistent winner, taking three RCCs, including Crufts 1970 under Phyllis Austin Smith of the great Braeval kennel.

The other major successes in this period were with the two apricot dogs, bred from their early stock, **Vanitonia Fire Alert** and **Fire Officer** who won three RCCs in the early 1970s. Graham and Roger's first interest in the Toy size was with the colours, especially apricots.

Lee Cox with the brown Toy Poodle Ch Vanitonia Lustful Hans.

Tom Isherwood with the Chinese Crested Ch Blandora Time Bomb via Vanitonia.
photo Johnson

At this stage we must leave the smaller size as they were taking a back seat to a new acquisition who was launching the Vanitonias in the Standard ring and was to be their first titleholder. This was Angela – the pet name for the black Standard bitch **Vicmars Boname** acquired from Vicky Marshall.

Roger had been inspired by Vicky's black dog **Ch Vicmars Balnoble Royale** and asked her to let him have a puppy when she had one of that quality.

Months later Roger received a call to say his puppy was on the train to Bristol, a little embarrassing for Roger as he had not told Graham about his plans in Standards. Graham was not enthusiastic but Roger went to the station, found the bitch tied in the guard's van and brought her home. Graham was still not persuaded and said that he would not put the Vanitonia affix on her, but a day later Angela was his firm favourite with her paws firmly under the table for good!

A great character at home, Angela did not like moving in the show ring and at her first championship show, WELKS under Barbara Peake, Roger looked in dismay at the puppy bitch class of 17 entries and Angela who would not put one foot in front of the other. Remembering her craving for dried fish, Roger ran to a nearby trade stand and then ran round the ring waving a large piece in front of Angela's nose. She won the class.

Her career took off, taking her first CC as a raw youngster under George Leatt at Scottish Kennel Club. A week later she took her second CC at Leeds and a few weeks later at Blackpool she won open bitch class of 17 under Ivan Strawson, to become the first champion at Vanitonia.

Roger had travelled to Blackpool with Josie McDermott and her black dog

The exceptional Standard stud dog, Swedish-bred Ch Harbovi's Heaven Can Wait for Vanitonia.
photo Pearce/Kennel Club Picture Library

Roger with the first Toy champion Vanitonia School For Scandal. She was a good brood too and a Pup of the Year finalist, something the kennel has achieved in four breeds, while Lee also won a heat with an English Setter.
photo Garwood/ Dog World

Roger winning BOB at Crufts with the Toy Ch Vanitonia Vandalizer.

Ch Josato Georgie Best who won the dog CC, BOB and the group that day, so it was a happy journey home. And it was Georgie Best who was chosen to sire Angela's first litter. She produced in this litter the white **Vanitonia Vanity Fayre**, who in turn produced the first homebred champion in the white **Ch Vanitonia Calamity Jane**. The first litter also contained the black Victoria Plum who produced **Ch Vanitonia Prunella Prune**, who took 13 CCs. The litter brother **Burlington Bert** was an influential sire and can be found in the pedigrees of many later winning Standards.

Boname came back to the show ring after her litter to take a total of ten CCs. She was mated next to Wendy Streatfield's **Ch Acadia Detonator of Leander**, one of the earlier imports from America who were to restyle the Standard Poodle in this country. From this litter two went to Australia where they took their titles and **Aus Ch Leander Luck Of The Irish** and

Aus Ch Leander Luck Of The Draw are behind most Australian-bred Standards.

In her next litter to **Ch Wycliffe Ovation for Vulcan**, Angela produced **Ch Vanitonia Proclamation**, made up by John Marshall.

Ovation proved to be an important dog for Vanitonia as, mated to Ch Calamity Jane he sired **Vanitonia Jane Eyre**, dam of **Ch Vanitonia Heavens Fury**, who went to Elisabeth Drake in Sweden.

Calamity Jane's litter to **Ch Dassin Diablo at Tiopepi** produced **Ch Vanitonia Joe Public** and **Am Ch Vanitonia Haysi Fantasi**, who in her litter before going to the US produced the dam of Sarah O'Higgins' group winner **Ch Vanitonia Heaven Help Us**. The litter sister of **Ch Heavens Fury** was dam of the sensational **Ch Vanitonia Queen's English** also owned by Sarah.

It seems appropriate, with all this talk of heaven, to mention the dog who has obviously been very influential for Vanitonia, and for the Standard Poodle in this country, the import from Sweden **Int Ch Harbovis Heaven Can Wait**, *from Elisabeth Drake's very successful kennel.*

Roger had been impressed with the movement of the Swedish Standards when he judged there and felt that the British Standards could benefit from this. He had handled the famous dog **Ch Twintops I'm No Party Player** *to win BIS at Stockholm in 1985 and it was his son, Heaven Can Wait, leading Standard in Sweden, whom Roger acquired.*

Not only did he have a good career in the ring, gaining 13 CCs, and being much admired for his movement, but he has proved a most valuable addition to the gene pool in this country and has so far sired seven UK champions. He is also sire of the white **Ch Maneetas Del Zarzoso Fuego Fatuo**, *bred in England, who had a specatular career in Finland and the US.*

Roger and Graham's other import was the white dog from the Spanish Del Zarzoso kennel of Juan Cabrera and Carlos Fernandez Renau, which has had a great influence particularly in the whites of this country. Juan and Carlos had great success in sending their bitches to the US for mating and they sent their black bred white, **Del Zarzoso Victoria**, *to* **Am Ch Eaton Entourage**, *a bloodline much admired by Roger, especially as it contained heavy line breeding to the beautiful black male* **Am Ch Longleat Alimar Raisin Cain**. *On top of these assets, Heaven Can Wait went back on one side to* **Am Ch Eaton Affirmed** *so the bloodlines had the potential to nick in well.*

Carlos and Juan offered the pick of the litter to Vanitonia, and he came over at seven months of age, rejoicing in the name of **Del Zarzoso Pardon My English**. *A big, masculine dog, he attained his title, and among his progeny was Queen's English.*

So the Standards put the Toys in the back seat, and it was not until

The Toy Ch Vanitonia Hypnotizer, owned by Alan Dredge.
photo Pearce/Kennel Club Picture Library

Alan Dredge's Toy Ch Vanitonia Holy Whisper.

Ch Vanitonia Holy Moses in Sweden with Tommy Östman.
photo Widholm

A large number of the Vanitonia Poodle champions have been made up by other exhibitors. This is one of the best known, Sarah O'Higgins' Standard Ch Vanitonia Queens English.
photo Steph

1980 that the first Toy was made up. The kennel had always retained a few Miniatures and most of the Toys now in the kennel trace back to three of these. The black bitch **Vanitonia Dolly Rocker of Pavlova** *had been mated to the resident stud* **Meliora Make Out** *several times but had produced no pups.*

Thinking she was barren, Graham and Roger decided to let her go to a good pet home, unconcerned that she had mated herself to Make Out on her last season. Several weeks later the phone rang; the new owners were concerned that Dolly had a bag of liquid hanging from her. A mad dash brought Dolly back to Vanitonia where she whelped four bitch puppies, all retained at the kennel, all growing to around the 12" mark, and all eventually mated to Toys to produce the current line.

Another small Miniature bitch, **Vanitonia Becky Sharpe**, *mated to* **Silvlandia Martin**, *produced the other stem line from which the present-day Toys descend, especially through the daughter and granddaughter of these*

two matings: **Vanitonia Polly Perkins** *and* **Vanitonia Lydia Languish**.

May Barlow gave Graham and Roger a lot of help and her **Ch Barsbrae Branslake Darty** *mated to one of the four foundation bitches produced* **Vanitonia Polly Garter**, *who won a RCC but has been of great importance as a producer for the kennel.*

Lydia Languish mated to **Tuttlebees Rather Royal** *produced the first Toy champion,* **Vanitonia School For Scandal** *who, mated to* **Ch Suraliam Boogy Woogy from Velveteen**, *produced* **Ch Vanitonia Holy Moses**, *top Toy Poodle of 1983 before going to Tommy Östman in Sweden in 1984 where he was Dog of the Year in 1984 and won the contest of champions in 1985. He was a top producer in Sweden and, mated to a few bitches before he left, he left behind four champion progeny. One of the bitches he mated was Polly Perkins and from this emerged* **Ch Vanitonia Holy Whisper** *who won 17 CCs. His other champion progeny*

Lee with the Sussex Spaniel Maladetta Martina's Double whom he handled to BOB at Crufts.

Ch Labamba Lawrence at Vanitonia winning RBIS at Scottish Kennel Club under Ken Sinclair.
photo Johnson

include the Windsor BIS winner **Ch Aedan Twice As Nice** and the good sire **Ch Starbase Timelord of Vanitonia**.

Vanitonia Holy Terror (by Holy Moses) was exported to the US and mated three bitches before he left. One of these matings was to **Vanitonia Polly Tickle**, another daughter of Polly Perkins by the litter brother of School For Scandal.

The dog from this litter, **Vanitonia Holy Riot**, although never shown, became a top stud dog. The bitch from the litter was the big winning **Ch Vanitonia Holy Psalm**.

A study of a Vanitonia pedigree reveals the close line breeding which has established their definite type.

Ch Vanitonia Scandalizer, litter sister to Holy Moses, was mated to Holy Terror to produce **Ch Vanitonia Vandalizer** who won 27 CCs, including Crufts twice beaten for BOB on the first occasion by his sister **Ch Hypnotizer**, making Vanitonia the first kennel to win both Toy CCs at Crufts. He too was a preotent sire.

Linebred on similar lines was **Ch Vanitonia Liquidizer**, BIS at BUBA in 1989. Mated back to Holy Riot, she in turn produced further champions.

Vandalizer's son **Ch Vanitonia Careless Whisper** was owned and bred by Alan Dredge who came to work at Vanitonia soon after leaving school and became a successful breeder and exhibitor in his own right.

The Vanitonia establishment is quite extensive. The kennel still retains a few Miniatures, including their only champion in this size, **Ch Idadoun Black Jermiah of Vanitonia**, bred by Mary Howarth. It also houses a few Cockers, Cavaliers (Roger and Graham had close links with the Alansmere kennel) and Miniature Schnauzers. It is immaculately kept and it is good to see the freedom the dogs have.

The organisation and administration of the pedigrees and records is managed by Graham: every litter bred here is recorded with names of pups, new owners and breeding history. Concern for healthy sound stock is paramount and all the stock is tested for progressive retinal atrophy. Eye certificates for all the stud dogs are available for all prospective users.

Although Graham titles himself the 'backroom boy' he is central to the success of the establishment with his organisation skills, his knowledge of breeding lines and his good eye for a puppy. Roger would be the first to acknowledge the great part Graham plays in Vanitonia's success story.

Since Frank wrote his article in 1991 much has changed at Vanitonia though not the flair for clever breeding. Tragically, Graham died in 1995 at the age of just 49. 'Backroom boy' he may have been but his astute business sense, humour and ability to get along with people were essential to laying down the successful foundation to the kennel. In spite of this undoubted eye for a dog, showing and judging never interested him.

Whereas everyone loved Graham, the more outgoing Roger was 'like Marmite', to use Lee's words. "You loved him or hated him – never a grey area!"

"I feel very fortunate to have known both of them, and they both shaped the person I am. Roger, of course, brought out my more

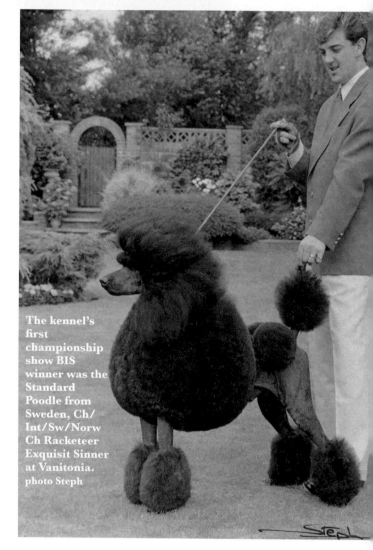

The kennel's first championship show BIS winner was the Standard Poodle from Sweden, Ch/Int/Sw/Norw Ch Racketeer Exquisit Sinner at Vanitonia.
photo Steph

flamboyant side, while Graham enouraged my more cautious side," says Lee.

A brilliant dog man with great flair and style, Roger was held in great affection by his friends; others he managed to rub up the wrong way and over the years he more than once found himself at the centre of controversy.

At times he was his own worst enemy and Lee admits he learned from him how not to deal with various situations! But Roger managed to survive battles, intense at the time, with both the Kennel Club and, later, the RSPCA, and even his worst enemy could not fail to admire the determination with which he battled against increasing disability through his very severe arthritis.

Ch Torpaz Talking Point at Vanitonia, the youngest Standard Poodle champion.
photo Hughes

The group-winning Standard Poodle Ch Vanitonia Eye Candy.
photo Harwood

Two influential imports: the Toy from Norway Solnes Erick The Viking is Vanitonia and (below) the Miniature from Spain Escandalo de Shikarah at Vanitonia.
photos Steph

Nor could they deny his enormous knowledge of very aspect of Poodles and their pedigrees – Tom recalls sitting with him going through the old years books, and Roger recalling every detail of every dog pictured.

He died in 2010 at the age of 69, secure in the knowledge that the future of the kennel say in safe hands with the partnership of Lee and Tom.

So, what was their background before they came to Somerset?

Lee was born into the sport. His parents, Roy and Dee, originally bred Pyrenean Mountain Dogs under the Maladetta affix, starting with a Carabrae from Brenda Judson. When Lee arrived they thought something smaller but similar might be sensible, Clumber Spaniels being an obvious choice. The first came from Brian and Frances Stanley and **Frastan Inca of Maladetta** won a CC at LKA '73 from Hubert Arthur.

Inevitably the children became involved in junior handling, but it was Lee's less 'doggy' sister Cheryl who won a semi-final of the junior handling competition on her only attempt, Lee having to be content with several second places!

Dee was working for Reta Goodger's Gamewood kennel of Clumbers and Shetland Sheepdogs and the latter was the first breed Lee ever handled.

Eventually, of course, he wanted a dog of his own, and his godmother, the formidable Ann Findlay of the Oldholbans kennel, gave him a Sussex Spaniel bitch. "I always had great ambitions," he admits, and decided to breed from her, becoming the first person to use the subsequently influential **Sh Ch Quintic Joby**. This produced **Maladetta Martina's Double**, who won two CCs, the first with BOB at Crufts '81 under Joe Braddon, shown by her nine-year-old breeder. Joe also did Clumbers that day, and BOB there was a dog handled by Lee's mum! Sadly Lee was deemed too young to handle his winner in the group.

The family later made up a Clumber, **Sh Ch Burtonswood Ballerina**, and won CCs with several others, **Maladetta Maestro** winning a huge number of reserves but never achieving his title.

Later, after the Coxes divorced, Dee (now Mrs Carter-Hunt), showed Cavaliers for some years with the Swaish affix. Today she has a couple of the Vanitonia Poodles as pets, often comes to look after the kennel when Lee and Tom are away, and still judges.

After his A-levels Lee went to work for Marks and Spencer as a management trainee, at the same time dabbling in professional handling. He campaigned John Nilsson's French Bulldog **Boristi**

Beatrice to her title, a breed which he and Tom now own thanks to a gift from Frances Krall.

He also showed an Oldholbans English Setter of his own who became the first of the breed to qualify for the Pup of the Year final, a breed he still loves.

He considered becoming a full-time handler until a chance meeting with Roger prompted him to ask if he could come and learn how to improve his trimming skills. Roger had recently had a hip operation and he and Graham were wondering if they would have to stop showing, but they soon realised that here was someone who could handle the dogs in the ring... And so Lee stayed on at Kaston Kennels.

Before he joined the team, he had always admired Poodles, especially Standards, from afar but hadn't been practically involved with them. Now he is besotted. "Much as I am still passionate about Clumbers," he says, "if I could have only one dog it would be a Toy Poodle. They are a wonderful, wonderful breed.

"Once upon a time it would have been a Standard, but now I'm getting older it would be a Toy." He is all of 40, by the way.

Tom feels the same about the Toys, too, in spite of his love for the Chinese Crested.

As for Tom, his family's involvement with dog was purely as pet owners, originally Rough Collies. When he was eight years old, his grandmother took him and his sister to Crufts. "From that moment on I knew I wanted to show a dog."

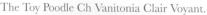

The Toy Poodle Ch Vanitonia Clair Voyant.

Ch Vanitonia Gloria May, daughter of Clair Voyant and dam of You'll See.
photo Croft-Elliott

The Japanese imported Toy Ch/Jap Ch Smash JP Rainbow Rider at Vanitonia, in the Crufts group ring.
photo Johnson

A Border Collie came next, with which the family competed in agility. Next they got a Papillon, the breed Tom had been captivated by at his first Crufts. The dog was 'enormous, nearly as big as the Border Collie' but he still managed to qualify for Crufts.

Young Tom nagged his parents to get a dog he could show more seriously and when he was 12 they bought a sable and white dog for £250. He rejoiced in the name of **Heavenly Sightseer**, and with Tom won two classes at championship shows and a third at Crufts – he has only recently died aged 15. They were also placed in the junior handling semis on their only attempt.

A little later Tom intended to go to college, but in the meantime wanted to get more involved in dogs and to learn about grooming. He'd already had some experience in grooming Poodles through his friendship with Marion Marston of the Seldoop kennel. He saw an advertisement for grooming tuition at Vanitonia in DOG WORLD ANNUAL, came down to Kaston in 2000 and never went home!

At the time the kennel was showing two Chinese Crested males. Once they were both made up Tom took over showing **Ch Blandora Time Bomb via Vanitonia**, and, just like Lee 20 years earlier, the first CC and BOB he won himself came at Crufts 2001, under Angela Draper-Andrews. They repeated this a year later, and qualified for the champion stakes final, the only Crested other than Nora some years later to do so.

Nowadays the partners would never argue about which dog to show. Lee says Tom had a special affinity with the Chinese Cresteds and that his handling skills with a free standing breed are far superior, whereas Lee himself prefers showing the stacked breeds. If necessary Tom will take in a Clumber or Lee a Crested, but generally they play to their strengths.

Tom sometimes shows the Poodles – indeed he won one of Graham's BIS awards when Lee couldn't return on the final day.

He recalls the first dog he was allowed to show at Vanitonia, after practising his trimming skills on her. He won a couple of junior classes and an open show group before she decided enough was enough! So Lee took over and the bitch became the famous Ch Clair Voyant.

Now let's resume the story of the dogs themselves. When we left the Standards, the kennel had had much success with the great-producing Swedish import Heaven Can Wait, known for his make, shape and soundness. Another of his progeny was the CC record holder and multiple BIS winner, Michael Coad's **Ch Pamplona Something Special**.

The next Swedish invader became the kennel's first BIS winner, the superbly stylish and typy **Ch Racketeer Exquisit Sinner to Vanitonia**. Roger was a frequent visitor to judge in Scandinavia, whose Standards were then he felt the best in the world. He saw Sinner as a youngster and asked Elisabeth Drake to try to convince his owner, the very distinguished breeder Margaret Vear, to let him come to England. She wouldn't sell him but agreed he could come for two years, as long as his co-owner Lotte Sandell could come over and show him. Once he was out of quarantine, she did so and made him up.

After his hip operation Roger could no longer show the Standards, so Philip Langdon showed him for a while, taking him to BIS at SKC under Andrew Brace. By 1993 Lee was in residence and took him over, taking CC and BOB at the International Poodle at their first attempt, and plenty more CCs, including one at Crufts. Then it was time for him to go home, "one of the saddest days of my life – I adored that dog".

But they still had his son ex the great Queens English, **Vanitonia Affidavit** – whose breeding typified their Standards the time, by Sinner ex a bitch by Pardon My English ex a bitch by Heaven Can Wait – who was little shown but who produced well. His sister **Exquisit Perfomer** won well for Michael Coad.

For an outcross they later brought in a Chorus Line dog from the US. Another big winner was **Ch Labamba Lawrence of Vanitonia**, who went back to Sinner of both sides. An enquiry to use Lawrence came from the controversial Pat Salama (Ashwell), a 'colourful character' as Lee describes her.

Roger and Lee debated about whether to go ahead but, feeling that the Torpaz strain which had bred on so well for other breeders probably wouldn't be around much longer, decided to say yes on the proviso they bought the whole litter. From this came **Ch Torpaz Talking Point of Vanitonia**, the breed's youngest titleholder at 12 months and a week. Of course, in their early days all these West Country kennels like Vanitonia, Torpaz and Sablecomb had worked together, all stemming from the original Vicmars.

Ch Vanitonia Back In The Red, the first red male Toy Poodle champion.
photo Croft-Elliott

Ch Vanitonia Back In The Red, the first red male Toy Poodle champion.
photo Croft-Elliott

To a champion bitch of the old Vanitonia lines Talking Point sired their latest Standard group winner, **Eye Candy**. Their latest venture is a complete outcross using the American-bred dog who spent a little time in Britain, **Ch Diego de Maya**.

Going on to the Toys, Careless Whisper was the successful stud dog when Lee joined the team. Among his progeny were the kennel's first brown champions, **Careless Hans** and **Lustful Hans**, and the latter's black sister **Village Gossip** was the first titleholder in Lee's name.

By then the line was very closely bred and it was time for look for something different. Once again they went to Scandinavia and **Solnes Erick The Viking** arrived from Solveig Naess, then based in Norway. After quarantine he hated the ring but somehow managed to get two CCs, he proved his worth through his descendants for Vanitonia and other kennels especially when his pups were put back into the old line.

His big winning daughter **Ch Vanitonia Clair Voyant**, mated to the good sire **Ch Montelle Just As Smart for Fabuleux**,

Ch/Sw/Norw Ch Vanitonia Tickled Pink, dam of Nora.
photo Walker

himself going back to the old Vanitonia lines, produced **Ch Vanitonia Gloria May** who won 20 CCs plus group places.

By then they had got to know Toshi Omura of the incredible Smash kennel in Japan, featured in the *Annual* a few years ago. And since then the two kennels have co-operated well, exchanging dogs more than once to mutual benefit. "If you let me have one of your blacks, I'll let you have a white," he said, and needless to say Lee and Tom jumped at the chance to have one of this astonishing strain of white Toys. "He has the same passion for the breed that we have, and the same ideas."

The strange aspect was that although Vanitonia had started all those years ago with whites, and Roger had a passion for the 'pastel shades', they had never made up a white Toy – the blacks dominated, with the occasional brown.

And so arrived the white **Ch Smash JP Rainbow Rider at Vanitonia** who had a great career including BOB at Crufts, two groups and an all-breed RBIS. Later they campaigned **Ch Smash JP Close Up** in the UK for Toshi who himself showed him to win a group at Windsor.

Nothing in breeding is plain sailing and sadly Rainbow Rider did not get the eye test result they had hoped for, so he was not used at stud and now lives happily as a pet with Lee's mum.

Toshi subsequently sent them a black dog, tested clear, as a potential stud – he had already sired a best of winners at Poodle Club of America, and had some Vanitonia lines behind him. While he was here, he sired two litters, out of Gloria May and her half-sister. Each contained one male puppy – the first, 'Graham', **Ch Vanitonia You'll See**, and the second a BIS winner in Russia and BOB at the World Show! Luckily they have collected his semen so hope he might prove more prolific for them in the future!

Poodle Graham's record is featured on our news pages – suffice to say only one male Toy had ever won a general championship show BIS in the UK, back in the 1960s, and now Graham has won eight! The first three came at consecutive shows within a fortnight in 2011. He may well end up number two all breeds for 2012 – he might have been able to add to his point score but Lee has been judging at a number of shows and once a dog has been shown in joint ownership he does not like to change it about.

Returning to the 'colours', Roger as we have seen has long had an interest in reds and apricots. He lived to see the birth of the red Toy, **Vanitonia Back In The Red**, by another Solnes import, but sadly didn't see him made up.

The kennel no longer has any Miniature Poodles, though two more champions have been made up since Lee came. They imported **Escandalo del Shikarah** from in Spain and he was the grandsire of the Harwood family's breed CC record holder **Ch Minarets Secret Assignment**.

Lee felt he'd like to make up a Miniature himself, along with the other varieties, and succeeding in doing so with **Riomella's Rio Rita for Vanitonia**. Later they went to visit Roger Bayliss in the hope of buying a stud dog, and came home with a bitch whom they made up, **Kertellas Double Dream of Vanitonia**. As they are no longer breeding Minis, they have let Jackie Kitchener have her and she has bred from her successfully, Bichons were kept for some years, and they bred a champion, **Vanitonia Takin Back My Love at Vanitonia** who was made up by Louise Stafford.

Today the kennel focusses on the Toy Poodle but Lee and Tom feel that in view of all the work that was put into Standards over so many years, it would be a pity to stop altogether, and an occasional litter is bred.

"We like to see other people winning with our stock, if they are prepared to do all the hard work..." says Lee. Roger took the same attitude and the number of other exhibitors who have made up Vanitonia Poodles is remarkable. It also helps keep more lines going than would be possible within one single kennel.

"Everyone has to start somewhere," says Lee, "and if someone is keen, who are we to say 'you can't'? Why shouldn't others have the same opportunities we had when we started?'

Tom with the kennel's three group-winning Chinese Cresteds: 'Nora', Ch Vanitonia Unwrapped – the breed's only UK general championship show BIS winner who has eight such awards, Ch Vanitonia Wots Occuring, who won two groups as a puppy, and Ch Zucci Highly Provocative at Vanitonia, the bitch CC record holder.

"Clumbers are a prime example. We desperately need some youngsters in the breed, otherwise in ten or 15 years it's possible there may not be any Clumbers left. So new people need to be encouraged, especially now that the world of dogs is at a low ebb. If that means sharing some of the success you've worked on, then so be it, for the good of the breed and the sport."

"Sadly not everyone believes in that – there's a big fear in this country that someone else might do better than you."

Ch Vanitonia Brace Yourself.
photo Walker

Sh Ch Vanitonia Wot A Liberty.

Indeed a large number of other UK exhibitors have made up one or more Vanitonia Poodles, in Standards Carol Charles, Philip Langdon, Arturo Sheppard, Jean Broomsgrove, Sarah O'Higgins, John Marshall and Sandra Dennison, and in Toys Ann Penfold, Malcolm Akers from the Isle of Man, Susan Crummey, Louise Wingham, Liz Spencer, Philip and Arturo.

In recent years Vanitonia has taken the Chinese Crested world by storm. How did it begin? Lee explains: "My partner at the time, Wayne, was fascinated by the breed and our friend Debbie Diamond was going to look at a litter at ther Blandora kennel and asked him if he wanted to go with her. Roger too was fascinated by them and asked if he could go. I said, 'Yes you can go but promise me you won't come back with anything. I'll kill you if you do.'

"Needless to say, Wayne and Roger came home and tried to sneak something in, and I knew full well they'd come back with a Crested puppy."

This was **Blandora Belles Are Ringing** who won a CC and puppy group. More important she 'got her feet under the table,' mixing well with the Poodles, and it all went on from there.

"If we're going to show with one, we might as well go with two," they felt, so they went back to Jeanette Sewell's kennel and persuaded her to see the brother **Blandora Rock N Robin**, who went BP at a club show first time out and became their first champion in the breed, going G2 at Crufts. Next came **Ch Blandora Time Bomb via Vanitonia**, and a couple from Nicky Moon including **Ch Zucci Highly Provocative at Vanitonia**, a group and Crufts BOB winner who still holds the bitch CC record.

Soon the homebred champions began to flow: we must mention **Vanitonia Brace Yourself**, twice top Crested, and **Wot's Occuring**, Crufts BOB 2012 and winner of two groups while still a puppy.

Then there was **Ch Only Annie Lusion**, a daughter of their first bitch, who produced **Ch Ticked Pink**. Catalina Gustafsson from Sweden saw the latter at Crufts and asked if she could show her over there. Roger was against the idea but Lee saw an opportunity of gaining new blood if they could bring her home in whelp to a Swedish dog. "Do what you want," said Roger.

So she won her Swedish and Norwegian titles and in the meantime Lee was judging the breed in Norway and gave BOB to a fabulous bitch, just what he was looking for and with points they needed in their own dogs. This was **Ch Sun-Hee's Temptation** from Sweden.

So he asked her owner if the bitch had any brothers. Yes, a champion dog, but his owner didn't want him used, and an unshown dog, **Tyson**, who had been used a few times. Lee never saw Tyson in the flesh, but did see photos, as well as admiring some of his progeny, so decided to take a chance when Tickled Pink came into season. It proved an expensive exercise, first getting her to the other end of Sweden to be mated, and then bringing her home which happened to be at Christmas time and cost £1,500!

A valuable litter, then, so what did she produce? A white powderpuff male and 'a pink hairless thing' – a big disappointment. "Told you so," said Roger. They decided to sell both as this wasn't what they'd hoped for – but the pink one had other ideas.

She developed into a total diva but, thinking she was destined for a pet home, they didn't take much notice of her until they put her on a lead at 12 weeks old. Most Crested pups are a nightmare to lead-train but little Nora set off like a train round the garden and 'my jaw dropped open', says Lee. "What have we got here?"

Vanitonia Unwrapped's first show was the breed club anniversary event with an enormous entry for American expert Dick Dickerson. "I stood at the side of the ring and the hairs on the back of my neck stood up," says Lee. She won the RCC and RBIS, then her first CC and BOB next time out.

By the end of the year she was a 'babychamp' with four CCs, two group places and four best puppy in show awards at general championship shows, already establishing herself as the darling of the ringsiders.

Brenda Banbury gave her the Pup of the Year final and so began an astonishing 2010 in which she became the first dog to take eight BIS awards at all-breeds championship shows within a calendar year, and topped the champions final. The Top Dog award was

Her brother Vanitonia U Bet I Am winning a heat of the Pro Plan/Dog World/Pup of the Year competition under Valerie Foss. He too became a show champion and between them they won 47 CCs. photo Johnson

closely fought, with the Kerry Blue neck and neck. To gain the title she had to be BIS at the last show of the year, LKA. Ann Arch, who had given her one of her BPIS awards, came up trumps and Nora was Top Dog, all before the age of two.

The decision was made to retire her there and then.

Their only sadness is that Roger died before he could see her in the ring. Now she's enjoying retirement. Her son by an American dog has recently been made up and they hope that in a future litter she might produce a hairless bitch to carry on.

After coming to Vanitonia, Lee went for a number of years without a Clumber. He kept up his interest and continued to judge them. After doing so at East of England he was so upset at the way the breed was going. Afterwards he was talking to Albert Wight who said: "The only way you're going to be able to do anything about it is not to moan but to have another one." A friend, Cherry Hicks, who worked with Hilda Monaghan of the famous Tweedsmuirs, told him she had a puppy available, so **Tweedsmuir Ladetta** joined the Vanitonias.

A lovely bitch who went back to the dogs Lee admired, she hated the ring, but proved an ideal foundation. He also admired the Kirkara dogs and their background so tried a combination few had attempted before, of a Kirkara dog, **Tommy Gunn**, to a Tweedsmuir bitch. Two puppies resulted; they kept both. The bitch, **Wot A Liberty**, won a CC from puppy, was made up as a junior and won a G4. The dog, **You Bet I Am**, qualified for Pup of the Year, took slightly longer to win his first CC but won a group with his second, his title the next week and ended up with three groups and a RBIS. Between them they has 47 CCs.

Hilda let them have a bitch pup, **Tweedsmuir Krystal Ice**, who was quickly crowned. So far, Wot A Liberty hasn't produced a litter – they live in hope – so they mated Krystal Ice to You Bet I Am, and from this a dog and bitch have already made a mark, the male **The Buck Stops Here** taking his title, two reserves and BPIS at National Gundog and BIS at the Clumber Club from his first six shows, doing the double with his sister at the breed show.

As a breed they remain Lee's first love, especially in today's difficult times with the health checks to contend with.

He feels he is lucky to have been brought up in the great days of the Clumber, and as a lad was encouraged by the breed's two great ladies, Rae Furness and Faith Gilham. He would often visit Raycroft, and was lucky enough to be invited to accompany Rae the first time she awarded best in show all breeds. She was a brilliant breeder and Lee still has her type in mind when he looks at any Clumber.

He feels the heyday of breed type was in the '80s, but eyes and soundness are better today, as they needed to be, and he hopes the breed will become more popular.

Clumbers are of course a 'high profile' breed and Cresteds were for a time, and Wot's Occurring was one of the dogs who passed the test at Crufts. Lee and Tom confess to being rather bemused by the concept, wondering what exactly is proved by checking just one dog at a show. And why just these breeds – after all many breeds have conditions which are tested for, and no account is taken of their health status. If there is to be checking, it should be across the board, they feel, and apply above all to stock that is bred from. They cannot understand, for example, how the Crufts Clumber failed when every other one tested since has passed. Bringing in the tests at Crufts of all places was, they feel, a huge mistake.

Today the kennel is no longer as 'extensive' as it was when Frank visited in '91. When Roger was first ill, they decided to let the numbers diminish and after he died Tom and Lee decided to keep it that way, no longer breeding to the same extent. For example when he arrived, there were around 25 Standard Poodles at Kaston; now there are three.

They still run a small boarding kennel, and Tom grooms dogs professionally, but Lee now works as recommendation manager for dog food company Purina, and is responsible for their trade stand at the dog shows.

Certainly they have proved incontrovertibly that cutting down on breeding hasn't diminished the quality of the dogs they produce!

Their most memorable dogs? Lee loved the Toy Holy Riot, not shown as he hated shows but 'as near perfection as you are likely to get', and later Clair Voyant, lovely to live with and such an important link in the line. And Nora, of course, refuses to be ignored...

From other kennels: the beautiful Clumber **Sh Ch Raycroft Sunny Jim**, the Finnish-bred Standard Poodle **Ch Canmoys Rubiazo**, 'the ultimate show dog', and inevitably the Lhasa **Ch Saxonsprings Fresno**.

An inspiration to Tom in his early days was the glamour boy American Cocker **Sh Ch Boduf Pistol At Dawn with Afterglow**, and more recently the Standard Poodle **Am Ch Dawin Spitfire**.

Health testing is a priority nowadays. As Frank pointed out in his interview, the Poodles have been eye tested for many years, but Lee admits that Roger was rather sceptical as to the value of testing for some of the other issues which Standards in particular have to worry about. Now, though, they do all the tests they can on all their breeds, and say that their latest Standard champion, Eye Candy, is the most health tested dog they have ever had.

They have recently joined the Assured Breeder Scheme. For some years they resisted doing so, feeling that they carried out all the requirements anyway, but the Kennel Club's Bill Lambert eventually talked them round. They do feel, though, that every applicant should be visited before they are accepted onto the scheme.

Lee awards CCs in nine breeds, having first done so in Clumbers at the age of 24, and has questionnaires in for more, having participated in the judges development scheme. He enjoys judging and feels it is one way to continue participating in the sport when eventually they cut down on showing. Tom was 26 when he first gave CCs, and is passed for Poodles and Cresteds.

They have judged frequently abroad and visit events like the Poodle Club of America feeling that otherwise it's easy to become insular and blinkered. It helps enormously to see what other breeders are doing and how they cope with any problems. Sometimes breeders overseas find it easier to be honest about their own stock.

Lee says: "You can talk to breeders in Britain about a problem and they say I've never had that in my line' when you know full well they must have done, as they all come from the same lines. You don't tend to get that attitude abroad. I can understand why

The kennel has also bred a champion Bichon Frisé, Louise Stafford's Ch Vanitonia Taking Back My Love at Louisianna, owned by Louise Stafford, pictured winning her third CC under Terry Burgess.

this happens – it you admit to a problem it becomes like a witch hunt. I wish the Brits could would stop the witch hunts and be more upfront about their breeding programmes."

All the Poodles and Cresteds run together and their accommodation is connected to the house; only the Clumbers are kennel dogs in the true sense. House dogs include a Pointer and a Frenchie as well as some older Poodles. Freedom and fresh air are considered priorities – the dogs can be out all day, with covered areas in case of rain, and there is a special room for bitches in season. They have full time help so the routine is just the same if Tom and Lee are away.

Lee does much of the basic trimming but admits that Tom is the master of doing topknots!

Do they go about breeding such different breeds the same way? In the Poodles, line-breeding usually works,and you can usually predict from the pedigree roughly what you are likely to get. Clumbers, too – Lee has known them since the '70s so has a pretty good idea what to expect from a mating.

Crested, though, are another story, and are virtually impossible to breed to type. There's no point in breeding them 'on paper'; the best results tend to come simply by using a dog who scores where your bitch happens to fail. They are so hard to breed consistently – which is why Lee and Tom feel that when they did manage to come up with something like Nora, it was a pity that such an achievement was by no means universally embraced by their fellow breeders.

What are their views on the dog world as a whole?

Sometimes, they feel, the KC needs to look at how things are done abroad – they'd favour a champions class, for example, to encourage people to carry on showing when one dog is dominating a breed. Optional benching, clusters of shows, grading, CCs for every breed with judges prepared to withhold – all possible ways, they feel, of making shows more appealing and/or more economical for the exhibitors. Yes, perhaps this might produce a few cheap champions at first (and you get those anyway!), but judges would soon get used to the idea of not awarding the CC if there was nothing worthy, just as they do in Scandinavia. Why would you travel more than a few miles for a non-CC entry, unless you are aiming for group places?

The Canine Alliance could well be a start, encompassing as it does some very enthusiastic people who with some good ideas.

Many of us are depressed about the future of the dog world but Lee and Tom feel that it's pointless being too negative. "Get up and do something about it, don't moan but try and find solutions. The future of pedigree dogs is in our hands".

All smiles after Nora's history-making eighth BIS win of 2010 which also gained her the Top Dog title. Pictured with Tom and Lee are judge Ann Arch and LKA vice-chairman Anne Bliss. photo Walker

The Dog World in 2012

Bath's RBIS was Jenny Griffiths' West Highland White Terrier Ch Karamynd Play It Again, pictured with chairman Muriel Iles, who has now retired after 60 years' service to the society, judge Clare Coxall and secretary Ben Ford.
photo Walker

RBIS at Boston was Melanie Spavin and Lee Raymond's Australian Shepherd Ch Allmark Ozzy Osbourne at Dialynne, seen with chairman Phil Kirk, group judge Sue Hewart-Chambers and Carol Baker of CSJ Specialist Canine Feeds.
photo Johnson

Two Cardigan Corgis have won RBIS awards in 2012; none had done so previously. At Southern Counties it was Lisa Croft-Elliott and Hanno Dijkhorst's Dutch-bred Ch/Int/Slo/Dutch Ch Floatin' Helen Heilin. With them are judge Zena Thorn Andrews, breed judge Annukka Paloheimo and chairman Dave Cavill.
photo Johnson

At Border Union Bill Browne-Cole's RBIS was Luke Johnston's Whippet Ch Danluke Dance Of Love, handled by his mother Helen. Left is show manager Marjory Macgregor and right treasurer Susan Webster. Luke himself had a great year, being one of the youngest handlers ever to win a group place at Crufts, with his Saluki.
photo Dalrymple

Phil Davies and Sean Crowley took RBIS at Windsor with the Kerry Blue Terrier Ch Perrisblu Kings Ransome, seen with commentator Jonathan Daltrey, judge Michael Quinney and Antony Bongiovanni of Royal Canin.
photo Johnson

Tom Johnston gave RBIS at Paignton to Valerie Smith's West Highland White Terrier Ch Faymar Fine Romance. On the right is secretary Aileen Hodsoll.
photo Farlap

Claire, Liz and (left) Mia Millward's Greyhound Ch/Int/Bel Ch Windspiel Northern Steel for Alouann was Jean Lanning's RBIS winner at Bournemouth. Committee member Clari Cross completes the line-up.
photo Harris

East of England's runner-up was the imported German Shepherd, Indo vom Tamaraspitze, shown by Steve Cox for Tina Jermey (right). Also in the line-up are judge Jeff Luscott, chairman John Orbell and committee member Vic Salt.
photo Walker

Richard Allan handled Franki Leung and Antonio Almeida's Wire Fox Terrier Ch Travella Star Craft to RBIS at City of Birmingham under Valerie Foss. With them are Pepe Haro Haro from one of association's twinned clubs in Spain and chairman Bill King.
photo Walker

IRELAND

Report and photographs: Joyce Crawford-Manton

Feelgood factor for Irish shows

Despite the continuing dire economic situation, the canine world seems to have steadied the ship in the past few years. Indeed at the majority of all-breed championship shows in 2012, entries were either up or at least on a par with last year. It seems that the exhibitors, while tightening their belts in other aspects of their lives, still want their regular fix of dog shows.

With the number of all-breed championship shows on the island now at 29, plus Belfast, although not with CCs for all breeds, bringing it up to 30, plus a further 11 group championship shows, not to mention all the breed club shows, plus the various special events and a myriad of open and limit shows, so vital for the training of judges, it is easy to see that the sport is very much thriving.

The biggest bugbear of the year has been the weather; at one stage it seemed that we would all be washed away. Luckily, the shows in Dublin have the advantage of holding their events at the National Show Centre at Cloghran, handily placed just beside the airport on the outskirts of the city, very convenient for bringing in foreign judges, something we have become very used to these past few years.

The mortgage on the building having now been fully serviced, plans are underway to add to the existing structure. What great foresight to have gone ahead with a purpose-built centre, originally opened for the World Congress in 1993 and celebrating its 20th anniversary in 2013.

Not so lucky are the clubs in the south and west who have no such purpose-built facilities; they had to struggle against the weather but still managed to pull off good shows. The shows in the north have had the luxury of the Kings Hall Complex in Belfast for a base but even here was not without problems as, with the sale of the surrounding grounds finally being agreed, and the new temporary building only completed the night before Belfast show, there remains uncertainty over what space will be available in 2013.

One northern based club, Newtownards, decided to move in May to a new facility in the town and was rewarded with one of the worst days of the year! Thankfully, the Irish Circuit was pretty much unscathed by the weather and a large number of visitors returned for the week-long festival.

The successes of Irish dogs in the UK and further afield continued, the more adventurous taking advantage of the more relaxed travel restrictions to bring home many major wins from Europe.

The promised change to docking in Northern Ireland, due in April, was delayed only temporarily, and having finally received Royal Assent in Parliament, will come into effect from January 1, 2013. The only bright note is that dogs docked before this date will be able to be shown for the remainder of their showing lives. Penalties for breaking this law are swingeing, fines and a potential jail sentence!

A meeting was held in September between the Irish Kennel Club General Purposes Committee and members of the affiliated clubs to seek views on restructuring the way clubs are represented at An Ard Chomhairle (General Council), and on setting up regional councils for the four provinces. The feedback will be discussed by the GP and further developments are expected next year.

James Newman and Séan Carroll's Papillon Ch/UK/Ger/Slo/Mont/Int Ch Denemore Iconsruben is in the lead to repeat his Irish Kennel Club Dog of the Year title, which he took in 2011. 'Ruben' took two BIS at Combined Canine international and Limerick and six reserves from ten group wins. He is seen winning the title Champion of Champions 2011 under Argentinian judge Dr José Vidal Monterro, now resident in Spain. In 2011 he had six BIS, two RBIS and 13 group wins.
photo Beggs

With just three championship shows left, the Siberian Husky, Jimmy Duggan's Ch Bedarra Cold Paws Warm Heart for Leorient, is hot on the heels of the Papillon, with three BIS from eight group wins. 'Flint', usually handled by Jimmy's wife Anita Foley Duggan, also took BIS at the Working and Pastoral Breeds Association of Wales. Home BIS came at Munster Canine, Dundalk where he is pictured with judge June Wall, at Dun Laoghaire.

It was 1997 when last a West Highland White Terrier took BIS at an Irish all-breeds event, so it was a thrill for Jane Jenkins when she saw her Ch Havasu Hugo Boss, piloted by breeder Ken Crockett, go BIS at the Irish Kennel Club international show. The next week 'Monty' took CC and BIS at the Northern Ireland breed club show.

It was a first for the breed when the Australian Shepherd Ch/Int Ch Hopscotch del Whymper dell G Jorasses, took BIS at Newtownards. Owned by Des and Joyce Manton, 'Gaby' has been top Aussie for the last three years. Judge was breed specialist Dr Marleen Collins.

Howard and Sally Tonks have been Pyrenean exhibitors for many years, and it has also been many years since a Pyrenean Mountain Dog clinched an all-breeds BIS, and that was one of theirs in 1999. Carlow gave them cause for double celebration as their Ch Shanlimore Maverick, just back from winning his third CC at Richmond, took BIS under Rosemary Daly-Meehan.

Another breed missing top honours for a long time is the Yorkshire Terrier, the last was over 25 years ago, but at Bray top spot went to Alan and Rita Fitzsimmons' Spanish import Ch Only You My Sky de Nemrac-Aniuq at Fitzelly.

Barry O'Neill and Sandra Stack's Basset Hound Ch/UK Ch Knockogue Arthurs Legacy heads group 6 and has two BIS wins (Hibernian and Kilkenny where he is seen with judge Willie Dobbin) from his 12 groups in 2012, and won his fifth CC at Belfast.

Dominating group 7 has been the English Setter Sh Ch Richecca Reach For The Skye, owned by Aidan McKiernan. 'Bailey' has two BIS from his six groups won, at South Tipperary and Bangor and North Down, where judge was Sally Burns.

In 2011 Colm and Rose Hastings' US-bred Old English Sheepdog Ch/Am/UK/Int Ch Lambluvs Live The Dream took all in front of her for group 1, and in 2012 she is well ahead with eight group wins. 'Sue' took BIS at Banbridge and Portadown where she is seen with judge Anita Foley-Duggan.

At the start of the year a young Bichon Frisé, Ashling Connolly's Ashmair Double Act, won the Eukanuba sponsored Irish Kennel Club Top Showdog Awards final, giving him his ticket to represent Ireland at the Eukanuba World Challenge. 'Beau' went on to win the Irish Pup of the Year 2011 under Croatian judge Bojan Matakovic (pictured). Now an Irish and UK champion, he has won five groups, BIS at Swords and twice RBIS.

Katie Kelly won the Irish junior handling final under Suzy Roffey and went on to represent Ireland at the international final at Crufts and at the European Show.

Tony O'Neill, secretary of the Irish Kennel Club, retired in September after over 20 years serving the club in many ways. Apart from taking on the job of show secretary of the IKC shows for many years, latterly he has been much involved in the promotion of the IKC National Show Centre, particularly bringing in outside, non-canine events. Tony was 'hands on' in the early days, taking the IKC 'roadshow' around the country, and was part of the IKC attaining full membership of the FCI. President Séan Delmar (left) presented him with a laptop.

Mary Crowley, vice-president of the IKC and very long time secretary of Dun Laoghaire CC, stood down from the post at the show in August. Chairman Nick Hammond presented her with a bouquet.

UNITED STATES

Bo Bengtson

Let's focus on the positives!

It is increasingly difficult to make any sense of the conflicting trends within the American dog sport. Why are we seeing a drop in American Kennel Club registrations, while entry figures in general are up?

Dogs are certainly as popular as ever over here, so why does AKC's share in the total dog population continue to shrink? If I may hazard a guess it might be that AKC is finally becoming what many have long felt it should aim to be: a sort of 'boutique registry' with fewer dogs, but a high percentage of these actively participating in organised events.

The exact number of registrations last year is not known for the simple reason that AKC no longer releases these figures. The all-time high was recorded in 1992, when over 1.5 million dogs were registered; by 2010 the total was down to 563,611 dogs, and the

One of the two candidates for the US' Top Dog 2012 title, English Springer Spaniel Gr Ch Wynmoor Champagne Supernova, handled by Robin Novack and pictured winning BIS at Sandusky Kennel Club under Sondra Esporite.
photo Booth

Narrowly in the lead as Top Dog in the US, the German Wirehaired Pointer Gr Ch Mt View's Ripsnorter Silver Charm, handled by Phil Booth to BIS at Scottsdale Dog Fanciers Association under Robert Shreve.
photo Rodwell

only indication we have that it was even lower last year is that AKC revenue from registrations dropped by $2 million.

If this continues AKC may eventually no longer live up to its proud claim of being the biggest purebred dog registry in the world, although for the time being that's almost certainly still true.

However, AKC has no plans on limiting its activities to just a select group of purebred show dogs. On the contrary, as AKC put it, "We're more than champion dogs. We're the dog's champion." That also means, increasingly, non-registered and even non-purebred dogs, which can these days participate in some AKC activities, although obviously not in conformation. This is still controversial in a few quarters, but it's clear that AKC's plan to include as many pet dogs as possible in its fold will result in their owners having a more positive view of AKC – and perhaps getting a purebred next time they buy a dog.

The increase in entries over the past couple of years is largely due to the success of the new grand champion title. There were 40,000 more entries in the champion class the year this title was introduced than the year before, and it's if anything more popular now than it was in the beginning.

Dog people love to chase titles, and while many of us can't take

this one all that seriously, it's unquestionably a boon to dog shows in the sense that more champions than ever are being shown in an attempt to 'Grand' them, as they say in the cat fancy.

The champion title has never been considered the ultimate pinnacle of a dog's show career in the US, as is often the case in the UK. With more than 100 new AKC champions per year in most breeds, over 200 in some, the title is simply a first stepping-stone to greater things for those deemed worthy of being 'specialled' – in other words, seriously campaigned. The rest used to retire once they achieved the 15 points required for the AKC champion title.

Now many of these former couch potatoes are dusted off and brought out again. It would be too complicated to explain exactly what's required for a grand champion title, so let's just say the genius of it is that you get points even when you don't win!

In fact, four of the top dogs competing for best of breed may be rewarded: BOB, BOS and the runner-up (or 'select') in each sex, provided they are already AKC champions. Yes, you need to be a regular champion before you can start collecting grand champion points, a source of much confusion and disappointment to, for example, owners of an outstanding youngster who wins BOB from the puppy class.

The success of the grand champion title may easily translate into more AKC titles in the future. There has been talk of junior champions, veteran champions, supreme champions (presumably multi-titled), etc. However, all those remain a pipedream as yet.

That relative rarity, a breeder-owner handled group winner at Westminster. Betty Leininger chose the Dobermann Gr Ch Protocol's Veni Vidi Vici, owned by Suzy Lundy, Dick Lundy, Jocelyn Mullins (handling) and Kevin Mullins, to top the working group. Sean McCarthy stewarded. The Dobermann is likely to end up number three all breeds for 2012.

Among the top dogs of all breeds for the second year, Affenpinscher Gr Ch Banana Joe v Tani Kazari is currently number one toy. He is imported from the Netherlands and shown by Ernesto Lara to BIS at Greenwich Kennel Club under Cindy Vogels. Owners are Zoila Truesdale and breeder Mieke Cooijmans.
photo Ashbey

Top hound is the American Foxhound Gr Ch Kiarry's Pandora's Box, handled by co-owner and co-breeder Lisa Miller to BIS at Detroit Kennel Club under Elliott Weiss. The other co-owners are Dr James and Jane Fitzpatrick and Harry Miller.
photo Booth.

In the lead as the year's top terrier, the Wire Fox Ch Afterall Painting The Sky, pictured after winning BIS at Santa Barbara Kennel Club with officials and members. 'Sky' is handled by Gabriel Rangel.
photo Rodwell

The Breeders' Showcase is a unique feature hosted by Santa Barbara Kennel Club. More than 120 teams of two homebred dogs competed. Winners were two Border Terriers, Gr Ch Meadowlake Simply Sinful and Meadowlake Pants On Fire, bred by Karen Fitzpatrick. Judges were Edd Bivin (left of winners) and England's Mike Gadsby (right). Far left is club official Desmond Murphy, Jr and far right, sponsor Purina representative Carol Grossman.
photo Rodwell

It is clear AKC has realised that mixing things up a bit and introducing new opportunities to compete can be a good thing. Seldom have we seen so many new features at regular AKC shows as in the past year. There's an unofficial four to six-months baby puppy class, group and BIS competitions especially for owner-handled dogs – in other words, the professionals who are such a big part of AKC dogs shows need not apply – and a reserve BIS award at all-breed shows.

The latter, an established and popular tradition in all other countries, has met with a mixed reception in the US. Most of us are happy to be recognised even if we don't win BIS, but some of the big shots would rather have nothing than 'best of losers' (as they call it). A few have even been known to refuse having a photograph taken.

All these new features are good, of course, but they can also be seen as a (rather belated) acknowledgment on AKC's part that regular exhibitors need more places to compete, since they are virtually shut out from the annual Top Dog race.

That this has evolved into a playground for the wealthy has been general knowledge among dog people for a long time. Common sense tells you that as long as points are simply cumulative you need to go to a lot of shows in order to achieve an impressive year-end total. And in the US there are A LOT of AKC all-breed shows:

The 2011 AKC/Eukabnuba show moved from California to Orlando, Florida. BIS went to the Standard Poodle Ch Jaset's Satisfaction, owned by Beth Harris, Michael Molnar and Jamie Danburg and shown by Ann Rairigh. 'London' is in the lead in the non-sporting group rankings for 2012.
photo Croft-Elliott

nearly 1,500 per year, plus untold specialty and group shows.

Nobody can hope to attend more than a fraction of all these, of course, but contenders for Top Dog, and their full-time professional handlers, must spend most of their time on the road, usually competing at something like 200 shows per year.

The cost involved is staggering: most handlers agree it can take from $200,000 to $500,000 to get even close to the top. That would include the handler's salary, and often a big bonus for every BIS, travelling costs – thousands of miles, sometimes by private jet – and extensive advertising campaigns in the glossy dog publications.

There's not much question that the top dogs are invariably excellent specimens of their breed, but what they possess in abundance even more than breed type is a willingness to go out there and show their heads off – not just on occasion, but every single time year-round. Perhaps this was not what dog shows were initially meant to focus on, but it's definitely what they are about at this level today.

It should be added that it does happen – not often, but enough to keep many people's hopes up – that less well known dogs take BIS over the top contenders. However, having a high win percentage doesn't help in the rankings unless a dog is campaigned consistently.

At the time of writing more than 200 shows remain this year, but according to most recent statistics it looks like a close race between two dogs for number one. The English Springer Spaniel **Gr Ch Wynmoor Chamagne Supernova** and the German Wirehaired Pointer **Gr Ch Mt View's Ripsnorter Silver Charm** have both defeated over 60,000 competitors in group and BIS competition so far during 2012, yet they are so close that a single defeat or victory could shift the balance.

The Springer is of course 'English' in name only; there's an established type difference between British and American Springers. He is known as Peyton and is handled by Robin Novack for a group of owners consisting of Celie Florence, Beth Fink, Dr Erin Kerfoot, Dr Kent Goodhue-McWilliams and Delores Streng. The GWP, Oakley to his friends, is shown by Philip Booth for Victor Malzoni of Brazil, well known as owner of some top dogs in the UK as well.

These two dogs illustrate two recent trends in the US dog sport. On the one hand the top campaigners are increasingly often owned by a consortium of 'sponsors', and on the other hand they are frequently owned by foreign exhibitors. Mr Malzoni, in fact, also owns the Wire Fox Terrier **Ch Afterall Painting The Sky**, who's top terrier and among the top ten of all breeds.

Most of America's major dog shows saw increased entries last year. The spring weekend in Kentucky remains in the lead: Evansville KC was the year's biggest show with 3,172 dogs in competition, more than 250 more than the previous year, while Louisville KC had 3,093 dogs on the previous day, also an increase.

The new year shows in Palm Springs in California had 2,964 and 2,693 dogs, respectively, an increase of 500-600 dogs per day! Others of the top ten shows, like Santa Maria KC in California and Dog Fanciers Association of Oregon, maintained their positions in spite of slightly lower entries.

By far the most imaginative of the regional all-breed shows, Santa Barbara KC, maintains a high profile in spite of lower entry totals. This year's figures of just over 1,600 dogs per day were still an increase from the previous year. With special competitions for best foreign bred dog, best 'bully breed' and especially the popular breeders' showcase, this year's shows once again made well-deserved big headlines.

The biggest increase of all, however, was noted by the American Kennel Club's own show, popularly known as AKC/Eukanuba, now back in Orlando, Florida with an impressive total of 3,064 dogs competing last year, all of them champions! There were numerous additional entries in the World Challenge and in the many other special events offered.

This was an increase of more than 1,000 dogs and augurs well for the 2012 event to be held in Orlando on Dec 15-16, especially as this

Best in show at Westminster Kennel Club in New York was the Pekingese Gr Ch Palacegarden Malachy, bred by Jim and Jean Smith and owned by David Fitzpatrick, Iris Love and Sandra Middlebrooks. His formal BIS photo is featured in Andrew Brace's interview with David on page 89. Here he is seen taking the toy group under Tim Catterson, his second such victory at Westminster. Edwin Hershey stewarded.
photo Ashbey

Houston Clark's choice in the herding group at Westminster was the German Shepherd Dog Gr Ch Babheim's Captain Crunch, shown by James Moses who co-owns him with Sheree Moses, Deborah Stern, Janet Lange, Carlos Navarro and Maria Deschamps. Steward was William Jackson. The GSD is the year's top winner in the herding group.
photo Ashbey

Patricia Laurans gave the hound group at Westminster to the Wire Dachshund Gr Ch Raydachs Playing With Fire v Gleishorbach SW, owned by Shirley Ray and Maria and James Sakoda and handled by Cheri Koppenhaver. Steward was John Everets.
photo Ashbey

year's show will be open for non-champions as well. Over the past 12 years this show has become the most colorful and international dog show extravaganza that the US can offer and attracts a host of foreign exhibitors with their dogs. BIS last year went to the black Standard Poodle **Ch Jaset's Satisfaction** ('London'), who continued to reign as the leading non-sporting dog through 2012 and is one of the top ten of all breeds.

So what about Westminster? With the advantage of 137 years of unmatched history, a prestige that no other dog show in the world except Crufts can compete with, plus unparalleled TV coverage and a prime location at Madison Square Garden in the middle of Manhattan, this show is still number one according to most aficionados.

The locations carries its own disadvantage, however, as space there is at a premium, and the number of dogs that can be housed has been limited to 2,500 for years. The news that breed judging at the 2013 show, to be held as usual the second Monday and Tuesday in February, will move to a much more spacious arena, with only groups and BIS finals to be held at Madison Square Garden, means that Westminster for the first time could increase its entry limit to 3,000 dogs. Non-champions may now also participate as long as they are 'major pointed' (which means roughly that they have a foot well up on the ladder towards the champion title).

Last year the biggest single-breed specialty event was, once again,

Winner of the non-sporting group at Westminster under Randy Garren was the Dalmatian Gr Ch Spotlights Ruffian, handled by Michael Scott for Jim and Barbara Lyons. James Stebbins was the steward.
photo Ashbey

Best in show at Montgomery County terrier show was the Lakeland Gr Ch Iron van Foliny Home, handled by Gabriel Rangel for Victor Malzoni, and bred in Belgium. Judge was Paolo Dondina from Italy who has had some of the most prestigious appointments in the last two years including BIS at Crufts, Westminster and the Winner Show Amsterdam in 2011 and the terrier group at Crufts 2012.
photo Ashbey

The Irsh Setter Gr Ch Shadagee Caught Red Handed returned to the ring after producing a large litter, and won the group at Westminster under Terry Stacy. Owners are Debra Burke and Nancy Lee Conner, and handler Adam Bernardin. Dr Bernard McGivern presented the trophy.
photo Ashbey

A second UK-bred group winner at Westminster, the Kerry Blue Terrier Gr Ch/UK Ch Perrisblu Kennislain's Chelsey, owned by, Ed, Lynn, Candace and Brock Yingling and Phil Davies from Wales for whom she had been number two all breeds in the UK in 2010. Handler was Bill McFadden, judge William Potter and steward Avery Bourke.
photo Ashbey

hosted by the Labrador Retriever Club of the Potomac, which had 752 dogs competing in the official classes. This means that the total entry figure, including absentees, multiple entries etc could be well into the four figures.

The national specialty shows for Collies and Golden Retrievers both had over 600 dogs competing, Shetland Sheepdogs and Whippets over 500 dogs, Boxers and Poodles over 400. Six breeds had specialties with 398-325 dogs: Rhodesian Ridgebacks, Flat-coated Retrievers, Siberian Huskies, Portuguese Water Dogs, Newfoundlands, Salukis and Great Danes.

With all the doom and gloom surrounding the dog world worldwide these days, there are some things to be happy and grateful for, even a few exciting events to look forward to in 2013 here in the US.

Bo Bengtson is Editor-at-Large, Dogs in Review. Photos by John Ashbey, Kim Booth and Kit Rodwell submitted by Dogs in Review.

Winner of the Eukanuba World Challenge 2011, held with the American Kennel Club/Eukanuba Show in Orlando, Florida, was the Australian Shepherd Ch Propwash Reckon, who qualified by winning BIS at the previous year's AKC/Eukanuba where he took the top prize of $65,000, having just arrived back from a stay in Italy. He was handled by co-owner Judy Harrington who co-owns him with breeder Leslie Frank. Also pictured are AKC's then board chairman Ron Menaker (who has since been succeeded by Alan Kalter), final judge Enrique Fillippini, FCI treasurer Rafael de Santiago and Jose Luis Ibanez of the sponsor. Runner-up was the Toy Poodle from Japan Ch Smash JP Moon Walk, owned by Yukiko Ormura and handled by her son Toshi. The UK's representative, Margaret Anderson's Lhasa Apso Ch Zentarr Elizabeth, was first runner-up (third) in the final, going on to even better things a few months later when she took BIS at Crufts.
photo Croft-Elliott

The David Fitzpatrick Story

Andrew Brace

A high school photo of David Fitzpatrick, aged 13.

SPEAK to anyone who is remotely involved with the Pekingese breed and the mention of David Fitzpatrick's name will result in a degree of awe and reverence for this American gentleman is acknowledged as being as fine a handler and presenter of a Pekingese as has ever been seen.

Earlier this year David handled the UK-bred **Am Ch Palacegarden Malachy** to win best at America's most prestigious dog show, Westminster Kennel Club, in his own inimitable style and in many ways this was the pinnacle of his career as a handler, breeder and owner of the breed to which he is clearly devoted.

David always wanted to own a dog as a small child but his parents refused to indulge him, mainly, David suspects, because he had a brother who suffered from many allergies. In the absence of a dog of his own, David would walk neighbourhood dogs and at one time hid a cat in his closet until it was discovered by his parents.

When he was 14 years of age, in 1970, David was visiting his Aunt Helen to help her clear out her garage when he stumbled across a copy of *Popular Dogs* magazine that fascinated him.

"I opened up this magazine and saw all these beautiful pictures of wonderful dogs and was completely blown away. In the small ads was one placed by a lady named Hermine Cleaver who lived in Newark, Delaware, around 15 minutes away from my home. She had Pekingese but I loved all dogs and maybe my breed of choice

may have been a Cocker Spaniel, but she lived so near that I wrote her a letter asking if she needed help with her dogs. I told her that I was interested in dogs and would be happy to help her in any way she needed.

"She took me up on the offer and very soon she was picking me up after school in her station wagon, taking me to the kennel, and there she taught me how to clean kennels, wash dogs, groom dogs and so on ... and I was getting five dollars a day for doing something I loved!"

The first dog show David attended was the Valley Forge Kennel Club to which his sister-in-law Betty had taken him. There he walked around looking at all the different breeds, but he started going to dog shows in earnest with Mrs Cleaver whose kennel name was Pencader. At the shows he helped groom and exercise her dogs and act as general factotum, rapidly becoming transfixed by the dog world.

David continued to help Mrs Cleaver for around six years, by which time he had graduated from high school and left full time

David's first ever group win came when he handled Ch Quilkin The Stringman under Anne Rogers Clark at the Longshore Southport show in June 1977.
photo Gilbert

Below: David winning BIS at the Pekingese Club of America show in 1981 with Ch Paladin's Sneaky Pete, sired by a Mingulay dog from the UK. The judge was Bill Bergum and also pictured are Geraldine Lee Hess (who incidentally awarded Andrew Brace his very first CC in Pekingese!) next to David and Dottie Schuerch.
photo Ashbey

education to work for her full time... "much to my family's chagrin", recalls David.

At the time professional handlers were licensed by the American Kennel Club and David had to apply for an assistant handler's licence which he duly obtained. This allowed him to show dogs that were in Mrs Cleaver's care, as she was actually a handler showing dogs for other people.

"Dutch by birth, Mrs Cleaver was a strict taskmaster and somewhat eccentric. She actually showed some of the first Shih Tzu when they were getting established in this country and handled for Gilbert Kahn among others. I remember one dog she had for him was an English dog called Chang of Kandu who became an American champion and she had several English Pekingese that she finished too."

When he was about 20 years old David was approached by Michael Wolf who at the time was working for the very wealthy Pekingese fancier and owner, Mrs Walter M Jeffords Jr, and asked if he would be interested in working for her.

David's finest hour... winning BIS at Westminster 2012 under Cindy Vogels with the UK-bred Pekingese Ch Palacegarden Malachy. Also pictured are the then president Peter van Brunt, chairman Tom Bradley and chief steward Sean McCarthy who is now the Westminster president.
photo Ashbey

In 1982 David handled a Sheffield bitch to win BOB in Pugs at Westminster under Bill Bergum.
photo Ashbey

The legendary Frank Sabella seen awarding David best of winners in 1986 with a Paladin dog he was handling for Dottie Schuerch.

David remembers: "We knew each other through the Pekingese, they weren't too far away and I guess they must have figured that I was a hard worker and I could groom Pekingese. So I moved back home and stayed with my parents for a while, the job with Mrs Jeffords being rather like a day job, then I would go to shows with them at weekends.

"I was a little cautious before I made the move a living-in job, but when I could see that it would work out I moved there full time. Bear in mind that I was thirsty for any kind of dog exposure and Mrs Jeffords kept around 250 dogs in a huge kennel property. To me this was doggy heaven and it wasn't just Pekingese that were kept... there were Pomeranians, Maltese, Yorkies, Pugs, English Toy Spaniels, Italian Greyhounds, Boston Terriers, French Bulldogs, Standard Poodles, Shih Tzu, Greyhounds, Lakeland Terriers and more that I have forgotten by now.

"And of course Mr Jeffords had a Foxhound kennel on another property as he was a Master of Foxhounds. It was glorious country and Rolling Hills Farm was a paradise and a wonderful experience for someone young and so eager to learn about dogs."

British judge Joyce Shipley awarded Ch Briarcourt's Coral Gable BOB at the Pekingese Club of America in 1986. On the left is Richard Thomas, father of actor Richard Thomas who played John Boy Walton in the famous television series.
photo Ashbey

David winning best of winners with Coral Gable as a puppy under the famous Anna Katherine Nicholas.
photo Ashbey

Michael Wolf was the primary handler for Mrs Jeffords and when the opportunity arose David had the chance to help out in the ring handling. He enjoyed his days at Rolling Hills...

"It was heady, being surrounded by eccentric people and so many dogs, and the Jeffords were people of great substance. Mr Jeffords' uncle owned the famous racehorse Man o' War and Mrs Jeffords was of course used to staff. I remember that she had come down to the place in the country on one occasion but minus any help. She called me over to the big house, clearly frustrated, and asked why she couldn't make a cup of coffee. She hadn't realised that you actually had to plug the coffee percolator into the electric socket; she had obviously never had to make a cup of coffee for herself before!

"She was a great present-giver and every Christmas sent lavish gifts to all these judges she had shown to, and she was so proud of the thank you notes she received. I used to help her with her Christmas list and sometimes was well aware that some of the judges on the list had died, but their widows may have still been around, so I just left them on the list and figured they would appreciate the gifts, which of course they did!"

After he had been there for about five years, there came the parting of the ways when Mrs Jeffords and Michael Wolf's association dissolved, somewhat acrimoniously. Both Michael and Mrs Jeffords wanted David to stay on with them and Mrs Jeffords offered various inducements but he opted to work for Michael. By now the AKC had stopped licensing handlers so David would be handling dogs in various breeds, many co-owned by Michael and

David's very first BIS came in 1986 when Coral Gable won under Keke Blumberg (now Kahn) at Skyline Kennel Club in Virginia.
photo Kernan

whoever happened to be financing the dog's campaign.

During this period David was still effectively 'the help' as he put it, but he maintains that these early days taught him a lot about conditioning dogs and also breeding as Michael was a prolific breeder.

In the early 1980s David felt that he had outgrown his position with Michael. "I didn't want to be an assistant for ever; I had decided I wanted to show dogs so the time had come to break out on my own. And Michael wasn't the easiest to deal with, but I did learn a lot there."

So David had some friends who lived outside of Washington DC, Art and Barbara Friedman, who had a kennel out of which he worked. From there he started to build a foundation as a handler.

"I started slow and handled a variety of small breeds for various

Ch Jo-Li Wind In The Willows won more than a hundred groups with David. Here he is winning a BIS under Michele Billings.
photo Meyer

Liz Stannard from Britain awarded Ch Briarcourt's Damien Gable BOB at the Pekingese Club of America show held over the 1992 Westminster weekend. Presenting the trophy is Bill Blair.
photo Tatham

clients. Then I had the good fortune to buy a Pekingese dog puppy for $400 from Joan Mylchreest named **Briarcourt's Coral Gable**." David immediately saw the potential in this dog who was clearly a cut above the average Pekingese.

"He had a lot of charisma, a magnetic way about him… you would look at him and he would look right back at you and had the IT factor. He was maybe a little high stationed for what we would want today but he was a solid, sound little dog… put him on the table and he was like the Rock of Gibraltar. Also he was the consummate show dog and you could stand ten feet away from him and he would just do it."

During his show career David owned Coral Gable in his own right but was then persuaded to let the infamous William McKay back the dog.

David takes up the story: "Rightly or wrongly I was persuaded to let this man back this beautiful dog. He paid his bills – usually in cash – and the dog got on a roll and won the group at Westminster in 1987, ending up as top toydog that year. Then in 1988 I showed him at the Garden again when he lost the breed – to one of Mrs Jeffords' dogs who was by Ch Belknap Kalafrana Caspar.

"Then all hell broke loose. It was pretty common knowledge that Mr McKay was under investigation for impropriety; he was effectively being accused of bribing judges. I was called in by the American Kennel Club for questioning about the various judges that had put me up with Mr McKay's dog. It was the biggest waste of my time because I knew nothing about what he was supposedly giving these judges, but the tragedy was that when I should have been enjoying campaigning a beautiful dog, the whole experience got soured.

"Moreover, the dog was due to be transferred back into my name but the AKC froze that and it took a few years to get it sorted, during which time the dog was not bred from. However there was a pot of gold at the end of the rainbow as the first puppy Coral produced after I got him back into my name was Damien".

After Coral Gable David did some useful winning with **Ch Jo-Li Wind In The Willows** for Joseph Joly III, sired by a St Aubrey dog, who racked up literally hundreds of groups. Meanwhile Coral had been used on a Briarcourt's bitch of predominantly St Aubrey breeding that David owned, but as he had not a registered kennel name in those days, the singleton puppy was registered with Joan Mylchreest's and thus **Briarcourt's Damien Gable** entered the world.

"Right from the start I could tell he was a good dog, and as a

Damien won the group at Westminster in 1994 under Bill Taylor, having won the same award the previous year under Jane Kay. He was top toydog in 1992 and 1993 and retired directly after his 1994 Garden win.
photo Tatham

David handling the BOB Yorkshire Terrier at Westminster in 1996, Ch Durrer's Steal The Show, under Margaret Young Renihan.
photo Ashbey

puppy he was one of those rare dogs that always looked perfect; he just never went through an ugly stage. When he was under a year old I took him to the Pekingese Club of America's roving specialties which were held in Texas. Terry Nethercott was actually the first judge and he finished in three shows in three days... is that what they call a hat trick? Vandy Williams was the second judge and Bob Jacobsen the third.

"He was such a beautiful dog and after finishing him I held him back until the Pekingese Club of America's show over the Westminster weekend when Liz Stannard made him best of breed. He won two groups at Westminster and was top toydog in 1992 and 1993, retiring at the Garden in 1994."

In the early 1990s David began using the Pequest kennel name on dogs that he bred and was building up foundation stock of his own. From Bert Easdon and Philip Martin he had a bitch in whelp to the Crufts BIS-winning Danny who produced two self-masked daughters who produced really well for David. "That was when I started to turn the corner with getting consistency," he claims, "and while Damien was a fabulous dog he wasn't necessarily a great

producer, not like the Yakee dogs that I had after him."

After Damien, David was showing a variety of different dogs in different breeds, finishing dogs and winning groups, before he got his next significant Pekingese, **Ch Linn-Lee's St Martin**, who amassed groups and bests in show. "He was a grandson of Ch Shih Go Idle Gossip, and came to me when he was about six months old. He won his first BIS at ten months and I actually showed him for three years, which is longer than I usually care to but he was an easy keeper and his owners, the Holcombes, were great clients.

"This little dog could walk in the highest grass or on rocks, it really didn't matter. He won loads of big bests in show and several PCA specialties and is now the top winning American-bred Pekingese of all time, a title that previously been held by Damien."

Then in 2003 David had the strangest telephone call. "This lady, Kit Woodruff, calls me up and says that she would like a Pekingese

David has handled Boston Terriers for several years and is seen here winning a group under Dennis McCoy with Ch El Bo's Yakee Doodle Dandy, who later came to the UK to Bert Easdon and Philip Martin.
photo JC Photo

David winning a non-sporting group in 1988 under Norman Patten with a Sweetkin's Chow Chow.
photo Alverson

David campaigned **Ch Linn-Lee's St Martin** for three years and made him the top winning American-bred Pekingese of all time. Here he is seen winning a BIS in 2003 under Betty Duding.
photo Kurtis

who could win Top Dog all breeds. I really didn't know who she was, but she had owned Pekingese for some years in Texas, and I remember thinking to myself 'who wouldn't want a Pekingese that could win Top Dog all breeds?!'

"Anyhow I did a little research and realised that she was in a position to finance the campaign of a top dog and before I knew where I was, I had a first class air ticket to Glasgow! Betty Tilley (formerly Dupras who lived in the UK for some time and won well with two Singlewell bitches, Twilight Mist and Meringue) had told me that Bert Easdon and Philip Martin had some very good dogs, some of which may be for sale, so off I went.

"Bert offered me this junior dog, a red dog with a black muzzle and not a ton of hair, but aesthetically this was one of the most beautiful animals I had ever seen. Bert is not into high-pressured sales-pitches so he basically handed me this dog and suggested I should groom him up as I could do a better job than he could!

"I figured the dog could win big, we agreed a lease, and I took

him back home in October, conditioned him up, took him to shows with me as a spectator and to be honest it took a while for him to get his head around showing, but eventually it all clicked into place and the following January I took him to some shows and he won three groups and a best in show which was won under Ric Chashoudian with Coco the Norfolk in the line-up. THAT was a memorable win, believe me!

"He wasn't qualified to be shown at Westminster that year, 2004, but he went to a specialty over the Garden weekend and won best under Bill Blair. His next show was Chicago where he won the group under Mrs Clark and best under Ron Menaker. Then it was just non-stop winning."

Jeffrey had arrived... aka **Ch Yakee If Only**. Despite all his major wins, he still was not top toydog as that year the award went to a white Toy Poodle, bred in Japan, handled by Tim Brazier and owned by the Sosnoffs. However the following year he went to Westminster where he won the toy group under Ken McDermott and then that was Jeffrey's year. He was Top Dog all breeds, much to his owner's delight, and ended up with 129 bests in show.

David reflects: "To beat the record held by Ch Chik T'sun of Caversham of 126 bests was phenomenal, and what was so wonderful was that Bill Taylor gave the dog five bests, as of course he and Nigel Aubrey-Jones were responsible for bringing over Chik T'sun."

Jeffrey sired several BIS winners for David and proved to be an excellent stud dog, "His puppies were just beautiful and so even," reflects David who sent Jeffrey back to Scotland after his lease was up.

The next Yakee that went to David was **Ch Yakee Playing Footsie**, again owned by Kit Woodruff. He won several BIS. David then started off with a Jeffrey son, **Ch Pequest Persuasive**, co-owned with her again, a very glamorous dog whose dam was also a Danny daughter, just as Jeffrey was a Danny son.

"He was winning everything in sight," remembers David, "22 bests in six months, and he had huge potential for Dog of the Year but sadly Kit died in June, and the terms of her will were such that the dog would never be shown again. That was sad."

Ch Pequest Match Point was another Jeffrey son, owned by Sascha M Rockefeller, who won around 25 BIS in one year of showing in 2007 after which he returned to his owner in New York City where he was one very pampered pet!

Afterwards David showed **Ch Linn-Lee's For The Good Times** to a dozen BIS, and he was out of a Danny grand-daughter that David had given the Holcombes.

British import **Ch/UK Ch Yakee If Only** winning the group at Westminster in 2005 under Ken McDermott.
photo Ashbey

A wonderful portrait shot of Ch/UK Ch Yakee If Only, son of the Crufts BIS-winning Danny, who became the top winning Pekingese of all time in the US with 129 all-breed bests in show to his credit, and like his sire in the UK, he was Top Dog of all breeds one year.
photo Weigand

David's latest hope, Ch Yakee Easily Persuaded, a son of Ch Yakee And Don't Forget It and Ch Yakee Follow This. He is seen winning a group in July under judge Polly Smith.
photo Ashbey

Ch Pequest Persuasive had won 22 BIS in six months when his co-owner died and he had to be retired. Both his parents were sired by Danny, Ch Yakee A Dangerous Liaison.
photo Weigand

As David is 'occupationally ineligible' to judge at shows in the US where champion points are offered because he is an active professional handler, his judging activities are restricted to judging match shows and sweepstakes, many of which may be well supported. As a result of the numbers of dogs and classes he had judged at these smaller shows David was able to accept an invitation to award challenge certificates in 2008 for the Ventura Pekingese Club, whose open show he had previously judged.

He pulled the second highest entry of the year next to Crufts and awarded the CCs to Palacegarden Baroque and Singlewell Trinny of Dragden, with the bitch winning BIS.

At that show David was very impressed by dogs from the Palacegarden kennel of Jim and Jean Smith. "It was a great experience," David says, "and really made me think harder than ever before when I had judged. The Smiths had one-piece dogs with good high tailsets, short necks, they were good, correct old-fashioned Pekingese and I appreciated it. They weren't over-coated and didn't all necessarily have the wow factor, but they were so very correct."

"In the parking lot after the show, I was going back to stay at Bert and Philip's, and I saw these people – who I had never seen before – who had shown these really good dogs. They were getting ready to leave and I approached them, told them how much I liked their dogs and asked if they had anything available. They didn't at the time, but I followed it up with an email and they eventually sent me some pictures of a dog puppy that was about five months old.

"I liked the photos and the pedigree, they had sent a video clip of him walking around their garden and I thought that the dog would suit, so I agreed to buy him. **Palacegarden Malachy** arrived in the US in June of 2008.

"I got him out of his crate, I put a lead on him and he walked up and down the sidewalk like a million bucks and I figured I had bought me a top dog!" smiles David as he tells the story.

"I took him home for him to grow up, I kept him socialised, took him around with me, letting him get all the experience without the competition and showed him twice at the end of 2009 and then in January 2010 I took him to Virginia when he won four groups and a best in show."

At this time David was Malachy's sole owner. He had in his opinion a top dog but he was aware that he needed a co-owner who could finance the campaign the dog needed.

For many years David had been a good friend of popular socialite and great dog fancier Iris Love whom he recalled mentioning that, if ever he had a great Pekingese, she would be interested in 'going on it', as the Americans would say.

Eventually he tracked down Iris who agreed to co-own Malachy but also wanted Sandra Middlebrooks to be a co-owner. Sandra had previously owned Charmin the Sealyham who had won BIS at Crufts, the World Show, the American Kennel Club National Championship and Montgomery.

The deal was done, Malachy had two new co-owners and David started campaigning him in earnest. "He won like crazy, was in close competition with the Smooth Fox Terrier in 2010, but didn't beat him so I went on with the little dog in 2011.

"I rested him in January so he could be in top form for New York as I knew he would have to look great to win under Frank Sabella who was judging the toy group, and then three days before I was ready to leave for New York I slipped on black ice and broke my left arm. I was just lying there thinking 'No, no, no ... not now, just before The Garden!'

"But I made it to the show, showed the dog but I was in such pain when Frank asked me to pick up the Pekingese. I had bought new jackets for the show and had to have the sleeves specially opened up – it was a nightmare but we won the group. Then we finished

Ch Pequest Match Point, owned by Sascha Rockefeller, won around 25 BIS before returning to his owner in New York City where he became a very pampered pet! Presenting the trophies are Sue Weiss, Estelle Cohen and Carol Reisman, and judge here is Don Sturz.
photo Phillips

the year with 113 BIS wins on the dog and we went off to Westminster again. Over the Westminster weekend I showed him to BIS at Progressive to get him warmed up and then we went for the big one."

As everyone knows, Cindy Vogels made Malachy best in show at Westminster, a great win for David, for Iris and Sandra, for the Pekingese breed and for the Smiths who were to be brought sharply down to earth at Crufts the following month when, having won BOB under Bert Easdon, their bitch failed to pass the much criticised vet check.

The days that followed saw David fulfilling a whirlwind of public appearances with Malachy. "Your life is not your own," David says, "The press were fighting to get close to him in the best in show ring, then we had a press conference, the Westminster party which goes on and on, then you have to have a private party and champagne for all your friends! I get to bed at 3.45, was up at 4.45, and then it was non-stop from 5.45 and you have no idea what's ahead for you with TV and guest appearances; it's a crazy schedule. For 48 hours it was total madness. And we got to open up the New York Stock Exchange!"

That was almost a year ago. This year David has had a quiet time, deliberately so. "After Malachy won the Garden I took a couple of months off, though we still were asked to do a few guest appearances for various kennel clubs and associated bodies. I didn't want to launch a new dog just yet but I have recently started to show a new Yakee dog I have, named **Easily Persuaded**, and known at home as Roger."

The Pekingese is not an easy breed to show, or to present. David is known universally as a master of his craft and the consummate professional. What is the secret?

"I don't wish to sound boastful but what probably gives me a bit of an advantage is the fact that I understand what the breed should look like, and why. Because of my background and the people I have been around, I appreciate the beauty of the breed. You need to understand how to keep and condition a coat, how that coat should be groomed, not using any damaging products, and maybe I bathe Pekingese more than some people would."

David is also one of the few American handlers who have never been tempted to race around the ring with his charges. How has he remained able to set his own stamp on Pekingese gaiting?

"I never pay attention to what other people are doing, I try to be at one with my dog and let the dog set the pace. The dog sets off and I will obligingly walk alongside; all breeds look so much better if they are allowed to move at the correct speed for that breed. It's also important to remain focused on your dog and not allow

people to distract you. When you get to shows like the Garden it's all too easy to get worked up and stressed, but I just try to keep myself to myself and keep calm."

David is a keen follower of Pekingese around the world, but notably in the UK. What does he feel about the way that the Kennel Club has dealt with the breed Standard and also the recent vet checks of the "high profile" breeds?

"I think it's disgraceful. The breed Standards should be the property of the parent breed clubs, like they are in the US, not subject to alterations at the whim of someone in an office who may never have owned a Pekingese.

"The reason most people fall in love with the Pekingese in the first place is because it IS an exaggerated breed with features that are not generic, but we still want to produce healthy, sound dogs that retain the characteristics of the breed we fell in love with."

Like many professional handlers, David sees judging as a natural progression from a lifetime of handling top show dogs. At 55 years of age he still enjoys breeding and showing a handful of dogs but he has never shown dogs at such a manic pace as some handlers so perhaps hasn't burnt himself out as he might have done.

"I would enjoy judging, of course, but you know, I really do enjoy what I'm doing too much. I guess in a few years I will have to think about slowing down and look more to judging, but I'm not quite ready to give up what I have right now."

After his Westminster win, David received hundreds of goodwill messages and congratulations. Among them, a senior stalwart of the American Kennel Club wrote: "I must say that I do not remember a more popular BIS win at The Garden. This is not surprising since our people in the fancy are so appreciative of you as a breeder/exhibitor and consummate dog person... you have set an example for all of our dog people, and especially our young handlers.

"As someone said before BIS went into the ring, 'David is the dog man that we wish we were and all aspire to be.' You certainly deserve all of the accolades you have received and I hope that it gives you a high degree of satisfaction to know that all of your hard work and passion has paid off."

There will be many people who I am sure are looking forward to seeing David packing away his tack box for the very last time and retiring from handling for good. When he does, it can safely be assumed that will make the transition from handler to judge seamlessly, and I am sure he will apply himself to that role with the same expertise, dedication and integrity that has earned him the reputation that he so richly deserves.

David at home with his Westminster BIS rosette and his latest group trophy from the 'Garden'.
photo Brace

CANADA

Mike Macbeth

What happened to the exective director?

One breed rarely represented at shows in the southern parts of Canada is the Canadian Eskimo Dog, whose distinctiveness is being challenged. The FCI wishes to consider the Greenland Dog and the Canadian Eskimo interchangeable, whereas the Canadian Kennel Club's position states that this is one of Canada's indigenous breeds and is unique.

The issue seems to be more a matter of principle than urgency. In the past three years, only 25 Canadian Eskimos have been registered with the CKC, and only one Greenland Dog.

There are dog people who are unique and dearly missed. Internationally known and popular all-breed judge Heather Logan died in June 2012.

When the CKC found itself (once again) in extreme financial difficulty in 1989, Heather, with extensive banking and financial expertise, volunteered as a '$1 a year' administrator and put the club back into a positive balance sheet within six months.

The 2008 honorary chair of the CKC, Heather made a heart-wrenching decision in June 2010 to resign her life membership as a public act of protest, the only honorary chair ever to do so. She felt her beloved CKC was then acting in what she considered contrary to good financial practices.

Over the past few years this Canadian report has been filled reports of crises and negative events swirling around the CKC. But after a November 2011 election, referendum and an executive search, 2012 started with renewed enthusiasm for a new beginning, with a new executive director, a new board of directors, and a new chairman.

At their first meeting, the new board wisely chose Michael Shoreman as chair. Mr Shoreman, with significant financial acumen, had recently retired as executive vice-president of the Royal Ontario Museum, one of Canada's premier cultural institutions, where he was in charge of a $350 million budget and a staff of 350. A CKC life member with over 40 years' experience as a breeder/exhibitor, he is internationally respected as an all-breed judge.

The new board of directors includes seven new board members (out of 12), including two former chairs in its make-up. The results of the members' referendum saw 46 new by-laws, some of which are meant to streamline efficiency. These amendments gained federal approval in August.

The CKC is unique in the world as it operates under the federal government's Animal Pedigree Act, and is frequently hamstrung for it cannot make by-law changes or accept new breeds without the approval of the Minister of Agriculture.

However, having settled outstanding impediments to progress, the CKC is now working amicably with the Ministry to formulate the rules of eligibility and establish an acceptable expedited process that will see more breeds accepted for registration.

The CKC's balance sheet is now healthier; cash and liquidity is strong, in large part due to savings from the termination of the CKC magazines *Dogs in Canada* and *DIC Annual*.

As in much of the world, registrations and average show entries continue to fall. One long-standing all breed club folded, creating a feeding frenzy as clubs requested the dates abandoned by others applying for the more desirable weekends. However, new initiatives helped to minimise a drop in entries. An experiment permitting

The battle for Canada's Top Dog is all but over, as it is impossible for any dog to catch the American Cocker Spaniel who earned instant prominence by defeating the 2011 US' Top Dog all breeds for BOB at Westminster. Back home, Gr Ch/Am Ch Mario n Beechwood's Midnight Express has broken the record for the most BIS awarded to an American Cocker. Ace, owned by Frank and Cathy Charest with his breeders Mark and Pam Ragusa, has 62 BIS from 55 different judges. In 2012 he as so far won almost twice as many top dog points as his nearest rival.

How many top dogs have interrupted a promising career to train in Finland for competitive moose hunting trials? Such is the life of the Karelian Bear Dog, Ch/Int/Multi Ch TsarShadow's I Speak Of War. After winning his Canadian championship as a puppy, Kosto spent a winter in Finland, but his youth put him at a disadvantage against older, more experienced moose hunting dogs. He joined handler Richard Hellman in Italy, and was an immediate and consistent winner, acquiring championships in Italy, Romania, Ireland, Gibraltar and Portugal, as well as international and European Winner titles. Back home with breeder Dawne Deeley, and now handled by Doug Belter, he has a breed record 37 BIS and is current number two all breeds. photo Miguel

multiple shows on the same day increased the number of shows (651 in 2011 and 612 in 2010) yet conformation entries fell slightly from 171,000 in 2010 to 169,100 in 2011.

Several new strategies seem to be helping to maintain revenues. All- breed clubs have three new options: classes for baby puppies, veterans, and a reserve best in show award. Other changes include discretionary four placements in puppy groups, a grand champion designation; and a Master Breeder and International Master Breeder programme.

Probably the most significant of the amendments to the by-laws is the relationship between the volunteer board and the paid manager who oversees the staff. Over the past two decades, so much power had been given to the chief executive officer,, including all control over money, that when the CKC faced bankruptcy in 2010 there was a groundswell to limit the powers of the CEO.

As the CEO designation was now toxic, the job title was changed to executive director (ED) which is also more appropriate for a non-profit organisation. The new by-laws clearly define the responsibilities. The ED will have operational control of the organisation but will report directly to the board, which will determine the club's strategic direction.

As the former CEO resigned in March 2011, a search began for a new administrator. In late 2011, as one of its final decisions, the retiring board hired the new executive director. Her tenure began the same day as the new board of directors, January 1, 2012.

And then, in September, the incredible news released via a short statement from CKC. The executive director was gone. The members were stunned. There was no explanation. The ED was chosen by the previous board after a significant employment search and began her probationary period with the full and enthusiastic support of the new board. Nine months later, the board chose not to extend her contract to permanent employment. Whatever changed was discussed in camera and no one is talking.

When the former CEO resigned in 2011, the competent and unflappable Leila Bahorie, senior manager of membership services, skillfully guided the CKC head office through the 2011 financial crisis. The 37-year employee has once again been installed as interim executive director. And as the CKC makes plans to celebrate its 125th anniversary in 2013, the search for a new executive director begins.

Currently in fifth place is Canada's top winning Welsh Terrier of all time. MBIS & MBISS Gr/Am/Can Ch Darwyn's I'm Not Arguing That, owned by Larisa Hotchin and shown by the Brazilian handler living in Canada, Milton Lopes. In 2010 he was the number two Welsh in the US behind his sire. Joe has won 29 BIS, including one in the US. Judge here is Mike Macbeth.
photo Photos-now.ca

In sixth place is the Alaskan Malamute Gr Ch/Am Ch Mytuk's Technical Knock Out CGN, whose sire was number two in 2007. Owned by Annette and Dave Milburn, he is handled by Jessie Clark. His total so far stands at 19 BIS. He is pictured enjoying weight pulling.

Current number three is the Borzoi Ch Taugo's Ulric, owned by Ken Cook and handled by Shannon Scheer. Boo has 16 all-breed BIS. It has been 35 years since a Borzoi in Canada has achieved this level of success in the show ring.

An interesting battle is brewing as two terriers are competing for top dog positions. Number seven at present is the New Zealand import, Ch/NZ Ch Whitebriar Jaw Dropper, owned by June Frazer, who with her late husband Tom has both bred and owned many top winning West Highland Whites and other top terriers. J D is handled by David Gignac, also from a well known Westie family. He arrived in Canada in mid May 2012 and he has accumulated 14 all-breed BIS and the national specialty.
photo Dogshots

Canada's Top Dog 2011 was the Pekingese, Ch/Am Ch St. Aubrey Niklaus of Elsdon CGN, owned by the legendary R William Taylor. That year he won 36 all-breed BIS and three specialty BIS, shown by Lynda Torrance. Bill Taylor has owned and bred Pekingese since the 1940s, and is honorary chair of the Canadian Kennel Club for 2012, a title conferred annually to recognise the contribution and importance of an esteemed member of the Canadian dog community. He and Niklaus (left) are seen here with the Peke's ten-year-old grandfather Ch/Am Ch St Aubrey Jubilation of Elsdon. Between them, they have 126 all-breed BIS.

In fourth place is the English Setter Ch/Am Ch Sagebrush Bullmtn's Judee, owned by Hilary Oakes and Bill Potts and named after Bill's wife Judee who died before the litter was born. She has won 11 BIS, shown by Hilary's daughter Sabrina or other handlers when Sabrina is at school. Judge here is Virginia Lyne.
photo French

FINLAND

Report and photographs: Paula Heikkinen-Lehkonen

The shows won't fit in the venues

While in many countries the kennel clubs have been worried about sinking registration and entry figures, that is not the case in Finland. In fact, many shows have been in trouble trying to fit all the rings into the venues and find more judges after the entries close. Although exhibitors complain about entry fees and other costs, they still go to the shows like mad.

It is a real problem to get indoor venues during the long winter season, because the shows are so big and there are not many large enough fair centres or sports halls. So most of the shows are held outdoors in the hectic summer season, and then the weather can be anything. This summer has been especially bad weather-wise, with more than enough rain.

Showlink, the subsidiary of the Finnish Kennel Club (SKL), had a nice hall where many smaller shows, such as breed specialties, were held. However, it turned out to be unprofitable. Although in the winter the hall was fully booked not only for shows but for judges' education sessions and exams, there wasn't enough use during the outdoor season, so the SKL decided to let it go.

The Showlink office was moved back to SKC headquarters, and a smaller hall is rented elsewhere. Unfortunately this place is too small for shows that need more than one or two rings. This is a big problem. There have been plans to buy or build a real kennel centre, which could house shows, trials, training classes, exams, offices, library and museum, but so far nothing has happened.

The discussion about health problems of purebred dogs is still going on vividly. Some newspapers now and then try to make a sensation out of this, claiming that crossbred dogs are healthier than pedigree ones, though according to the statistics of the insurance companies this is not true. Still, it seems to be difficult to change the image in the eyes of the general public.

Some carefully planned and controlled crossing with another breed has been done to enrich the gene pool in certain breeds, under supervision of the SKL and breed club.

In the future it might be possible to produce more DNA tests to find out if the dogs are carriers of certain hereditary diseases. Dr Hannes Lohi, internationally respected scientist, has worked with his team in co-operation with the SKL to find the genes which cause certain defects. Dog people have been more than generous in giving blood samples of their dogs , and many clubs have organized match shows etc to raise money. Dr Lohi says that studying the genetics of the dogs can help also to find the genes which cause similar hereditary diseases in humans.

We lost one of our most experienced all-rounder judges, Ritva Raita, at the age of 82. She had judged all over the world, and her judging career lasted over 50 years. However, life must go on, and some new all-breed judges have been qualified: Leni Finne, Harri Lehkonen and Harto Stockmari, all widely experienced and internationally known.

The most successful breeder and exhibitor of the year is without any doubt Tuula Tikkanen, whose Smooth Collies are high on all three lists, Showdog of the Year, Veteran of the Year and Breeder of the Year. She even has a possibility of winning all three contests. Her bitch Int Ch Timonan Veronica Velvet (far left) is the current leader in the top dog list, and her elder kennelmate Int Ch Timonan Neat Nefertiti (left) is pressing hard on the veteran list. With her breeder's team, consisting of four homebred dogs, she has done a lot of winning. However, the life of a top breeder is not just celebration. Tuula's young bitch Timonan Xyliet Xylona was BOB at Crufts and was planned to stay in UK for more shows, but suddenly died of a mysterious illness soon after Crufts.

Another breeder who is high in several fields is Juha Kares, whose Chic Choix dogs of various breeds have won the Showdog of the Year contest more than once. The Lhasa Apso bitch Int Ch Chic Choix Cleopatra Eurydice (pictured with Sanna Koppola) is the current star, but Juha has been successful with his Lhasas in breeders' groups as well and is leading the breeders' list at the moment.

I can't remember if one owner has ever before had two dogs of different breeds among the top ten, but Sari Laitinen has had this incredible luck in 2012. She is co-owner of the Smooth Fox Terrier Texforrier Get Off My Cloud, who is usually handled by the breeder and co-owner Molli Nyman, while Sari's Lapponian Herder Int Ch Suukkosuun Shamaani has kept this domestic working breed in the limelight. Sari is a breeder of Manchester Terriers, but is interested in other breeds, too.

Another youngster who has enjoyed tremendous success has been the Newfoundland Wave Seeker's Fly Me To The Moon, owned by breeder Outi Lius and Erkki and Leila Selin.

The Björkman family has been at the top with Smooth Dachshunds for several years, and their newest star is the young dog Unita's The King.

Leader of the veteran table is the Schnauzer Int Ch Chivas Grand Calvera, a Czech import owned by Anne Mäkimaa. He started his career as a youngster and is still going strong at nine years, winning not only the veteran stakes but also 'real' groups. Besides the Smooth Collie, the other top veterans are the Afghan Hound Int Ch Neliapilan Kuutamokeikka and the Pyrenean Mountain Dog Int Ch Chenespace Insigne.

Another strong candidate for the Breeder of the Year award is not Finnish but the Swiss breeder of American Cockers, Laurent Pichard. He has sent several dogs to Finland and a team of very capable young ladies has prepared and handled the dogs. The leading figure of this team, Sanna Vartiainen, had a baby during the year, but that hasn't stopped her from grooming the dogs and coming to the shows. Tarja Hovila with her Adamant's English Springers, double winner of this contest in the past few years, has been doing well but hasn't been quite as eager to show as before.

The late Ritva Raita.

Also among the top ten are Mikko Ylitalo, Arja Hirvelä and Michaela Ståhlberg's Afghan Hound Ch Agha Djari's Blue Blood (pictured), the Irish Red and White Setter Redwhitesilk Dynamite, the Affenpinscher Ch Mambo Jambo v Tani Kazari and the Azawakh Azamour Wahid.

NORWAY

Espen Engh

A year of consolidation

With more than 75,000 members, the Norwegian Kennel Club (NKK) is one of the largest voluntary organisations in the country. After a rather stormy period, 2012 has been a rather uneventful and consolidating year under the leadership of our first woman chairman Siv Sandø.

The main current political challenge may be to find a meaningful role for the regional level of the NKK, as the club is made up of 13 regions to cover our vast geographical distances. An attempt to delegate the organisation of the international shows to the regions has met with only moderate success, and most of the shows are still organised by the NKK centrally.

The NKK also forms an umbrella over about 225 dog clubs. During 2012 our dog clubs collectively experienced a moderate drop in membership. In the first months of 2012 there was a significant drop in registrations as well, but during the summer and autumn numbers have picked up, and it now looks as if 2012 may end up as a record year for the number of dogs registered. Likewise, entries at the major shows have increased significantly in recent months.

In addition to the 11 big international shows, there is an ever-increasing number of smaller championship shows almost every weekend. Year after year the number of CCs in each breed has increased; there are more CCs available in many breeds than there are dogs registered per year.

Finding space in the calendar has become a challenge, and in recent years shows are even organised between Christmas and New Year's Eve. Many of the smaller among the about 500 championship shows have been struggling with significant decreased entries, probably reflecting the fact that there are simply far too many shows.

A report from a working group appointed by the NKK board suggests quite substantial changes with a marked reduction in the number of CCs available per breed and breed classes without CCs at championship shows, much like the British system. However it remains to be seen to what degree, if at all, the proposals will be put into effect. It is expected that the clubs will put up a fight to keep their CCs.

Commercial dog training is a big business in Norway and is conceived by many local dog clubs as potential competition for the same market. A long time NKK project aiming to establish some formal co-

©Roger Sjølstad

After several years with the same dogs dominating the show scene, 2012 has seen several new faces winning bests in show at the majority of the 11 international shows organised annually in Norway. With just two more shows to go, the Kerry Blue Terrier Int Ch Shylock Navigator to Edrus is in a very comfortable lead on the Top Dog table. Bred and shown by Helge Kvivesen, he is a grandson of Norway's Top Dog in 2007, Helge's Russian import Int Ch Link to Shyloch Iz Goluboi Legendy. He is owned by Charlie and Eva Lejdbrandt in Sweden.
photo Sjølstad

operation with and possibly certify the most qualified of the commercial trainers recently stalled without any positive result.

After several years with few new judges coming up, it is encouraging that there are more than 50 applicants for the educational course for potential championship show judges. The extensive training of judges in Norway, as in the other Scandinavian countries, has met with the approval of most other countries and has produced some of the most widely travelled international judges.

Indeed the Kennel Club, London, has accepted our judges education as a substitute

The latest in a long line of top winners owned by Dag Løken of the Tiny Jewel kennel, Ch Dan-Star-Kom Neverending Tiny Jewel, is among Norway's top dogs for 2012, currently in second place. Himself a multiple BIS winner, the Pomeranian also has two BIS-winning daughters.

The Cocker Spaniel Ch Rainstorm Latest News recently won his UK show champion title, taking the CC at the Cocker Spaniel Club. At only 20 months old, he has already won 17 CCs in four countries and three BIS at spaniel specialties. He is owned and bred in Norway by Marianne and Ørjan Ullebø.

The Cardigan Corgi Int Ch Golddigger Cymraeg Ci, owned by Lars Hallblom and bred by expatriate Norwegian Christine Sonberg in Belgium, is currently third on the Top Dog list in Norway. A champion in five countries and a multiple BIS winner, he has won a CC in the UK as well as the RCC at Crufts.

Int Ch Voulez Vous Hidden Rock, bred and owned by Anita Byklum and co-owned and usually shown by Maud Nilsson, is pictured winning one of her six specialty BIS under Michael Coad. The Miniature Poodle is many generations Norwegian breeding on her dam's side and is among Norway's top winning dogs in 2012.

Int Ch Mementos Kelly, bred by Torunn Sørbye and owned by her and Lene Bjerknæs, is among Norway's top winning dogs in 2012. The result of insemination with frozen semen from Int/UK Ch Carpenny Walpole, the dual-purpose black Labrador bitch has won a first prize at a cold game test.

Friedrich Birkmar of the Estava Rain Akitas has been one of Norway's top exhibitors over the last decade. This year his British-bred Int/UK Ch Redwitch Adrenaline Junkie is among Norway's top dogs of all breeds. Junkie won the CC both at Crufts and the World Show in 2012 and his son Estava Rain Hold The News was made up in the UK this year.

The Pharaoh Hound Int Ch Antefas Q-Lahn has been a top winner over many years with more than a dozen BIS. Now handled by Bjørn Erling Løken for owner Sonja Tørres, he is Norway's top veteran all breeds for 2012. He is pictured winning best veteran in show at Oslo International under French judge Jean-Jacques Dupas.
photo Sjølstad

For the third year running, the famous German Shepherd Dog Ch Zanta av Quantos won Norway's Top Dog competition in 2011. The only dog ever to win this competition three times, this multiple BIS-winning bitch may well be Norway's top winning show dog of all time. It came as a terrible shock that Zanta perished in the Woodhaven kennel fire in Ireland in August 2012 along with the same owner's Pembroke Corgi. Still very much in her prime, Zanta was in Ireland to be shown there, and her death is a great blow to the breeding programme of owner/breeder Tor Johansen.

for half the numbers of dogs otherwise required to award CCs in the UK. This same agreement on reciprocal recognition of judges between the KC and the Norwegian, Swedish and Finnish kennel clubs also aims to have a positive effect on the influx of British judges to our countries.

During 2012 another Norwegian FCI all-breeds judge, Svein Helgesen, was approved as the sixth all-rounder currently residing in Norway. There are also several Norwegian all-breeds judges living abroad.

Plans are well on their way for the FCI European Show at the Norwegian Trade Fair Centre between Oslo city centre and airport on September 4-6, 2015. It will no doubt be by far the largest dog show ever in Norway with an estimated entry of 13,000 dogs, half of which are expected to be local.

The venue, the largest exhibition centre in Norway, already hosts our final show of the year, the Dogs4All extravaganza which has already attracted up to 6,500 dogs. To train for the big event in 2015, the 2014 Dogs4All will be a double show over three days in November.

Much to the delight of the dog show people, NKK has been granted an exception from our Dog Act to allow American Staffordshire Terriers, Dogos Argentinos, Czech Wolfdogs and Filas Brasileiros to be shown at the European Show in 2015.

These breeds are sadly otherwise banned from being imported and shown in Norway. We also have good reason to believe that we will get a dispensation from our Animal Welfare Act to allow dogs that have been legally docked and cropped in their home country to be shown at this one event. Showing docked dogs has been illegal for more than 20 years and cropped dogs for 60 years.

The requirement for a rabies antibody test was abolished from January 2012 and made travelling with dogs to and from Norway much easier. Required treatment against echinococcus remains, however, and with the recent advent of the parasite in Sweden, the regulations for parasite treatment are likely to become more stringent.

Under the umbrella of the Nordic Kennel Union (NKU), the kennel clubs of Norway, Sweden, Denmark, Finland and Iceland have for many years sought to harmonise regulations and practices and meet frequently at administrative and political level. Among the fruits of this work are the current common show regulations in all five countries and recent harmonisation of the recognition of new or non-FCI-recognised breeds. On behalf of the Nordic countries, Norway has undertaken to seek FCI recognition for the Lancashire Heeler with the assistance of the KC.

SWEDEN

Dan Ericsson

Kennel club and breeds co-operate on health

The Swedish dog world has been fairly quiet throughout the whole of 2012. No new major decisions or rules have been implemented by the governing bodies of the game and the number of registered dogs has remained at a similar level to previous years.

Show entries have however dropped somewhat possibly as a result of the present global economic climate. So also has participation at trials and other doggy events, but this has luckily not caused a dramatic decline in interest and activity overall.

Health in pedigree dogs continues to be a major topic and 2012 has been no exception. The newly formed Kennel Club committee has had a busy year revising recommendations to judges and breeders alike, all done in close co-operation with concerned breed clubs.

The launch of a DVD pertaining to breathing in the brachycephalic breeds (also available on YouTube.com) has been a great success and it is hoped that the DVD will help all to understand specific problems these breeds are faced with, not least in the show ring. The next similar project will cover movement as it is felt that many judges fail to observe and penalise lameness in the ring.

The coveted BIS award at the Wortd Show in Salzburg went to the renowned American-bred Saluki **Ch Shiraz California Dreamin'**, owned in Sweden by Niklas and Ingunn Eriksson. He is known worldwide for his phenomenal career spanning several years and he crowned his many wins by claiming the top spot in Salzburg under FCI president Hans Müller.

On a sadder note, the Swedish dog fraternity mourns the death of Elisabeth Matell of the Cracknor Norfolk Terriers. Although resident in the UK for over three decades, she did a lot for Swedish dogs internationally helping to promote dogs and people, but, perhaps more importantly, she was a source of inspiration to all Swedish dog fanciers. The terrier world will certainly be the poorer for losing one of its great breeders and ambassadors. On a personal note, I would also like to pay tribute to Elisabeth for a friendship that lasted uninterrupted for more than 40 years.

The Swedish Kennel Club has invited all Swedish championship judges, in total about 280, to a seminar about health in pedigree dogs in November. No fewer than 260 judges will be attending, and this will be an excellent opportunity for Swedish dogdom to gather and exchange views in our constant striving for health and perfection in pedigree dogs. The seminar will be funded by the kennel club and is held in the Stockholm area.

Sweden looks forward to welcoming judges, breeders and exhibitors to our shows and other events in the new year.

Despite declining entries, competition at the very top has been extremely fierce and the famous evergreen Wire Fox Terrier Ch Crispy Legacy, owned, bred, trimmed and handled by Agneta Åström, has once again dominated the Swedish show rings. He is now coming up to six years of age, but is, it seems, in top form. He has enjoyed huge success in previous years and was Rainer Vuorinen's choice for BIS at the prestigious Stockholm winter show in 2011. He cannot now be beaten as Top Dog for 2012. He is pictured winning BIS in Sundsvall under Dan Ericsson.
photo courtesy Hundsport

The Wire's closest rival was the Standard Poodle Ch Aleph's American Idol, bred in the US by Elizabeth Brown and Paula Morgan who own him in partnership with Charlotte Sandell whose Huffish Poodles have been so very successful. Charlotte has piloted several Standard Poodles to Top Dog in Sweden before. American Idol has made a name for himself not only in Sweden, but around the world in 2012 gaining BOS at the Poodle Club of America and he also won the group at the FCI World Show in Salzburg, Austria. He won all three BIS at Högby triple international shows, and is pictured with judge Birgitta Svarstad.
photo courtesy Hundsport

For the second year running the industrious Stockholm Kennel Club hosted the annual Puppy of the Year competition, held at the beautiful Grand Hotel in the centre of Stockholm. The cream of Sweden's pedigree puppies gathered for an enjoyable, festive afternoon in wonderful surroundings to see Dr Göran Bodegård (holding rosette) select the British-bred Old English Sheepdog Kerjalee Showtime Girl, owned by the very experienced Ingela Wahlström, as Sweden's Puppy of the Year 2012.

It is hoped that this event, ably run and presided over by Marina Reuterswärd, known to many judges as the organiser of the previous Champion of Champions event held at the same venue, will continue for many years to come. Sweden is indeed indebted to the club with Mrs Reuterswärd in charge for providing the dog game with such festivity and panache. Also pictured are Dan Ericsson and Swedish Kennel Club chairman Nils Erik Åhmansson.
photo courtesy Hundsport

The much sought-after award for Top Breeder, always highly contested in Sweden, was won by Helene Hulthén and Maria Söderqvist's Cameron Soft-coated Wheaten Terriers in 2011. These two talented young ladies have won everything possible within their chosen breed, but have also done wonderfully well at group and BIS level and it was no surprise to see them top this competition last year. For the second time, they have also won top terrier in Sweden, with the young bitch Ch Cameron Rockferry, pictured with Helene winning a group place under Svante Frisk.
photo courtesy Hundsport

A top winner of 2012 is the Australian Terrier Ch Jaskarin Bravo owned by Saija Walldén, seen winning BIS at Avesta under Blaz Kavcic.
photo courtesy Hundsport

The Badavie Salukis, owned and bred by Maria Nordin and Maria Brandén, finished a close second to the terriers in the breeders' competition in 2011. The Badavie breeders must be admired for retaining outstanding type and quality for years and have been great favourites for the top spot for many years. In 2012, they seem likely to go one higher and are indeed on top of the list as we go to press, followed by the equally acclaimed Almanza Flat-coated Retrievers, owned and bred by Ragnhild Uhlin and Susanne Karlström, another kennel of great fame and one that has had major impact on the breed internationally.
photo courtesy Hundsport

The year's leading gundog is the Flat-coated Retriever Caci's Win-a-Latte, breed by Carina Östman and shown by Mikale Persson.
photo courtesy Hundsport

BIS at Östersund was the Irish Water Spaniel Ch Whistle Stop The Wind On Fire, shown by Sussie Narfström who co owns her with Gregory Siner and Connie Philipsen. She is sister to Britain's top gundog of 2012.
photo courtesy Hundsport

Raglan
a kennel of international significance

Dan Ericsson's Raglan kennel of Scottish Terriers, based in Sweden, has certainly made an international impact, not least in the UK with a top winner and a top producer. Well over 100 champions have been bred since Dan started in the breed as a animal-mad schoolboy more than 40 years ago, after his grandmother persuaded his parents to let him have a dog.

Over the years he has benefited from the guidance of the best possible mentors, starting with the leading Swedish breeders of the day, and then visiting Britain where experts such as Elsa Meyer, Betty Penn-Bull, the Owen family, Maureen Micklethwaite and Nellie Holland ensured he was steeped in the breed's lore and history.

Subsequent success has encompassed top terrier and even Top Dog awards, and continues today.

Dan is also establishing a line of Labradors which has produced several titleholders including three generations of homebred champion bitches, and in the past has bred and shown Pekingese including the famous UK import Ch Lien Ru's Boi of Hyldewood, obtained from Hilda Garwood.

He started young as a judge in 1976 and is now passed for all breeds, officiating worldwide. He chairs the Swedish Scottie and Labrador Clubs and finds time to sit on Kennel Club committees too.

Here is a selection of his most important dogs.

Dan's first Scottish Terrier, born in 1970, became Ch Torsloch Terzette, bred by Birgit Norman, at whose kennels he spent much of the school holidays. She was by Ch Gaywyn Marquis, a UK import. Mated to the UK import, Ch Gillson Grand Monarch, she produced Dan's first homebred champion, Raglan Rio Rita, pictured.

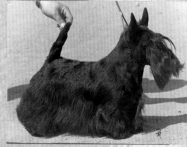

Ch Raglan Rebecca, a daughter of Regatta, owned by Monika Knutsson-Hall (Floreo), with whom Dan has worked very closely in their breeding programmes. Ch Floreo Althaea, a daughter of Red Rarity, was one of Dan's best bitches.

Ch Raglan Regatta, a BIS winner by a Rio Rita son ex a Ravita daughter. photo Roslin-Williams

In the early '70s Dan wrote to Elsa Meyer of the famous Reanda kennel in England, asking if he could visit to help with her dogs. She agreed immediately and so began a friendship which lasted the rest of her life. From her Dan had his second foundation bitch Ch Reanda Ravita, a group winner and BIS at the Swedish specialty.

Ch Raglan Red Rarity, top terrier 1977, was a son of Ravita, sired by Terzette's brother.

The kennel's best male, Ch Raglan Rory, Sweden's Dog of the Year 2001 and top terrier ever with 25 group wins. He was by Ch Kantorns Johnny Walker (UK-bred Ch Balgownie Brilliance ex a Raglan bitch by Venturesome) and was the only puppy produced by Dan's UK import Ch Bruiek Spellbinder. "The sort of dog one dreams of," says his owner, and he had some great progeny too.

In Britain Dan got to know all the great Scottish Terrier breeders of the day, many of whom had enjoyed decades of success. None more so than another of his mentors, the inspiring Betty Penn-Bull, and ever since he has tried never to stray too far away from the Kennelgarth lines. He imported Ch Paddington Bear of Kennelgarth who was a BIS winner and the kennel's greatest stud dog, producing among others six group-winning bitches.
photo Undén

Another great English kennel was Gaywyn, owned by Muriel Owen and family, and Ch Gaywyn Venturesome joined the Raglans at five months. A group winner, he too was an excellent sire, especially to daughters of Paddington Bear.

The French import Ch Sweet Romeo du Moulin de Mac Gregor, bred by Ruth O'Connor and the only wheaten owned by Raglan. He proved a valuable outcross and his daughter Raglan Roman Empress produced three UK champions for Pam Pagram.
photo Böös

Ch Raglan Royal Serenade, a daughter of Paddington Bear ex a Rebecca daughter, is Dan's choice as the best bitch he has bred. She was top terrier in Sweden in 1996 and was BOB on Miss Penn-Bull's last judging appointment.
photo Undén

Dan had always admired the Brio dogs of Jane Miller in England so was especially thrilled when she showed interest in having one of his dogs. UK/Sw/Norw Ch Raglan Rose Maiden at Brio was by Rory ex a bitch by UK-bred Ch Tamzin Toy Soldier ex a daughter of Paddington Bear. RBIS at Crufts 2004 and runner-up Top Dog all-breeds '03 were just a few of her achievements. She is seen being handled by her breeder to BIS at Windsor, with Leonard Pagliero, judge Ole Staunskjaer, Terry Thorn and Jane.
photo Johnson

Ch Raglan Referee, a son of Paddington Bear, winning BIS at the Swedish specialty under Muriel Owen.

Ch Raglan Royal Prospect, Sweden's top Scottie 2002, by Rory ex a Paddington Bear daughter, seen winning BIS at the Swedish Terrier Club centenary show under Harry O'Donoghue. A good producer too.
photo Böös

Continued overleaf

The kennel's big star in the 1980s was Ch Raglan Royal Commander, top terrier 1984 and '85. He was by UK import Ch Noonsun New Generation (by Ch Kennelgarth Edrick) ex Ch Raglan Rich-and-Rare, younger sister to Rio Rita.
photo Undén

Ch Raglan Roslin-Williams, second in the group at the 2003 World Show, a full brother to Rose Maiden. He was sold as a puppy to Marina Guidetti in Italy for whom he had a spectacular career before returning to Sweden after her early death.
photo Undén

Jane Miller also had Raglan Royal Connection with Brio, by a Venturesome son ex Royal Propect. He has produced seven UK champions, including Chs Brio Exquizite and Inquizitive out of Rose Maiden, and current Pup of the Year winner Ch Stuane Florette.
photo Llovall

Raglan today: At the Swedish Scottish Terrier Club's recent 40th anniversary show judged John Herd from Scotland. BIS was Dan's Melscot Heron at Raglan, bred in Croatia by Ch Raglan Rising Generation. BOS was Heron's daughter Ch Raglan Rosemary Smart (ex Raglan Ruccola, by Ch R Ricardo ex Ch R Royal Prospect) who won her title on the day and became the 138th champion bred at Raglan.

Dan had always been interested in Labradors and now has several at home. Foundation bitch was Ch Guideline's Eden Wall, dam of three champions.

Ch Raglan Braveheart, a son of Eden Wall and a particular favourite at home.

DENMARK

Vibeke Knudsen, the Danish Kennel Club

The Danish Kennel Club (DKK) celebrated a very unusual jubilee in September. Jørgen Hindse, who turned 70 in August, has now been president of the club for 35 years.

The club's seven general committee members are elected directly, ie all of the organisation's 33,000 members may vote. The general committee members are elected for four years at a time and they then elect their officers. All positions of trust in the DKK are voluntary and unpaid.

It must be said to be a fantastic achievement to be elected nine times – so far! Besides the office of president of the DKK, Jørgen has had a fine career as managing director of an international production company and he is also the president of the Europe Section of the FCI.

The DKK's close co-operation with the pet insurance company Agria has given access to a treasure trove of data about what dogs really get sick from – and what they die of. Agria's veterinary expert on this field, Brenda Bonnett, has prepared some really good material regarding the individual breeds. This material has now been placed at the breed clubs' disposal via the DKK.

In a number of cases the material shows that the diseases that the dogs have traditionally been examined for before breeding are not the diseases that in reality cause the biggest problems. The DKK works according to the motto 'sharing and caring' in order to share information so that the individual club and breeder can do their best for the dogs.

On this basis the general committee has throughout the year carried through meetings and discussions with more than 50 breed clubs in order to simplify and revise the breeding demands that are made on the individual breeds.

In January 2012 the DKK held a large conference for about 140 show judges. It included a number of workshops with great importance attached to conditions that influence the dogs' health and well-being: movement, muzzle, eyes, skin, coat. You can see more at www.dkk.dk/ Dommerkonference-2012 (mainly in Danish, but there are some video recordings).

All over Europe it is a problem that pedigree dogs, which have often been imported illegally, are sold to buyers who have not really thought about what a pedigree is, or whom they are dealing with.

The puppies are often sick and are frequently put to sleep. They have been badly socialised and imprinted and they risk spreading diseases because they originate from areas where serious illnesses like rabies often appear.

The DKK has entered a co-operation with the Danish Veterinary Organisation and the Danish Veterinary and Food Administration to make the public aware of these problems. This has been done with the campaign 'Check the puppy' (in Danish: 'Tjek Hvalpen', www.tjekhvalpen.dk), which has been received very well in the media and among other things resulted in so called 'go-cards', free postcards distributed in cafés.

In the competition for the popular title Dog of the Year the Standard Poodle Abica's Miles Ahead is leading. He was bred by the Danish sisters Kirsten and Marianne Nielsen and has Mikael Nilsson from Sweden as co-owner. But nothing is certain until the first weekend of November, where over 10,000 dogs come to Herning to compete for the titles Danish Winner (Saturday) and Nordic Winner (Sunday).

Many foreign exhibitors remember the World Show in Herning in 2010 as a very well run show and have wanted to return to the traditional finish of the show year which in Denmark always takes place in Herning.

The Danish Kennel Club president for 35 years, Jørgen Hindse, in action at a breed club show

Current number two in Denmark is Bodil Rûsz, Sue Huebner and Michael Laub's Puli Ch Cordmaker Hurdy Gurdy.
photo Heikkinen-Lehkonen

In the lead in Denmark's Dog of the Year competition is the Standard Poodle Int Ch Abica's Miles Ahead, bred by Marianne Nielsen, who also breeds Afghan and with whom he lives. He is owned by her sister Kirsten, Mikael Nilsson from Sweden and Kathy Arnold. Mikael won BIS at Crufts 2002 with Ch Topscore Contradiction. Miles is also top ranked in Sweden and is a BIS winner in Denmark, Sweden and Finland, with eight such awards and 12 group wins.

FRANCE

Anne-Marie Class

Kennel club and vets join forces on microchipping

Life in the dog world is unbelievably diverse so I asked some French key figures for their opinions about 2012.

Serge Sanchez is editor of the French magazine *Vos Chiens*. There are lots of publications about dogs in France. The French Kennel Club (SCC) has *La Revue de la Cynophilie* which communicates about all aspects of the dog world including scientific articles. But *Vos Chiens* gives us all the results of the shows and main working trials. What were the most significant events of 2012? Serge says: "In one sentence, the re-election of Christian Eymar-Dauphin

BIS at Paris under Luis Pinto Teixeira was Gwen Huikeshoven's Petit Basset Griffon Vendéen Dehra Amazon Bvlgari.
photo Vos Chiens

Montluçon's BIS winner was Vincent Loubet's Wire Fox Terrier Slicey Heart Of Mine.

as SCC president and of his team with interesting future prospects, and the French Championship Show in Metz in July. This event was memorable as the Societé Canine de Lorraine is one of the most dynamic canine societies. The organisation was perfect and there were many working trials and demonstrations of herding dogs, police dogs, search and rescue dogs, guide dogs for blind people and so on, all day long.

"Another matter was the achievement of Thierry Thomas in Salzburg in freestyle and dog dancing. Thierry does his training three times a week in a village hall 15 miles from his home."

BIS in Bordeaux under Frank Kane was Ivan Martinez Santome's French Bulldog Cinania Muhammad Alí.
photo Vos Chiens

Sports other than showing are very popular in France. This is Michel Picaut's Commanche, a member of the French Mondioring Team, pictured at the World Championship.

Could you tell us about the Grand Prix that you created in 1984? "Some 30 years ago, with my wife Evelyne, we were Welsh Terrier breeders and had bought two in the UK, both top dogs of the year. We admired the British dog world's organisation and when we created *Vos Chiens*, we drew our inspiration from the British example.

We take into account many results; CACIBs and reserves give points as well as the Club Show (Nationale) CACs.

There is the Grand Prix and the Top Dog; the Grand Prix involves breeders with their kennel name's victories and Top Dog one dog's results".

What changes have you noticed? "Concerning shows, we can see the same passion as many years ago. I do not feel there are fewer exhibitors despite the economic crisis. And there are still enthusiastic breeders. A new phenomenon now is the increasing number of professional handlers; 30

Sandy Lejeune's Coton de Tulear Ever Smiling des Fleurs d'Aloes was France's Top Dog 2011 and probably in 2012 too. She will represent the country at the Eukanuba World Challenge.
photo Vos Chiens

The climax of the year was the French Championship Show in Metz in July. The location was chosen because of its geographical position close to the rest of Europe.

After the four-day World Show in Paris with its 37,000 entries for two shows on one site, a figure never reached by any other show, the 2012 French Championship with 6,814 dogs seemed like a 'picnic', and the show came up to the expectations of the SCC, proving an excellent collaboration with the Societé Canine de Lorraine. All went well; the one disappointiment was that there were fewer visitors than expected, because the Tour de France chose that weekend to arrive in Metz, and the summer holidays were starting. That's an issue for 2013: how to attract the general public to shows?

There was a 'Discover Dog Village' and a game teaching children the right way to behave with a dog.

It was a very British final with BIS going to Avril Lacey and Stan Szyczewski's white Puli Weetoneon Artic Storm and reserve to Nic Burnikell and Bart de Croo's Dogue de Bordeaux Emberez The Big Show who was also best of the French breeds. The Weetoneon kennel has been resident in France for several years. Pictured with the winner are judge Laurent Pichard, SCC president Christian Eymar Dauphin and Elisabeth Castellotti offering the vase of the French Republic President.

The 2013 show is in Marseilles on June 1 and 2.
photos Horvath

years ago, there was only one, Pierre Boestch, now there are a dozen.

"Shows are better and better organised but I feel that with the disappearance of cages, there are fewer visitors. I have regrets with gundogs which are a national heritage in France with so many breeds but owners do not show them so much."

For Christian, the most important topic of the year was the management of the national dog identification file which the SCC has run since 1974. With the expansion of microchipping compared to tattooing, the vets and the SCC joined forces to manage the file together. The SCC and a vets' union (SNVEL) signed an agreement and created ICAD, Identification of Domestic Carnivores. Two years ago, they created an association to promote pets.

If the Ministry accepts the ICAD application, 80 people will work in this organisation which will be located in both the SCC and SNVEL buildings. Last year there were 740,000 new

identifications, compared with 202,131 LOF registrations. The English Setter is by far the highest in group 7: with 6,135 registrations, it is a very popular breed for hunters in France and with a dynamic breed club.

The dog scene is not only about shows and many enthusiasts prefer to work with their dogs. Last year saw 560 agility competitions with 163,476 entries, 79 hound trials involving 4,700 dogs, 96 field trials involving 6,626 dogs, 87 hound competitions involving 4,363 dog, 348 obedience events involving 9,285 dogs, 442 police dog activities with 8,603 dogs and 127 tracking tests with 2,572 dogs.

Then there are herding tests, earth dog trials, dog dancing, search and rescue tests, 'cavage' (truffle searching) etc.

A new project was born in 2012 to federate all these working events and a meeting is organised in December. Pierre Rouillon, new SCC committee

member, is in charge.

There were 30 CACIB shows with entries between 1,500 and 3,500 while the French Championship Show draws around 7,000; 55 CAC shows and 250 club shows. In total, 187,967 dogs were entered.

The main shows with more than 3,000 entries were Paris 3,041, Bordeaux 3,272, Montluçon 2,664 plus 800 club show entries, Orleans (3,106) and Metz in November.

The main issues and challenges for 2013 are the management of the file with the new collaboration, the improvement of relationships with the general public, the increasing involvement of scientists in breeding and much more.

GERMANY

Dr Wilfried Peper

Entries thrive but registrations crash

In 2012 the general assembly of the German Kennel Club (VDH), a remarkably developing show-scene and a negative record of registration figures appeared to be the topics of major importance.

At the general assembly, held in April 2012, all members of the board stood again. All of them were re-elected, mostly by unanimous votes. The well prepared modifications of the statutes found similar majorities.

The German show scene was constantly developing and improving although the ring discipline of too many exhibitors is still close to a catastrophe.

The 21 international CACIB shows and nine national all-breed shows, most of them organised as 'combi-shows', kept their high level of entries and visitors – two of them drew much more than usual: Bremen with its splendid show venue and Karlsruhe which replaced Stuttgart. The reason for this most favourable change was the financial conditions at the old place. Furthermore Karlsruhe is much better located for exhibitors from the neighbouring countries.

In May the VDH European Winner and National all-breed show were undoubtedly highlighted by the British Dog Festival, which had been organised as part of this prestigious event.

In 2009 the VDH and the Kennel Club had agreed upon the most innovative concept of a British and German Dog Festival to be held in 2012.

For all British breeds additional Kennel Club CCs were offered according to the KC regulations by 32 British judges, invited by the KC and in co-operation with the breed clubs concerned.

On Friday 40 British breeds were present, five on Saturday and 18 on Sunday, with entries more than 41 per cent higher than the year before. Impressive figures, proving it a successful and innovative show concept. It should be continued with partners which are country of origin of a considerable number of breeds.

The final contest of the festival, best British exhibit in show, was judged by Albert Wight, who gave the top honours to the Border Collie.

Gerald King, the official representative of the KC, as well as all the British judges,

BIS at the Europasieger was the Leonberger Amicus Optimus Antonius, owned by Natalia Kuharskaya from Russia.
photo Roberto

The Dortmund British Breeds festival was part of the National show held with the Europasieger. Overall BIS was the Samoyed from Denmark, Gitte Nielsen's Cabaka's McGee Of Calle.
photo Roberto

In a remarkable double, BIS at both the Bundessieger and at the concurrent national show was the British-bred Petit Basset Griffon Vendéen Soletrader Bjorn Borg, for Gwen Huikeshoven from the Netherlands. The same day, his granddaughter Peek A Boo was winning one of her many BIS back home!
photo Roberto

were extremely pleased with an event which had been much more than a show, while demonstrating successful international co-operation and improving mutual understanding.

The traditional Bundessieger show, for the last time organised in combination with a national show, was as attractive as always and ended with a sensation: Soletrader Bjorn Borg, a Petit Basset Griffon Vendéen who can be regarded as the incarnation of the breed Standard and perfectly presented by Gwen Huikeshoven, excelled as BIS at the Bundessieger and at the National show.

Next year all shows directly organized by the VDH (VDH European Winner, Leipzig and Bundessieger show) will be double international shows.

As a remarkable contrast to the German show scene the the number of VDH-registered puppies crashed down again. After the dramatic decrease in breeding activity between 1996 and 2000, a period of a slight increase and some years of constancy, a new crash has to be mentioned.

From 2010 to 2011 the registrations rapidly decreased from 85,252 to 80,554. The VDH does not breed, but as a kennel club it provides helpful services. The German economic situation can hardly explain a development like this. At present the problems are quite obviously caused by and in Germany's most powerful breed clubs, their breed-relevant structures and policies.

In 2001 Christopher Habig, a former president of the VDH, wrote: "A crisis is the best push to get all those things done which had been underestimated for a long time. That is to say, the dog world in the 21st century must be run by capable representatives who are supported by efficient structures."

As far as the German breeding-scene is concerned it seems to be a long way to Tipperary. On the way it cannot be helpful to ask the frogs if some swamps must be drained.

BIS at Erfurt was Noel Baaser's Basenji C-Quest Jokuba Dandy Shandy.
photo Roberto

At Lingen BIS was Renata Bogucka's Irish Setter Meldor Sett Estor Of Magic.
photo Roberto

Silke Eberhardt's Lagotto Romagnolo Kan Trace Cesare was BIS at Hannover.
photo Roberto

Neumünster's pole position went to the Mastiff Wizard Varvary Skifii, owned by Olaf Wienholz.
photo Roberto

The black Dwarf Poodle Pan Tau von der Hutzelscheweiz, owned by Anne Birgitte, Ute and Stefanie Schilling from Denmark, took BIS at Leipzig.
photo Roberto

The British-bred Cavalier King Charles Spaniel Miletree Constellation, owned by Klaus Vorderstrasse and Markus Kirschbaum, took top spot at Dresden, and again at Bremen.
photo Roberto

BIS at München was the Basset Hound Nhabira Favourite, owned by Rinus Versluis from the Netherlands.
photo Roberto

Jacques Sousa's Dogo Argentino Flash des Larmes du Soliel was BIS at Offenburg.
photo Roberto

Nürnberg saw a French victory for Iris Sablery's Australian Shepherd Energies Paparazzi de Costys du Tomberg.
photo Roberto

Rostock show was topped by the Weimaranaer Grey Classic's Ipanema Girl, owned by Edwin and Kristina Lenaerts from Belgium.
photo Roberto

Saarbrücken's BIS winner was the Longhaired Dachshund Vincent vd Taunushöhe, owned by Ilknur Bräutigam.
photo Roberto

BELGIUM AND LUXEMBURG

Climax to the FCI centenary

Report and photographs by Karl Donvil

Brussels show a week before Christmas had a very nice entry of 3,574 dogs, though this was 400 fewer than the previous year. Under Norman Deschuymere BIS went to a Belgian breed from a Belgian owner, Jan Roosens' Swedish-bred Papillon Siljans Truly Yours. Jan was placed in the group at Crufts with a Papillon a few years ago.

Kortrijk 2011 felt the impact of the many shows and festivities held that year and the entry number dropped back to 3,066. The show has always had a close bond with the UK which contributed 112 entries. Monique van Brempt's winner was the Siberian Husky Snowmist's Quidditch Seeker, owned by Kim Leblanc and Benny van Gorp.

Next year at Mouscron there will be some changes as Raymond Deconink will hand over his position to a new president. For 2012 he can look back to another successful show with a slightly increased entry. Harry O'Donoghue (right) judged BIS and winner for the second year running was the American-bred Pug Winsome Gold Standard owned by Bjorn Erling Loken and Trond Tørres from Norway and handled by Christine Sonberg. Laurent Heinesche (second left) judged the group. The Pug later won the Masters Trophy, a gala champion of champions-type event held with Liège show.

This year the Lovanium Trophy show at Leuven lost its president Eddy Vogeleer; his successor is Rudy Feyaerts. At the 2011 show Christian Stefanescu gave BIS to Bart and Carine Bauwens-Roobrouck's Leonberger Hakuna C.Bora Z Miloticek shown by junior handler Inneke Vanseer.

The Flanders Dog Show at Gent, Belgium's unique and famous biennial 'one-day-CACIB-show' is still very popular and gained slightly in entries. Under Liliane de Ridder-Onghena, Jacques Houben won BIS with his Welsh Terrier Heinerle von der Hohen Flür, bred in Germany.

This Schaal der Kempen at Hoogstraten was another success although it did not equal the record entry of 2011. Norwegian exhibitors returned home with several podium places including BIS. Norman Deschuymere chose the German Shepherd Zanta av Quantos, owned by Tor Johansen. A top winner at home for several years, she was tragically later among the victims of a kennel fire in Ireland.

At the Ambiorix Trophy show Piotr Kroll gave BIS to a Clumber Spaniel just a few days over a year old, Kornell van de Hompele Pomp, owned by Johan and Ingrid Vandeborg-Vanormelingen.

Antwerp's Brabo Show has a new goal, to become the '(Facebook) Like This' show, providing big rings, plenty of space for a drink and a snack, a pleasant main ring and so on. There was a small increase in entries. Hans van den Berg gave BIS to Dominique Delabelle's Whippet Hannah di Mahana, from the Netherlands. Her dam Daydream di Mahana had won the same award in 2007 under August Dewilde, this year's group judge.

Lommel, a small one-day CAC show, drew a record entry of 1,353 dogs. One reason might be the new breeding regulations of the Belgian Kennel Club which say that both parents of a litter need to meet the minimum requirements for breeding, gaining a minimum qualification of good at a Belgian show under a Belgian judge. A show like Lommel is the best opportunity to enter your dog if you need that qualification as a CAC show has more Belgian judges officiating. Laurent Pichard's BIS was the Cardigan Corgi, UK-bred Gowerston Jazzsinger for Pemcader, another success for Christine Sonberg. He is the sire of the breed's first male and female group winners back home.

Genk drew a big increase of entries to 1636. Vincent O'Brien gave BIS to a dog who had crossed the English Channel, Julie Sheridan's Newfoundland Hanningfield Touch Of Magic, a group winner at home.

The Royal Fox Terrier Club of Belgium celebrated its 125th anniversary when Falaën, a small village in the Ardennes, was the place to be for no fewer than 139 Fox Terrier fanciers from throughout Europe. Margaret Hughes gave BIS to the Wire Crispy Legacy, owned by Agneta Aström from Sweden.

Two years ago the main hall of the venue for Liège Golden Dog Trophy Show burned down. This year a new roof was ready just in time to celebrate the 75th anniversary of the Syndicat d'Elevage Canin de Liège.

Liliane de Ridder-Onghena gave BIS to the Miniature Poodle Kudos Lykke Li, owned by Mikael Nilsson from Sweden and handled by Biagio Cellamare.

At the end of 2011 Brussels concluded the festivities of the FCI centenary with the Champion of Champions Show, only the third ever held. The FCI held some interesting seminars the previous day. The emphasis was on the welfare of the dogs and how to get rid of any kind of exaggeration. Only a limited number of entries were allowed, 150 per FCI group, and it worked perfectly, with 893 entries counted.

After the initial round, the 64 finalists were judged in a knock-out competition by Ermanno Maniero from Peru for the FCI Americas Section, Hiroshi Kamisato from Japan for the Asian and Horst Kleibenstein from Germany representing the European section.

Eventually the Pembroke Corgi Andvol Pinkerton, for Olga Shilova from Russia, was awarded Vice-Champion of Champions and the Golden Victor was the Irish Wolfhound Absolute Roan Inish Tullamore Good Stuff, owner Petra Tomasovicova from Slovakia.

The winners were invited to the gala dinner in one of the most beautiful concert halls of the city, where a great many VIPs came over from all over the world to hand over gifts and congratulate Hans Müller as president of the FCI. I think the FCI can look back on a thrilling year to celebrate its 100th anniversary. Besides the dog shows there were lots of other events like field trials, racing, coursing, agility etc.

Luxemburg's spring show drew 5,184 entries, representing 271 breeds and 35 nationalities. Enrique Filippini's BIS was the UK-bred Akita Ruthdales U Cant Touch This, from the famous Dutch kennel of Marcel Huls.

Mechelen show suffered from a heatwave, Sunday's temperature peaking at 36.9 degrees. Andrew Brace's BIS was the Canadian-bred Miniature Smooth Dachshund GrandGables Ms Just A Tease owned by Philippe Meier from the Netherlands.

Luxemburg's autumn 2011 show was reset to November, but there was a big rise in entries to 4,656. Impressive prize money was on offer for the first time. Jorge Nallem chose for BIS the Pomeranian Fon's Flying To Dan-Star-Kom who came from Russia with his owner Liudmila Komyakova and went home with 700 euros.

Luxemburg's September 2012 show experienced a serious drop to 3,841 entries. Marina Ostrovskaya made it yet another victory for Christine Sonberg, this time with the Pug bitch Kingpoint Catwalk, born in Finland.

THE NETHERLANDS

Haja van Wessem

All pups to be microchipped at seven weeks

The decision of the Dutch government that as from 2013 all puppies have to be microchipped at seven weeks is a small step forward in the battle against the puppy farmers and the not so very careful breeders of purebred dogs.

A small step indeed because the decision does not include mature dogs and because there are, as yet, no sanctions. Moreover, if the breeder lets the puppies go at an earlier age – as most puppy farmers do – there is nothing to be microchipped!

Breeders of purebred dogs have to register their puppies and have them microchipped by the Dutch Kennel Club in order to obtain a pedigree for them but the harm is done by the breeders of 'lookalikes' who are sold without a pedigree or with a fake pedigree and by the puppy farmers who sell the pups with a pedigree but who don't want to know about health checks and tests.

A bigger step forward would have been a microchip obligation for each and every dog. The Dutch KC said in a press release that it was pleased with the government decision but also that it regretted there was no mention of investigation and enforcement of the law. The fact that the microchipping is obligatory only for puppies means that it will take years before a total identification and registration has been accomplished.

The consultations of the Dutch KC and delegates of the breed clubs about health and welfare regulations for breeders go on and on and no firm decisions have as yet been made. In view of the government's decision to control dog breeding – it is the state's secretary's intention to scrutinise two different breeds each year – it would seem advisable to speeds things up a bit.

The Dutch KC came up with a plan to have all parents and puppies in the litter DNA-identity tested by the club's official who does the microchipping of the puppies. This plan would improve the welfare of pedigree dogs.

The plan met with general disapproval of the breed clubs because it was insufficiently detailed about what the costs would be for the breeders and who the future owner of the swabs would be. It was found unacceptable that the breeder would have to pay for the taking of the swabs and the analysis by the laboratory, whereas the laboratory would be the sole owner of the swabs. Also, it was not clear how the DNA establishing of parenthood would contribute to the welfare of the dogs.

The Kennel Club committee took this plan back for further detailing and will present it later in 2012.

Winner of the Dog of the Year Show was the British-bred Akita Ruthdales U Cant Touch This, bred by Matthew Bostock and Janet Armstrong and owned by Marcel and Lene Huls in the Netherlands. He was Top Dog in 2010 and third in 2011. At the time of writing, the end of September 2012, he was runner up to Top Dog 2012. This yeas he had two RBIS wins.
photo van Wessem

Best in show at the Winner Show, Amsterdam, in 2011 was the British Petit Basset Griffon Vendéen Soletrader Peek A Boo who is by 'our own' Cappuccino van Tum Tum's Vriendjes, owned by Sara Robertson and handled by husband Gavin. Breed judge was Dr Paolo Dondina (holding the large rosette) and group judge Gunnar Nymann from Denmark. RBIS was also British-bred, the Cavalier King Charles Spaniel Miletree Constellation bred and owned in Britain by Peter and Ruta Towse and co-owned by Klaus Vorderstrasse and Markus Kirschbau from Germany. He was also BOB at Crufts 2012.
photo van Kempen

Top Dog 2011 was the Irish Wolfhound Pitlochry's O Brian-orak, bred and owned by Conny Fernhoudt-Schildt. This was not Conny's first Top Dog: in 2008 this award was given to the homebred Pitlochry's Catweazle. Conny has been in the breed for over 30 years and she won the group at Rotterdam this year with a son of Catweazle.
photo van Wessem

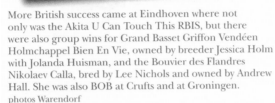

More British success came at Eindhoven where not only was the Akita U Can Touch This RBIS, but there were also group wins for Grand Basset Griffon Vendéen Holmchappel Bien En Vie, owned by breeder Jessica Holm with Jolanda Huisman, and the Bouvier des Flandres Nikolaev Calla, bred by Lee Nichols and owned by Andrew Hall. She was also BOB at Crufts and at Groningen.
photos Warendorf

Reserve BIS at the Dog of the Year Show was the Lagotto Romagnolo Gleska Goody Goody, bred in Sweden and owned by Camilla and Katrien van Gemert. She was top gundog in 2011 and is in the lead for that award this year.
photo van Wessem

After the success with Cappuccino Gwen Huikeshoven came back with a new trump card: her homebred Grand Basset Griffon Vendéen Fido Dido van Tum Tum's Vriendjes won BIS at Leeuwarden.
photo van Wessem

Top Dog at the time of writing is the Deerhound Cairnesund's Pearly Prince, bred in Denmark and owned by Jasper and Ineke de Vos-Brugman.
photo van Wessem

Pembroke Corgi Otreks What Dreams Are Made Of, bred in the US and owned by Jan Snijder, won BIS at Tilburg and reserve at Rotterdam. Jan was very successful with his import Belroyd Kingbird and his homebred Corgis under the prefix Pennies from Heaven are doing equally well.
photo van Wessem

Philippe has several top winning Dachshunds. Perfect Painted Ballistic She Goes, was RBIS at the Gundog show and at Rotterdam he won BIS with the bitch Cyberdachs Mini Mona Lisa (pictured), bred in Hungary. This youngster also won the group at Alkmaar and has several impressive wins in other countries. Philippe breeds Dachshunds under the Swissking affix.
photo van Wessem

At Uden, one of the few shows that wasn't drenched in rain, group 4 was won by a multi-titled Miniature Dachshund bitch Grandgables Ms Just A Tease, bred in Canada and owned by Philippe Meier. She also won the group at the Dog of the Year show and Eindhoven.
photo van Wessem

An unusual success was the group win of the Sussex Spaniel Julius of Tonispada at Norriss, bred in Luxemburg) and owned by Chris Wakefield from the UK who is a regular visitor to our shows.
photo van Kempen

ITALY
A wind of stagnation

Costanza Ferraris

The Italian show calendar is always full of events. The number of shows seems to increase year by year. Is it a reaction to the decreasing number of entries? The kennel clubs organise two shows on the same weekend and, when possible, also a few breed specialties. New titles also appear.

The number of entries fluctuates between 1,000 and 2,000 per show. In the past you saw many exhibitors running after the Cajelli Trophy for the Italian Top Dog but now this competition is becoming less important. At the end of the year you don't have any idea about which dogs will be the top three and it is difficult to obtain updates.

The magazines which covered shows are disappearing little by little. *I Nostri Cani*, the official magazine of the Italian Kennel Club, publishes only the results with photos sent by the kennel clubs. There is no official photographer and not all the shows have their own professional photographer.

The Cajelli Trophy is calculated on points from podium places at international shows. The count is done by the Italian Kennel Club (ENCI) and the results are published between March and April of the following year without any fanfare, just a page with a list of names and numbers but no photos.

In previous years the names of the three winners were already known at the end of the year. The final shows of the season saw a real race down to the last point. The international show of Milan, the first of the year, saw the winners crowned. There was great excitement among the exhibitors. The atmosphere was a bit like the one you breathe at the end of a school year, waiting for the final results.

This led on to two other points competition being set up. That more successful was the Top Dog, for each breed. The second one, organised by ENCI, died the same year it born. To earn points you had to show your dog at specific shows chosen by ENCI.

Even exhibitors' international travel plans have changed in the last few years. Instead of going to Spain, Portugal, France or Belgium, Italian exhibitors prefer to show their dogs in the 'new' countries such as Slovenia or Croatia, closer to Italy.

Among the year's BIS winners other than those pictured were: we can mention the Bulldog **Rembombory Trichet** (Lucca), Neapolitan Mastiff **Claus del Nolano**, UK-bred Lakeland Terrier **Nujax Rising Sun at Saredon** (Pisa), Alaskan Malamutes **Rohan del Biagio** (Forli) and **Million Dollar Boy del Whimper DG Jorasses** (Caserta), Chow **Moima Alberto Tomba** (Alessandria), Smooth Chihuahua **Hillside Rendezvous** (Modica) and Maltese **Cinecittà Quentin Tarantino** (Torino).

Winner of the Cajelli Trophy for 2011 was the Saluki Delborghino Oscardelarenta, pictured with owner Leonardo Galliano. Runner-up was the Akita DeKaner's Wolverine Revenge, ownd by Francisco Garcia, who was BIS at the Spanish centenary show and at the 2011 World Show in Paris, as well as at Pistoia in 2012.
photo Ferraris

The Cajelli Trophy also has a section for Italian breeds won in 2011 by the Bracco italiano Ribot, handled by Francesco Vasanella for Paolo Codeluppi.
photo Ferraris

BIS at San Remo under Brenda Banbury was the Pomeranian Upstart Fora Sun Blush owned by Riccardo Gentili and reserve the Bearded Collie Ho in Mente Te del Cuore Impavido, owned by Filippo Ripolo and handled by Olga Klimova. The Beardie was third in the Cajelli Trophy for 2011 and in 2012 took BIS at Erba, while the Pomeranian was also BIS at Ancona.
photo Ferraris

In 2011 Italy celebrated 150 years of unity. At the end of 2011, ENCI organised a show where a special title was offered to all the CAC winners in the national breeds. Dr Francesco Balducci, ENCI president, gave BIS to the Maltese Rhapsody's Saturday Night Fever, owned by Tonia Holibaugh from the US, reserve to Ivano Panciroli's smooth Segugio Italiano Gea and BIS3 to the Spinone Tina dell'Adige owned by the dell'Adige di Poli kennel.
photo Ferraris

BIS at Insubria under Edd Bivin was the Samoyed Cabaka's Bobbie of Storm Cat, owned by Pierluigi Buratti.
photo Ferraris

The international show calendar started as usual with Milan, one of the few shows which attracts foreigner exhibitors. BIS judged by Kornelija Butrimova was the Pembroke Corgi from Russia Andvol Pinkerton, handled by Olga Shilova for Olga Shuvalova.
photo Ferraris

Reggio Emilia and Modena combine to make a double international show. At the former Paolo Dondina awarded BIS to Roberto Tasselli's Kerry Blue Terrier Balboa Ray Ban, second to Stefano Paolantoni's White Miniature Poodle Calais B dell'Alberico and third to Francesca Zampini's Azawakh Azamour Ayman. On the second day, BIS at Modena under Francesco Cochetti was the Miniature Poodle. The Kerry's other victories included Cremona and Arezzo and the Azawakh won at Livorno.
photo Ferraris

Amiong the breeds which could be discovered at the Italian breeds show was the Segugio Maremmano. Even though it has about 2,000 registrations per year, it is seldom seen at shows. Most belong to hunters, not really interested in dog shows. BOB was Ziro, owned by Matteo Rigati.
photo Ferraris

At the Spaniel specialty in Germany: Susan Young gave the BOB Cocker to Roxicocker Sovereign, owned by Roxana Opris from Italy, who went on to RBIS under Marjo Jaakkola.
photo Ferraris

On the Sunday at the World Show best breeders group was was the Newfoundlands and third for the Bernese Mountain Dogs, a big surprise was for the judge Otto Schimpf when he discovered that the handlers came from the same Italian kennel, Starry Town of Maurizio Mauro and Gabriele Guidi.

At Italian victory at the European Show in Bucharest for the UK-bred Lhasa Apso Zentarr Morgan, owned by Stefano Paolantoni (seen with an orange tie) and handled by Javier Gonzalez Mendikote. Also pictured are Yolanda Nagler, Romanian KC president Christian Stefanescu from Eukanuba, Petru Muntean and group judge Francesco Cochetti. The Pepper and Salt Schnauzer Amor di Schnauzer Wild Boy and the Wire Dachshund Magica Roma also won their groups for Italy. At this show ENCI delegates made a presentation to promote the 2015 World Show which will take place in Milan.
photo Ferraris

IBERIA

Marcelino Pozo

Two years ago I began talking about the economic crisis which has not spared the world of dogs. The recession will take a long time to recover from and continues to affect breeders, kennel clubs, exhibitors and magazines. May I encourage you to not lose your enthusiasm and confidence.

Gibraltar

The Gibraltar Kennel Club again captured the attention of exhibitors from southern Europe with the chance to win two CACIBs in one weekend and thereby achieving a Gibraltar champion title in the various classes.

The two international shows, the 36th and 37th, were held at the Victoria Stadium with a total entry of 1,608 dogs, surpassing other years. As always the club appointed an excellent panel of judges.

BIS on the first day at Gibraltar under Ann Ingram and RBIS on the second day under Peter Green (pictured) was Juan del Pino's West Highland White Terrier Hormiga Atómica of New Gryffindor.
photo Pozo

On the second day BIS was the British-bred Akita Redwitch Relight My Fire, owner Alvaro Cosme.
photo Pozo

Portugal

The Club Portuguese de Canicultura had a calendar of 12 CAC shows and 12 with CACIBs.

Two of the most important shows are Oporto's International Norte, won by the Portuguese Water Dog Way To Glow da Pedra Da Anixa, and Lisbon, won by the Maltese Azzaros Fend.

Portugal's current Top Dog is the Bracco Italiano Nicodemo del Tavuliddaro, winner of multiple groups, owned by by Elsa and Miguel Colaco, and pictured winning a group in Luxemburg.
photo Donvil

Second in Portugal's rankings is the Bullmastiff Ruppert da Casa Alto Cristelo, owner Ricardo Manuel Miranda.
photo Pozo

In third place is the Samoyed Cabaka's Valiant of Gucci, owned by Pedro Brito, who was BOB at Crufts.
photo Brace

Fourth is a Portuguese Water Dog, a breed which often features well at Portuguese shows. This time it is Way to Glow da Pedra da Anixa owned by Isabel Nobre.
photo Pozo

Spain

The dog show calendar of the Spanish Kennel Club (RSCE) was composed of 24 national and 28 international shows, two of which carried the obligatory point for the Spanish championship. One of them was in November in Talavera and the other the 84th spring international show in Madrid which was again held in the Juan Carlos I Fair Centre after its success there the previous year. It drew an excellent entry of more of 4,000 dogs.

Spanish exhibitors did well at the Salzburg World Show, highlights being second in group for the Affenpinscher Pramada N Coachlight's Naughty Nestor owned by Araceli Fernandez and third for Enrique Boza's Miniature Wire Dachshund Alpheratz Just Do it.

Heading the ranking for Top Dog in Spain is the Pomeranian Ch Sunterra's Izziling Hot, owned by Julio Martínez de Marigorta, who will represent the country at the Eukanuba World Challenge.
photo Pozo

Currently in second place in the Top Dog list is the BIS winner at the Madrid international show, the Dogo Argentino Casper Fantasma Blanco de Cueva de la Mucheres, owned by Antolin Crespo and Jairo Cuartas.
photo Pozo

The British-bred Beagle Dialynne Legacy, owned by Albert Abajo, is in third place. His English Springer Sieger's Match Point is also in the top ten.
photo Brace

In fourth place, the same position as two years ago, is the Maltese Azzaro's Fendi, owned by Tiziana Saracini.
photo Pozo

One of the Spanish native breeds features among the country's top ten, the Garafian Sheepdog Zeus, owned by Armando Paz.
photo Pozo

Each year one of Visitacion Echerria's Bearded Collies is high in the Spanish rankings. This time Double Scotch Black Pygmalion, handled by Luis Gerez, is in fifth place.
photo Pozo

Blanca Ferrer's Pug Los Chato's del Turia Who's Your Daddy was BIS at Granada and features in Spain's top ten.
photo Pozo

It is well known that dogs are the hobby of Queen Sophia and for the second year she visited the Madrid show, walking through the halls enquiring about the breeds and watching the morning's activities.
photo Pozo

During the main ring programme at Madrid Carlos Salas presented three Spanish native breeds, the Carea Leones, Carea Manchego and Xarnego Valenciano.
photo Pozo

AUSTRIA

Maria-Luise Doppelreiter

Salzburg was the centre of the dog world

The highlight of 2012 was of course the World Dog Show in Salzburg. The total entry of 18,607 dogs, plus more than 5,000 dogs at the club shows in the park of Anif Castle, representing 55 countries, was a bit lower than expected, but a good number considering that docked dogs are not allowed at our shows any more.

Junior handling was a big event with over 60 juniors each day. In connection with the show there were also competitions for heelwork to music and freestyle, as well as the World Championship for obedience. Some clubs also organised their own shows, so that some of the breeds were shown over three days.

With fewer than 150,000 inhabitants Salzburg is much smaller than Paris, where the last World Show was held, but I think the town and our kennel club coped quite well with the organisation. There were some traffic problems in the mornings, the main reason being that exhibitors didn't book their parking tickets in advance so that they blocked the motorway leading to the fair centre where the show was held.

Most of the rings were big enough, with lots of space round them for the exhibitors and their dogs. The showground was clean over all three days, and it was comfortable for all.

Judges were very well entertained; the highlight for me was Saturday evening when we had a lovely dinner in the archbishop's residence, and afterwards an impressive organ recital in the church nearby.

Three great days with friends, I hope we will all meet again in Budapest 2013!

This was the most important, but not the only show in Austria in 2012. The show season of 2011 ended as usual with the Wels double show, at which the Austrian Superchamps were announced: the male Pug **Picador's Gogol**, owner Sabina Chiesa Folbrecht, and the female Golden Retriever **Sequins Speedwell**, owner Verena Arminger.

The 2012 season started in February in Graz, followed by Wieselburg (April), then after the Word Show came Klagenfurt in June, Oberwart in July, a double show in Innsbruck in August, and the Bundessiegerschau, our Crufts qualifier, in Tulln in September. In December we will have the double show in Wels again with the Superchamp competition. The entries were a bit down after the World Show, but we still have more than in other countries.

By a points system the most successful dogs from each FCI group are declared Austrian Show Winner; owners must enter their dogs before a deadline and they are published on the homepage of the kennel club (ÖKV).

Group 1: Briard **Ed Stuart La Mia Amici**, owned by Martina Riedmann; 2 Hovawart **Pablo Ex Mercator**, Peter Czermak; 3 American Staffordshire Terrier **Carmichael's Get Out Of Jail**, Manuela Boitscheff; 4 Wire Dachshund **Ella von der Zirbenleiten**, Susanne Wazek; 5 Iceland Dog **Töfra Tryggur Aron**, Susanne Götzinger.

6 Beagle **Glossy Gambler von der Thurnmühle**, Friderke Grünke; 7 Irish Setter **Castello Alin de Lon**, Bernd Kvarits; 8 Cocker Spaniel **Queen of Hearts Made In Austria**, Hanna Krenn; 9 Pug **Anjos Toyota**, Sabina Chiesa-Folbrecht, the only dog to repeat a 2011 win; and 10 Whippet **Moskito's Bonanza**, Andrea Mücke.

Leader in group 8: the Cocker Spaniel Queen of Hearts Made In Austria, owned by Hanna Krenn. She was also best of day at Salzburg in 2011.

At the World Show in Salzburg junior BIS under Agnes Ganami Kertes was the Toy Poodle Shantaram Hands Off, handled by Marie France van de Welde and owned by Alessandra Giuliani from Italy. With them is Austrian Kennel Club president Michael Kreiner.
photo RBT

The Tulln Bundessieger Show as usual had a very good entry. The showground is popular with visitors and exhibitors, dogs can run on grass and there are many stands, as well as delicious food for the humans. BIS was the American Cocker Spaniel Räuberlein's Dance With The Stars, owned by the sisters Verena, Rafalea and Cristina Eitel from Germany. Jonah's sire Ch Räuberlein's Shooting Star won BIS at Tulln some years ago, and goes back six generations to Ch Sandy Hill's Chico v Horbach, the first American Cocker imported by the breeders from the US in 1974.
photo Deya

WORLD SHOW

Saluki strides out to win the World

The 2012 World Show took place in Salzburg, Austria, and drew almost 19,000 dogs.

Best in show was the Saluki **Shiraz California Dreamin'**, owned by Nicklas Eriksson from Sweden, and reserve the Pembroke Corgi **Andvol Pinkerton**, owned by Olga Shilova from Russia.

The other group winners were: Newfoundland **Starry Town Bob Prin**, Maurizio Mauro, Italy; Smooth Dachshund **Norden Liht Unkas**, Anastasia Krylova, Russia; UK-bred Basset Fauve de Bretagne **Shiroblam First Slip**, Elisabeth Strömberg, Sweden; Siberian Husky **Snowmist's Quicksilver Speigas**, Kim Leblanc, Canada.

Standard Poodle **Aleph American Idol**, Charlotte Sandell, Sweden; American Staffordshire Terrier **Don King Of Ring's**, Natalija Zeljic, Serbia; Weimaraner **Grey Classic's Ipanema Girl**, Edwin and Kristina Lenaerts, Belgium; and English Springer Spaniel **Linmoor Zimply Zalient**, Katarzyna Ksiazek, Poland.

photos RBT

SWITZERLAND

Costanza Ferraris

Come to Geneva in 2013

In 2013 the European Show will take place in Geneva. For 2012, the Swiss show calendar started with the double show at Lausanne which takes place during the Animalia weekend, one of the biggest animal events in Switzerland. The first BIS was judged by Leif Wilberg who selected the Dutch Affenpinscher Billy Bongo v Tani Kazari, owned by Mieke Cooijmans and Frank Rossier, while the following day Ron Menaker gave the BIS to the Hungarian Old English Sheepdog Bottom Shaker My Secret (pictured), owned by József Koroknai. A little later he won the group at Crufts.
photo Ferraris

On the second day at Fribourg, BIS under Ann Joe Sampaio was Didider Coton's Afghan Hound Jacosta Gold But Not Copper, from France, a Swedish-bred dog with a great record including BIS at the sighthound specialty in Courtrai 2011. The Lausanne and Fribourg shows in the French-speaking part of Switzerland are organised by the Société Canine Vaudoise.
photo Ferraris

At Fribourg BIS on the first day was judged by Rita Kadicke-Skadina. Her choice was the American Cocker, Very Vigie Farouk, owned by Isabelle Talon and handled by Hugues Schuh. Only 15 months old, he had already won numerous young BIS.

It is very rare to see a Swiss hunting breed on the podium but at Fribourg the Lucerne Hound Fiona v Weisshorn, owned by Emil Isenring, won the group under Christine Rossier.
photo Ferrais

Aarau one-day international show is only two years old but already a great success. BIS under Christine Rossier was the Italian Welsh Terrier, Cunnings Diana owned by Giuseppe Avvenuti. On the right is chairman Barbara Muller.
photo Roberto

The St Gallen double CACIB show opens the season in the German part of Switzerland. First day winner was the Russian Pug, Predery Pug Eralash Show Man, owned by Kunitsyn and Ryabukhina, while Sunday's winner is pictured, the Whippet Over the Moon Absolute Mann, owned by Fabrizio Manni from Italy.
photo Ferraris

POLAND

Janusz Opara

This year season's highlight was the Euro Sighthound Show, organised back to back with the Sighthound Breeds Club of Poland and Polish Greyhound Club specialties in the beautiful, historic surroundings of Czestochowa. The panel of renowned breeder-judges attracted a stunning entry from 20 countries.

BIS at both sighthound shows under Gerard Jipping and Knut Blutecher (pictured) was the Afghan Hound Al-Nacira Bint Roula von Haussman owned by Elisabet Leven and Sven Westerblad from Sweden, seen with the second day RBIS, the Whippet Sobresalto Ndringhete Ndra owned by Annalia Rovani and Arnoldo Cotugno from Italy .

Those who know Maciej Lipiec, president of the Sighthound Breeds Club, have no doubt this unforgettable weekend would not have been possible without his passion and dedication to the club over the last few decades.

photo Milian

Where breeding stock must have
show successs

This has been yet another year of steady entries at most shows and growing interest in other activities with dogs.

Shows play an important role in our breeding system. Our current rules impose on each brood bitch and stud dog strict demands of being successfully shown at three shows under three different judges after reaching full maturity, that is after 15 months of age. One of the shows has to be an international event or the breed specialty; the qualifying grading for males is excellent, for females excellent or very good.

It really takes a good quality specimen, both in conformation and disposition, to fulfil these demands. Still, it is not a formula for breeding good dogs.

Not allowing poor quality dogs to be bred from is a good attitude to breeding but, as anywhere in the world, real success comes from the combination of a true talent, knowledge and dedication in a breeder; this cannot be produced by any rules.

While a minority of show committees decided to adjust their entry fees to the growing costs of organising their events, the vast majority opted to sympathise with their customers – the exhibitors – and did not raise their entry fees. Listening to ringside chat proves the latter decision is the right one and their entries endorse the preferences of the exhibitor.

There were 15 international shows in 2012 well spread throughout the country and our show calendar. In spite of our winter weather, which can be a deterrent, we have expanded our show season and have no real break from past traditions.

Countless breed specialties and all-breeds shows offering CCs do not leave much room in avid exhibitors' calendars. Still more and more Poles make the trip to Crufts, the European Show and the World Show. This has been a year of significant success for Polish exhibitors at these prestigious shows and we have noticed growing interest in gaining the Crufts qualification for 2013. Not only does our qualifying show attract bigger entries but qualifying shows in neighbouring countries get a steadily growing numbers of entrants from Poland.

Delegates to the Polish Kennel Club representing regional clubs, their numbers depending on the membership, will be designated during clubs' general meetings by the end of March 2013.

In May they will all discuss the future of our organisation at the kennel club's two-day general assembly. We across our fingers that clever decisions will be made and the right people voted for to lead us steadily through the challenges of the future.

The Polish Greyhound has been known for centuries but the efforts to get the breed recognised by the FCI were no less dramatic than the nation's struggle for independence. It feels good to see the breed growing in popularity at home and abroad. At the specialty BIS was the bitch Gudelka Arcturus, seen with the best dog, Artur Litwa's Incitatus Arcturus, who had also been RBIS at the first sighthound show, and the best junior Nachylek Arcturus, all bred by Bianka Horbatowska.
photo Milian

HUNGARY

A question of survival

Gábor Szalánczi

For the Hungarian Kennel Club (MEOE) 2002 was all about survival. The full story is very complex, but briefly, the MEOE was attacked by the Hungarian Dog Breeding Association, which claims to care for lot of breeds, but without breeders, dog shows or any dog activities. It was founded by a few people who were removed from the MEOE a long time ago.

Unfortunately they had a good personal contact in the Hungarian Agricultural Ministry, and a few years ago a ministry order wanted to control all dog breeding (as with farm animals), and obtained the right to give a licence for pedigree dog breeding to clubs or associations.

The MEOE fought for years against this order, with much success, and the constitutional court ruled for the MEOE. But then the animal breeding laws were changed again, and the MEOE had to start fighting once more. The last battle of this war was in the spring and summer of 2012, when the MEOE was given until July 1, 2013 to come to an agreement with the ministry and the HDBA.

The World Show 2013 can therefore go ahead, and we await the resolution of this difficult situation next year. We hope a successful World Show can be a strong plus point for the MEOE in the negotiations.

The HDBA needs the FCI licence, because the law requires membership of an international organisation for breeding, and the FCI has declared its support for the MEOE. The MEOE has more than 10,000 members, successful shows and competitions, lot of breed clubs and, most important, FCI membership.

The HDBA has few people (fewer than 100), five to ten clubs, but no shows or competitions, but the right from the ministry to run things. At this moment is no legal dog breeding association in Hungary, because both sides are missing rights or licences. The MEOE thanks all the dog people for their support by letter and on the internet.

In August, the Hungarian Parliament changed the animal welfare law. The most important aspects were a total ban on ear cropping and tail docking is allowed only until seven days. The MEOE has not changed its rules and so far these dogs can still be shown in Hungary.

Thanks to the economic crisis, entries are declining; the average for CACIB shows declined to 1,000-1,100 dogs, the national shows 5-600. In 2012 were held 15 international and 24 national shows. The number of pedigrees issued also went down.

Best in show/day winners other than those pictured included: **Heartily Bart Simpson**, Jack Russell Terrier from Serbia; **Skipper's Wish You Were Here**, Newfoundland; **Devils and Fairies Flash Of The Blade**, Staffordshire Bull Terrier, who won the Champion Show; **Evak's Shalimar**, Silver Min Poodle from Russia.

Bernegarden's Wish Upon A Star, St Bernard from Slovakia; **Fon's Flying to Dan-Star-Kom**, Pomeranian from Russia; **King of Helluland Feel The Win**, Newfoundland from Slovakia who won the group at Crufts; and **Weimpoint Keepgoin**, Pointer.

The Pointer Weimpoint Keep Smilin', owned by Kristina Pilatus-Lenaerts (Belgium) and Dorottya Záhonyi-Ábel (Hungary), was junior RBIS at the World Show (pictured with judge Agnes Ganami Kertes), and group winner and junior group 2 at the European Show. photo Gabor

The big winning Old English Sheepdog Bottom Shaker My Secret, owned by József Koroknai and handled by Zsolt Hanó, won the group at Crufts, the first time a Hungarian dog had achieved this. photo Gabor

Twice BIS at one weekend at Komarom: the Welsh Terrier Nagant from Michael, owned by breeder Denk Csaba with Bob Krautscheid from the Netherlands. Nagant won the RCC at Crufts. photo Gabor

BIS on both days at Szekesfeherva was the Lhasa Apso Sayonara Thinker of Golden Sprite, owned by Zsuzsanna Csizmadia. photo Gabor

The Golden Retreiver Dewmist Silk Screen had in the previous years won everything possible. In 2012 he beacme a veteran and came back to win a BIS at Debrecen, judged by Gabriel Valdez. Owner is Sandor Kozak and handler Zsolt Hanó. photo Gabor

The year's greatest success a Hungarian-owned dog was RBIS at the European Show for the Afghan Hound Oudry Gandamak, owned by Csilla Bakos. photo Gabor

THE EUROPEAN SHOW

photos Paula Heikkinen-Lehkonen and Harri Lehkonen

The biggest show ever for Romania

The FCI European Winner Show took place in Bucharest, Romania. Although the entry was somewhat lower than expected, with over 6,000 dogs it was the biggest show ever held in the country, and drew praise for its organisation.

Best in show was the Lhasa Apso Zentarr Morgan, owned by Stefano Paolantoni from Italy and his British breeder Margaret Anderson, and handled by Javier Gonzales Mendikote. For Margaret this represented an unusual double, owning and breeding the BIS at both Crufts and the European Show.

RBIS was the Afghan Hound Oudry Gandamak, owner Csilla Bsakos from Hungary.

BIS3 was the Flat-coated Retriever Caci´s Win-a-Latte, owned by Carina Östman from Sweden.

Group winner: the Kerry Blue Terrier Rollick´s Super Hero, owned by Ivana Bilic and Igor Mioc from Croatia and hamdled by Ante Lucin.

Group winner: the Russian Black Terrier Oskar Yablunevyi Tsvit, owned by Irina Yablonka, Ukraine.

Group winner under Barbara Müller: the Crufts group-winning Old English Sheepdog Bottom Shaker My Secret, owned by Joszef Koroknai from Hungary and handled by Zsolt Hano.

Group winner: the Basset Hound Bassjoy Crazy Night, owner Mariano Galan from Spain.

Group winner: the Wire Dachshund Magicaroma, owned by Annaluve Saletti from Italy.

Group winner under Claudio de Giuöliani: the Pharaoh Hound Reedly Road Illuminated, owner Maria Evteeva from Russia.

Group winner: the Pointer Weimpoint Keep Smilin, owners Kristina Pilatus and Dorothya Zahauj, Hungary.

THE BALKANS

Compiled by Ante Lučin

BULGARIA

It has been a very good year for the Bulgarian dog world. Let's start with the biggest success of our junior handler, **Stanislav Petrov**. In very strong competition at the World Show in Salzburg he won the title 'Best Junior Handler of the World' making all the dog people here very very proud.

The leading Bulgarian dogs who are giving us so much joy are the Bullmastiff **Ch Game Keeper's Play My Game** 'Teddy' and the Dalmatian **Ch United Spots Quinlan** 'Tott'. The Bullmastiff has won many BIS throughout Europe, in Italy, Switzerland, Greece etc, and his last big success was at the qualifying event for the Eukanuba World Challenge were they took the qualification and Teddy will be the representative of Bulgaria at this great event in Orlando, US.

The Dalmatian has had many BIS in all the Balkan countries.

This year we had about 30 shows in Bulgaria. The entries are increasing and we are happy about that.

The Bullmastiff Ch Game Keeper's Play My Game winning under Frank Kane.

The best event again was the Black Sea Winner Shows, this year held at St Konstantin and Elena resort on the Black Sea. This combination of shows and holiday attracts a lot of dog people from the whole of Europe. Again it was a great event with many world renowned judges and a perfect holiday on the sandy beaches.

Next year we hope even more exhibitors will visit our beautiful country, with great natural history and nice dog shows.

PLAMEN BACHOVSKI

The Dalmatian Ch United Spots Quinlan.

Stanislav Petrov, best junior handler at the World Show.

MONTENEGRO

Ten all-breed shows took place over three days in Montenegro in the spring, offering the chance to gain five national titles. Supreme Champion was the Basset Hound from Belgium, Nhabira Iceman, owned by Fonie de Vadder and Licua van Buggenhout and handled by Edwin Lenaerts.
photo Guy

Montenegro is a small country situated in the south of Europe but it has a very long tradition of organising dog shows. It holds five international and five national dog shows every year.

It can boast beautiful scenery and wildlife, and offers good shows as well as the chance to visit to some places that will take your breath away.

The shows usually start in early spring and for years Bar has opened the season. The Adriatic Cup is in early May and as a rule most people choose this place to show their dogs. The season lasts until late autumn and ends in the northern part of the country.

The number of exhibitors ranges from 300 to 1,200 and most of them come from abroad. The Kennel Club of Montenegro has very good relations with regional kennel clubs. The judges are well known professionals and are carefully chosen. The KCM also organises specialty shows and has very active clubs around the country.

The Montenegrin Mountain Hound is a national breed and the club pays special attention to improving the quality and increasing the number of high quality dogs. A specialty for this breed is organised once a year.

We can be proud that a lot of our breeders visit other countries

CROATIA

Croatia is a country with a dog-breeding tradition of more than 110 years with the first international show held in the capital city of Zagreb in 1932.

International shows in Croatia are traditionally organised in the same cities throughout the country. For several years, they have been run as double CACIBs which is one method recognised by large number of organisers to attract more exhibitors.

In 2012 16 International shows were organised, visited by 11,000 exhibitors from all over the world.

In early March in Zagreb we had two shows won by the Dalmatian from Croatia **Dalmino Vodoo Vision** and Maltese from Italy **Cinecitta Dakota Fanning**.

Four shows were held in a Zadar in May together with an International Champion of Champions topped by a Shiba Inu from Russia, **Orienta Hoshi Naomi**. The four BIS winners were: Flat-coated Retriever **Almanza Positive Privilege** owned by Croatians, Miniature Dachshund from Russia **Kinchville Cecina Mumbo Jumbo**, Siberian Husky from Montenegro **Icily Zone Rock** and Tornjak from Croatia **Lord** who was supreme BIS.

Later in May in Varaždin, winner of both shows was the Lhasa Apso **Chic Choix Orlane Insider** from Finland.

In June winners of the Umag shows were Newfoundland from Italy **Indian Bay No One Like You** and also from Italy, the Saluki **Del Borghini OscarDelaRente**.

The summer was devoted to the Split shows billed as 'Four Summer Night Show' with two national and two international shows, the latter won by the Deerhound **Baylind Kielland** from Norway and the Maltese **Richelieu's Richie Rich** from Sweden. Supreme BIS was

the winner of one of the national shows, to an English Springer Spaniel from Denmark **Sieger's Pure Gold**.

At Osijek in September the winners were a Lhasa Apso from Hungary **Sayonara Thinker Of Golden Spirit** and Alaskan Malamute from Hungary **Kids Of The Snow-Storm Over The Rainbow**.

The show season begins and ends in Zagreb in March and November. At the time of writing, the latter shows haven't been held so we'll mention the winners of 2011's autumn event. Winner of the specialty shows held on Friday evening was an American Staffordshire Terrier from Croatia **Lion King Diva Sting**, and the BIS were an Akita from Hungary **Orient's Pride Thor of Woly Point** and Pointer from Belgium **Seasyde As Good As Gold** who was supreme BIS.
PETRA BUVA, Croatian Kennel Club

Champion of Champions, the Shiba Inu Orienta Hoshi Naomi.

Supreme BIS at Zadar, the Tornjak, Lord.

BIS at both Varaždin shows was the Lhasa Apso Chic Choix Orlane Insider.

Supreme BIS at Split, seen with Sean Delmar, was the English Springer Spaniel from Denmark Sieger's Pure Gold.
photo Brace

to go to shows and have a lot of success. We have World and European Winners and also winners at specialty shows for certain breeds.

Tourism is one of the main industries in Montenegro and a lot of hotels are pet-friendly so that people who do not want to leave their dogs at home can spend wonderful summer holidays together with their pets.
SANJA VRETENICIC

One of the BIS winners in Montenegro was a locally owned dog, Alabai Don Markon's Middle Asian Shepherd, Avatar.
photo Guy

SERBIA

The end of Serbia's show calendar for 2012 will be marked by the country's biggest biggest show, the international how in Belgrade in November. We expect more than 1,000 dogs to be entered.

The Serbian Kennel Club with help of local city and breed clubs organised 25 international shows and more than 100 national or specialty shows. The National Championship for German Shepherd Dogs drew 250 dogs and that for Dobermanns 200.

As usual the average number of entries was from 300 to 600 depending on their importance.

Almost the same as the previous year the number of registrations was about 34,000 which confirms that despite the big economic crisis in Europe, popularity of 'man's best friend' in Serbia is not going down.

Our kennel club was honoured to organise the World Championship for English Pointing Dogs and that for Continental Pointing Dogs, the Saint Hubert World Championship, the Meditereanean Cup and the European Championship for Pointing Dogs. We had the pleasure of hosting 22 delegations from countries all around the world.

Breeders from Serbia had very successful results at the biggest shows in Europe. At the World Show in Salzburg the American Staffordshire Terrier **Don King Of Ring's** was again BOB and won the group. The Dobermann **Maxim di Altobello** was BOB while the Longcoat Chihuahua **Microschihuas Furious'N'Extravagant** was Junior World Winner as was the Gordon Setter **Rising Sun Midas Touch** and the Dogo Canario **Ana Casa del Goxy**. Jack Russell Terrier **Heartily**

Bart Simpson won the CAC.

At the European Show in Romania the Jack Russell was Vice European Winner while the same owners' **Knotteliten Visit Norway** at only ten months was Junior European Winner and BOB.

Smooth Chihuahua **Microschihuas King Of The Rings** was Junior European Winner while the same kennel's Longcoat, mentioned above, was European Winner.

The Mastiff Chriss and German Wirehaired Pointer **Ziro Fantastic of Mikli** were both BOB.
NEMANJA JOVANOVIC

The young Jack Russell Terrier Knotteliten Visit Norway was BOB at the European Show.

SLOVENIA

At Ljubljana in January took place Slovenia's first weekend of shows. The Saturday drew 1,220 dogs from 28 countries. BIS was the Jack Russell Terrier **Mr Energyzer di Sutri** from Italy. On Sunday the entry was 1,243 dogs from 31 countries and winner was the black Medium Poodle **Grace the Event Starring Moravia** from the Czech Republic.

Narje national show, held in April at Vrbljene by Ig drew 604 dogs and was topped by the Old English Sheepdog **Ch Reata's Kobayagi** from Croatia.

The Hunting Kennel Club Cerknica ran a national show at Kozarišče for the hunting breeds, won by the Cocker Spaniel **First Anthony Schonez**.

At Koroška national show in May BIS from 379 dogs was the German Shepherd **Cindy od Žekša** from Slovenia. Hrušica national show saw the American Staffordshire Terrier **Beatrice Long Step** take both BIS and best young dog from 345 dogs

Winners at Bled international show was the pepper and salt Miniature Schnauzer **Gentleman de Illyria**, who was supreme BIS, and on Sunday the English Setter **Elitiste Rodney Mr von der Guldegg**. Each day there were about here were 924 dogs from 21 countries

At Lendava international in July, from 527 dogs, 18 countries, BIS was the Rough Collie **Midlands-Corner Happy Dreams** from Germany.

In August the Slovenian club for Great Danes organised its first specialty, with award nominations for junior CAC and title Slovenian Club Winner 2012, at a beautiful site, Betnava mansion in Maribor, where 96 Danes from nine countries were presented, won by the was brindle bitch **Burj Khalifa della Baia Azzurra**.

Next day the Kennel Club of Trbovlje held its twentieth anniversary national show. The anniversary was complemented by the 55th anniversary of the club's foundation. the Golden Retriever **Blue Sky Happy Company** was chosen as BIS, under a tent in a terrible rainstorm.

The Slovenian club for sighthounds was also celebrating 20 years, with a special show and an international coursing competition in September. At the Eurocup Show there were 67 dogs won by the Afghan Hound **Pablo Picasso Gandamak**, while the coursing competition, opened by president of the Slovenian Kennel Club Blaž Kavčič, was won by a Whippet **Czukaseri Zsivany Dynamite**.

At the Maribor and Pohorje weekend of international shows (915

and 861 dogs, 33 and 32 countries) the BIS winners were the American Staffordshire Terrier **Atractive Lady Diva Sting** and Newfoundland **King of Helluland Feel The Win**.

The international shows in Koper-Capodistria drew almost a thousand entries, won by the Azawakh **Azamour Ayman** and Siberian Husky **Deep Impact della Vanisella**.
SAŠO and BARBKA NOVAK

At Ljubljana BIS winners were the Jack Russell Terrier Mr Energyzer di Sutri and Medium Poodle Grace the Event Starring Moravia.

Bled's BIS winners were the Miniature Schnauzer Gentleman De Illyria (supreme BIS) and English Setter Elitiste Rodney Mr von der Guldegg.

Koper's BIS winners were the Azawakh Azamour Ayman and Siberian Husky Deep Impact della Vanisella.

Winners Worldwide

At Vietnam KA's first international show, Jackie Perry's BIS was Le Duy Bao's Pomeranian Dream Team Moon Walker.

At Jakarta international show, Indonesia, BIS under Andrew Brace was the Beagle Ch Blessed Champ Akiko.
photo Benny

BIS at Hong Kong KC under Bill Browne-Cole was Franki Leung's Kerry Blue Terrier Ch Hotspice's Forever Blue Jeans.

Czech Bloodhounds have made an impact on British lines recently. A BIS winner at Brno under Miroslav Vaclavik was Martina Kilvarová's Arosa od Hadiho Potoka.
photo Szalanczi

Valerie Foss' BIS at the Barbados KC was Wayne Welch's UK-bred Rottweiler Ch Juffther Dream Lover.
photo Greenidge

The UK-bred French Bulldog puppy Kingfriend Mr Wow was the most consistent winner at four all-breeds shows run by the breed club in Thailand. He is owned by Frederick Tan from the Philippines.
photo Brace

Judging in Ecuador, Andrew Brace gave BIS to the Shar-Pei Ch El Yoce e'General's Energy, owned by Ilaria Bondi de Ciabatti.
photo Kuzelj

At the Eukanuba World Championship Show in Malaysia, Andrew Brace's BIS was the Australian Terrier living in Japan, Cliftop Gunna Be A Star.
photo Chuah

A BIS winner in Bratislava, Slovakia under Hiroshi Kamisato, Diana Rogozhina's Rhodesian Ridgeback Tina Treading Harley Leo, from the Ukraine.
photo Szalanczi

RUSSIA

Breed specialties show the way

Alexey Kalashnikov

At the new year show, The Golden Collar, Top Dog of the year is traditionally chosen. It was the Tervueren Pyrytuulen Yllatysnim, owned by Tarmo Makkonen, a Finnish citizen who has lived in Russia for many years.

The was an indication that the selection of Top Dog is beginning to be done in a civilised fashion in Russia, resulting in a marked increase in the value of this title to breeders, especially as the owner is someone for whom dog breeding is nothing more than a hobby.

'Sepi' was given to Tarmo by his brother, who owns a Finnish Belgian Shepherd kennel. He is a champion in many countries and in Finland has passed all the required tests for working dogs.

The Eurasia show took place in March. Formerly it was in February, but the tendency for shows to be held during the warmer months is taking hold in Russia.

It was conducted according to the manner accepted on the Continent with a double CACIB over the two days. It took place in a rather compact facility with about 6,000 dogs shown each day, effectively the same 6,000 dogs, each shown twice.

Only all-rounders judge at shows such as Eurasia, many of them with close ties to their kennel clubs. Formerly their critiques were discussed in detail on internet forums after each show and posted on Facebook. Nowadays most large European shows don't require written critiques which is a great relief to the judges and leads to speedier judging.

Another tendency is for small breeds to become more popular, although the statistics from Eurasia don't bear this out, perhaps because when choosing to acquire a large breed the owner more often decides to obtain a show-quality dog and to exhibit it frequently. Biggest entry was in Miniature Schnauzers of all colours with 217 and Labradors 202. About 50 breeds were represented by just one or two dogs.

BIS first day under Monique van Brempt was the Alaskan Malamute Skywalker Sausimayok (above left) owned by Ekaterina Chebotareva and Evgeniya Girina, a champion in 12 countries with seven BIS. Runner-up was Janita Januskauskaite's Maltese Sensation of Lovely House (left), who took top spot on the second day under Kari Jarvinen when reserve was the Pomeranian Fon's Flying to Dan-Star-Kom for Liudmila Komyakova and Sujitra Peeyachaiprapha.

The Pride of Russia award went to Tatiana Chistova's Russian Black Terrier Dorofey iz Russkoi Dinastii (below), judge Elena Agafonova.

At the World Show in Austria about 2,000 dogs from Russia took part, many with success in breed and group including two group winners, the Pembroke Corgi Andvol Pinkerton, owner Olga Shuvalova, and Smooth Dachshund Norden Liht Unkas, Anastasia Krylova.

National breed club shows are especially important because in most cases the judges are specialists. Their organisation should serve as an example for the CACIB shows, possibly because there is no commercial element involved and because many breeders volunteer to work at them.

The Russian Canine Federation has liquidated the Terrier Soyuz show, one of the most interesting terrier specialties, in a move toward all single-breed shows. To all intents and purposes, the RCF has attempted to take control of all the national club shows, although it has not been successful in every case.

Finnish expert Olli Kokkonen judged at the Leonberger club show where BOB was Rua Soleil Gordon Guinness (left), owner Svetlana Borodina.

Frederic Maison, a noted specialist from France, judged the 73 dogs at the Irish Wolfhound specialty. BOB was Tsarskaya Prihot Victoria (below left) for Natalia Beresneva.

The Day of the Giant Schnauzer had Jeanette Seltz Halter of France judging in the grounds of the Forest Fields, a country residence outside Moscow.

A feature of these shows are the many informal events rarely seen at CAC and CACIB shows, for example the contest for most beautiful head among the Irish Wolfhounds, the parade 'Adopt a Schnauzer', the contest for best attack dog etc.

The participation of Bo Bengtson of the US at the sighthound show was a treat for breeders and he received glowing reports from the participants. He also judged Dachshunds where his BIS was Elena Grishina's Miniature Wire Magik Rainbow Brabus (below right).

In spite of the many problems experienced by clubs and show organisers, an understanding of what is most important in breeding dogs is reflected in the success of certain breeders.

For example Giant Schnauzers from the Gloris kennel of Olga Seliverstova have won at the most prestigious shows. At Crufts 2010 her Ch Gloris Shock Dog won the BCC; in 2011 her Gloris Lincoln was BOB and in 2012 Gloris Santa Barbara, owned by Giovanni Bonifacio, won the BCC. Pictured below left is the best veteran at Eurasia, second day, Gloris Cancan, with judge Wayne Burton.

Another breeder who has achieved great success internationally is Valentina Popova whose Scottish Scotch Terrier Filisite Brash Celebration took RBIS at Crufts 2010 and in 2011 won the DCC.

Then there are Dobermanns from the Zoosfery kennel (Evgeny Rozenberg), the Pekingese from Sunrise Dragon (Elena Artemenko), represented below right by Natalia Romanyuk's Ch Billi Boy iz Sunrise Dragon, and the Dachshunds from Gudwil (Vera Gubina) – seen below is Elena Grishina's Ch Gudwil's Terrific Timothy Dalton.

These and others have worked to influence positively the development of their breeds in Russia and their achievements are an example to new breeders.

Translated by Linda Bruce

Another show that stands out is the hunting dog show put on by the Moscow Society of Hunters and Fishermen, a picnic-like event at the beautiful Kolomenskiy Park in Moscow. There was no BIS, but instead a parade of winners. Each dog's score was a sum of several elements: his hunting certificate, his pedigree and his performance in the show ring. The judges were all specialists from the club.

ISRAEL

Making a mark at Crufts

Text and photos by Yossi Guy

Ch Bugsy, a Cocker Spaniel owned by Marius and Judith Wolff, with the background of the Dead Sea before winning the first ever Crufts qualification at the CACIB show in Arad.

Bertiebulls Satsuma, a Bulldog owned by Avi Mallach, Tomer Ouzan and Eitam Ben Harosh, went BIS at the CACIB show in Arad, seen with breed judge Prof Zeev Trainin. This was Israel's first Crufts qualifier, attracting a 20 per cent larger entry than the previous year's show in the same venue.

Inna Blayvas' Multi Ch Bat Yerushalaim Shel Zahav, the top winning Canaan bitch of all time, is the first ever Crufts BOB from Israel. She has been twice World Winner and European Winner, along with many other titles. She was the first Canaan to be BIS at an all-breed show.

Luis Pinto Teixeira visited Israel to judge several specialty shows. and is pictured with the BIS Miniature Pinscher Mor Bat Chen, bred by Shimshon Berger.

The largest CACIB show in 2012 took place in Acre. Tali Lin's Kerry Blue Terrier Serbrjanyi Veter Garmonika went BIS under Avi Marshak.

Israel's first registered Kangal dogs, with the background of a Turkish building in the town of Acre. The first pair of these watchdogs, previously known as Karabash, was imported from Germany where they had been confiscated from Turkish immigrants. The two are registered in the external stud book as the breed has not yet been officially recognised by the FCI.

Dorit Dembin's Cairn Terrier Ch Happy Beit Dembin was 2011's Dog of the Year and represented Israel in the Eukanuba Challenge preliminary in Bucharest.

In January, a CACIB show took place at a kibbutz in the centre of Israel. Agnes Ganami awarded BIS to a Cane Corso Ch Dorian Gray Gerassi Corso, owned by Lazar Gerassi.

Margaret Jones from Canada judged a toy club specialty show putting up a Cavalier, Seminal Five On Bridge, owned by the Orlev Family. The Orlevs were among the three Israelis who participated at Crufts 2012.

GREECE

Lila Leventaki – George Kaninias

Which British Akita will be Top Dog?

Since June we have had new show titles in Greece:

Grand Greek champion, any Greek Champion who accumulates an additional three CACs.
Greek show champion, for breeds which require working trials but for which trials for those breeds do not exist in Greece. They need six CACs.
Junior champion of Greece, requires two JCACs.
Veteran champion of Greece, requires two VCACs.
Greek reproducer champion, every male or female who has at least three champion offspring.

The Greek Kennel Club hopes that these new titles will help increase entries at shows. Unfortunately, the general assembly did not approve that a foreign champion can become a Greek Champion with only one CAC, instead of the three currently required. This would have certainly increased the number of foreign entries.

Greece had the honour of organising the Mediterranean Winner Show where Play The Game, the Bullmastiff pictured right, was BIS under Carla Molinari. this year. Reserve was the Old English Sheepdog Aryakas Geocosmic, third the Papillon Lenskyi Aragaon and fourth the Brittany Viktor.

Mediterranean **Winner**

At the time of going to press, Greece still has two more national shows to look forward to. In the top two spots of the Greek Kennel Club's point system are two British-bred Akitas, Ch Ruthdales Super Model bred by Matthew Bostock and Janet Armstrong, and owned by Socrates Gasparinatos and Ch Mynyddaf's King Of The Ring, bred by Wilkes and Birch and owned by Panoloulos Vasilis. Both have won BIS four times at international and national shows. Two things are certain: the winner will be British-bred and will be an Akita!

2012 has been the year of the Bullmastiff in Greece. Of the eight international and three national shows which have taken place so far, a Bullmastiff won the group eight times! Six times it was Ch Game Keeper's Play My Game, handled by Fabricio Manni for Todor Baev from Bulgaria, who almost every time was also BIS. They are pictured here with Frank Kane. The other two group winners were from Greece: Ardhub Cant Touch This, imported from the UK, bred by Lynn Mc Groarty and co-owned with her by Giannis Roussos and Maridespi Georgala, and Ch Gioko Grammy who was bred in Greece and owned by Konstantinos Gkalitsis and Alexia Kamenou.

JAPAN

Mai Ozeki

The probable all-breed number one dog for 2012 is the Siberian Husky Misanga JP Lavender owned by Sachiko Nomura. He was BIS dog at FCI Japan International, which is the biggest show of the year, and is going to represent Japan at the Eukanuba World Challenge this year.

Unlike the previous year with one of the biggest earthquakes in history, we have managed in 2012 without any big disaster. The areas affected by the earthquake have been fixed little by little and people are moving back to some of those areas, which is very good news for us all in Japan.

The results of the London Olympics had a big role in encouraging our citizens with the largest number of medals in the history of Japan. The wrestling team especially amazed us with four gold medals.

However, when talking about the dog world, the situation is a bit different: The entries have been dropping dramatically for several years. One of the main reasons besides the economic circumstances is that foreign-bred dogs have strict restrictions when it comes to entering shows.

The Japan Kennel Club states that if a dog was born in another country and has won either an FCI international champion/foreign champion title or more than five bests in show, it is not eligible to be shown at local shows. These make up about 75 per cent

of the shows each year. That makes it almost impossible for foreign-bred dogs to be ranked within the top 20 all-breeds and those who own such dogs have less interest in showing them.

Hopefully the situation will change as we need more people to be interested in dog shows.

As for Japanese dogs overseas, we have had great news everywhere. In particular, Japanese Shetland Sheepdogs, Borzois, Papillons, Jack Russell Terriers and Chihuahuas have had wonderful results everywhere. Of course, Toshi Omura's Smash Poodles have won many awards everywhere including **Smash JP Sakura**, who is most likely to be number one Toy Poodle in the US this year.

Above all, a Japanese Boxer, **Hi-Tech The King of Sherry Shoot J**, bred by Shinjo Teragaki and Masao Hanabusa, won BOB at the American Boxer Club. We all know how competitive it is at ABC and yet a Japanese Boxer won at such an important show. Rumour has it that he will be campaigned in the US for the next few years. We wish him best of luck there.

Likely to end up among the top dogs of 2012: Hiroko Hiyama's Shetland Sheepdog Kencherry's Vip Room.
photo Nakashima

A big winner of 2012: Yuka Isaka's Giant Schnauzer Montesol JP's Evelin Star.

Among Japan's successful show dogs of 2012: the Borzoi Majenkir Magnus O'Blyss, owned by Mai Ozeki.

Another dog likely to be in the rankings for 2012 is the Toy Poodle Magic Fantasy JP Second Movement, owned by Akemi Kishida, pictured winning RCC at Crufts under Peter Young.

Also among the big winners of 2012: the Whippet Dieu Pater Sprit JP Lafaea Wheelr, owner Yuka Isaka.
photo Yakamura

2011's all-breed number one dog was Kimiko Oya's Borzoi Paradise Queen JP 101, who will probably be ranked within the top ten again this year.

MONACO
All change at
Monte Carlo

Report and photography by
Costanza Ferraris

IT WAS on the eve of the 2011 Monte Carlo dog show that Princess Antoinette of Monaco, the president of the Monaco Kennel Club, died leaving the club without its pilot. Her daughter, Baroness Elisabeth-Ann de Massy, took her place just a few days before the show.

Since then many changes have happened. The most important was connected with specialties that are organised during the show. Their CAC is double counted. That means that with one CAC the breeds with a specialty can become a champion in a single show. Normally, to become a Monaco champion, your dog needs two CACs.

Guests of the weekend were the local firemen with their dogs, demonstrating how they work together.

This year they were 400 more entries. The kennel club had to use a second tent to host all the rings. Several improvements had been made to the show and the BIS received the trophy from Princess Charlene of Monaco.

The BIS line-up at Monte Carlo: RBIS, Grand Basset Griffon Vendéen, Jour de Noel van Tum-Tum's Vriendjes, owned by the Huikeshoven family from the Netherlands and handled by Francesco Vasanella; president Baroness Elisabeth-Ann de Massy: BIS, the Miniature Poodle Dior Generation Top, owned by Nathalie Bourgeois from France and handled by Vincent Loubet; Princess Charlene of Monaco, judge Lisbeth Mach and the president's daughter Melanie de Massy.

The specialty held with the show was for British sheep dogs. Brenda Banbury gave BIS to the Anyway Any How of Fool's Paradise, owned by Sjaack Meyer from the Netherlands.

Each year the philatelic office issues a stamp connected with the specialty. For 2012 they chose a Rough Collie belonging to the Italian kennel di Cambiano, painted by Collette Thurillet.

AUSTRALIA

Lee Pieterse

Welcome to the supreme champions

A NEW 'supreme' title is now available for Australian dogs who have already achieved their grand champion status (1,000 CC points). Requirements for supreme grand champion are the grand title, plus three all-breeds bests in show, or ten best in group/specialty best in show – three different BIS judges or ten different group/specialty judges giving the awards.

The last requirement is a CC after July 1, 2012, so we have been treated to seeing a steady stream of top dogs, already grand champions, coming out of retirement to take that last CC for their new supreme grand champion awards.

Good news for those who are involved in sending or bringing dogs to Australia. The powers that be have decreed that quarantine will be reduced to ten days. How that number was conceived is a mystery to me.

The government in New South Wales, the most populous Australian state, has created a Companion Animals Task Force which has, as its main recommendation, asked for the compulsory registration of all dog breeders.

This plan, and the tightening of the breeders' code of conduct, is a serious attempt by the government to deal with the problem of unwanted companion animals and unscrupulous puppy farmers.

Most reputable breeders have no issues with this concept or with the associated inspection of their kennels.

However, nowhere do the task force recommendations ask for a higher standard of care from the purchasing public or even provide for a serious education on how this could be achieved.

In other words the message is: "If there is a problem with unwanted companion animals it's all the fault of the breeders!"

Last year I discussed the merits of judges researching their potential winners on the internet. This year there have been a couple of kerfuffles about exhibitors who, inadvertently or otherwise, assist that process by distributing information about their dogs in cyberspace.

The concept has gone even more viral with the use of Facebook. Some are even calling for a ban on advertising show wins on Facebook.

Many of us 'friend' lots of people without giving much thought to future involvement with them. So, on Facebook, you could inadvertently send a picture of your dog to a 'friend' who is contracted to judge your breed at a forthcoming show. Indeed, one of your Facebook friends could send your dogs' photo and win information on to one or many of their judging friends.

Surely using email and Facebook for publicity is no different to advertising in a magazine? Is not the line only crossed by intentional contact between the exhibitor and the judge who is about to judge his dog?

A difficult but interesting issue which is guaranteed to keep the indignation meter on high alert!

Top Dog 2011 in the DogzOnLine pointscore was the English Setter **Gr Ch Bridgewood Front Page News**, featured in last year's *Annual*.

Australia's top shows are the Royals and in 2012 the majority of these have been won by Australian-bred dogs. However, there were exceptions including the year's first Royal, Canberra, won by Dan and Olivia Ciguenza's US-bred Alaskan Malamute Gr Ch Wolfmountains Icemile Warrior. Judge was William Russell and the entry 1,716.
photo Cabal

At Sydney Royal, from an entry of 3,589, Göran Bodegård chose as BIS Leanne and Christophe Duval's Beagle Ch Beagelee Archangel. Both he and his dam were conceived by artificial insemination using semen from dogs in the US.
photo ffire

Front runner in the 2012 Top Dog pointscore is Fran Matthews, Glen Vernon and Ron and Diane Besoff's Dalmatian Sup Ch Paceaway at Rosemount. He is so far ahead in the standings it seems unlikely that any other dog will catch him. A champion by 13 months, he has 75 BIS and was number three all breeds for 2011. He is pictured winning BIS at Brisbane Royal under Hassi Assenmacher-Feyel from an entry of 2,154. He also took BIS at the first two of the Spring Fair shows in Sydney under Erwin Deutscher and Sean Delmar.

photo Mayfoto

At Adelaide Royal BIS was Esther Joseph and Michael Looby's Gordon Setter Sup Ch Triseter Celtic Ice, a multiple BIS winner. The entry was 3,331 and judge was Colette Muldoon.

photo Matschke

Melbourne Royal's BIS was Elizabeth Lasry's Shetland Sheepdog Sup Ch/Can Ch GrandGables Home Town Hero, bred in the US. Now eight years old, he has won BIS at Melbourne Royal previously, along with another royal BIS, royal groups, specialties and all-breed BIS. Judge was Luis Pinto Teixiera. Entry was 3,580, about 350 down on last year.

photo Ibiza

At Perth Royal Adrian Landarte's BIS from 1,261 dogs was Helena Fitzgerald's Border Collie Gr Ch Borderfame Moon Dancer AD, JDX.

photo Animal Images

Darwin Royal's BIS under Andrew Burt was another conceived by AI, Judy Clifford's Bull Terrier Ch Sarajeni Joker Jane.

Sue Wright's German Shorthaired Pointer Sup Ch Moruada Californication was the Hobart Royal BIS. He has been handled by a number of people throughout his career, on this occasion by Cheyenne Schelcht from the US. He has twice been RBIS at royal shows and is a multiple all-breeds and specialty BIS winner. Judge was Jorge Nallem and the entry 688.

At the third of the Spring Fair shows Michel Bouchard's BIS was Cheryl Le Court's Siberian Husky Ch Suthanlites Twilight.

photo Cabal

Sunbury with 2,286 entries is arguably Victoria's most prestigious non-royal show. BIS under Mario di Vanni was Sue Huebner and Penelope Kelly's Hungarian Puli Gr Ch Cordmaker Topsy Turvey.

photo Ibiza

NEW ZEALAND
The fight for docking continues

Rosemary Hubrich

The past year seems typical of the dog world in general in these challenging times, with most of the hardcore continuing as usual, despite a general downward spiral.

Membership and New Zealand Kennel Club revenue continue to decline at about eight per cent each year. NZKC has made considerable cost reductions and continues to look for further savings. Fortunately, obedience and agility maintain a more vigorous following. An NZKC survey indicates that most people who do not renew membership, do not because of cost and the general unfriendly culture of dog showing...

NZKC has three venues, all of which strive to break even. Late in 2011 the management committee for the show venue at NZKC headquarters near Wellington disestablished itself, handing control to the NZKC director/secretary. It is an old and demanding building and much needed to be done before the NZKC National show was held there in October 2012. It is hoped that a considerable saving on venue hire was achieved.

Given support of NZKC president Owen Dance and executive council, the management committee of the NZKC Auckland Exhibition Centre produced a nearly on-budget performance. There were considerable donations from clubs, plus fundraising by way of a raffle and a spectacular sky-diving effort by the committee off the Auckland Sky Tower!

At the NZKC annual conference of delegates, a popular remit to pass was that which will entitle all-breeds clubs which own or operate their own property, to hold an annual benefit show to assist with maintenance and upkeep. This already applies to the three NZKC show venues. Constitutional change that might help to revitalise NZKC was not much advanced at the conference, as usual.

The Animal Welfare Act came up for review, regenerating concerns regarding tail shortening and breed-specific legislation. NZKC encouraged members to petition their MPs.

The NZKC stance on tail shortening supports freedom of choice; it does not wish to lose breeders and exhibitors of traditionally docked breeds, as has happened in other countries when tail shortening was banned. Breeders may register puppies with tails shortened by an accredited tail bander, docking using rubber rings – the NZ Council of Docked Breeds administers a tail banders' accreditation programme.

Publicity in support of a ban came by way of a member's article in the *NZ Dog World* (NZKC magazine). A spirited response came from the Docked Breeds Council and supporters who worked for years to maintain the right to shorten tails.

Eukanuba Challenge winner for 2012 was the Australian-bred Miniature Poodle Gr Ch/Aus Ch Westpriors Black Giorgio, owned by Yvonne Smith and John Stanton. Giorgio has won 17 BIS since his arrival in New Zealand in mid 2011.
photo Supashots

BIS under Ricardo Saldana at the NZKC National Show was the Canadian-bred Samoyed Gr Ch/Can/Am/UK Ch Vanderbilt's One Cool Cat, owned by Gary and Lynn Carleton and Jessica Bello.
photo Supashots

The young British-bred Ch Palacegarden Lancelot of Parkavon, owned by Keith Brown and Robbie Gray, was a home-town winner of the Supreme Dog contest, held in Christchurch. Judges were Shona Prebble, Wayne Burton and Stephen Meredith. Later in the year he also won the Dog of the Year contest in Auckland.
photo Supashots

Runner-up in the competition to find New Zealand's Eukanuba Challenge winner was Sandra Macklin's American imported Schipperke Gr Ch/Am Ch Tumbleweed's On The Road Again, who has eight BIS.
photo Supashots

SOUTH AFRICA

Greg Eva

Dateabase helps breeders plan for health

The South African dog scene remains strong despite the general financial situation in the world. The levels of registrations seem to have consolidated and there is a growing support for Kennel Union of Southern Africa-registered dogs as a result of our recording various health statistics. These will assist in the future by providing a database as a guide to breeders when planning healthy litters.

KUSA is presently closely involved with the Department of Agriculture with regard to the Boerboel and its stabilisation as a recognised breed.

The new judges learning programme is nearing completion and, by all accounts, this should assist the up and coming judges in their endeavours.

The worldwide financial problems have reached South Africa and we can expect a less than smooth passage over the next months. However, the dog world will no doubt continue to provide an interest to those people who want to have purebred, healthy dogs.

KUSA's National Dog of 2012 was Heidi Rolfes' Maltese Ch Fabulous Moments Valentina's Magic, seen with president Greg Eva, sponsor Audrey Hauptfleisch and judges Augusto Benedicto Santos III and Luis Pinto Teixeira. The Maltese was also RBIS at the International Africa Show and BIS at Goldfields Kennel Club.

Werner Cesperdes gave BIS at KUSA's International Africa Show to Melissa Matthys' Staffordshire Bull Terrier Ch Monetrouge Flying Solo. President Greg Eva is on the right.
photo Bellstone

TKC Supreme Dog 2012 is Denise Edmondson's Samoyed Ch Annan Burning Ambition.
photo Bellstone

KUSA National Showdog of the Year 2011 was Chris and Erna Aucamp's Canadian-bred Shih Tzu Ch Winterholme's Love Story at Dunstars, pictured with Greg Eva. Among the Shih Tzu's 2012 successes was BIS at the KUSA Championship Show and Reserve National Dog.

Leading the KUSA Showdog of the Year 20102 at the time of going to press was Clair van den Bergh's Afghan Hound Ch Aviva T'Scaramouch, seen winning a BIS under Christine Davies.
photo Bellstone

Obituaries

Inevitably the world of dogs has lost some of its most respected personalities during the past year. We are able to mention just a few of them here; to the friends and families of them and others we have lost go our thoughts and sympathy. Their contribution to the dog scene will never be forgotten.

The sudden death of **Elisabeth Matell** was an enormous shock to all. An unforgettable personality, she was devoted to the Norfolk Terrier, having owned her first while living in her native Sweden. In the UK, she bred the breed's first BIS winner and CC record holder, 'Betty', followed closely by 'Coco', Top Dog in the US who returned home to take BIS at Crufts. She worked for DOG WORLD for nearly 30 years and was meticulous about the advertisements she created for the paper and this ANNUAL.

Marjorie Henley Price founded the Canine Concern Scotland Trust which has done so much for the image of the dog over the past 25 years. Over the years she served as chairman of trustees, administrator and life president. Her dynamism and persuasive manner made the trust an immediate success, not least through its Therapet visiting scheme and schools education campaign.

photo Farlap

Denise Courtney was the long-time secretary of Bournemouth show which this year at last achieved its ambition of holding its show on its own land. Formerly an exhibitor of Afghans and Deerhounds with the Zarheid affix, she judged the hound group at Crufts.

Dick Terry was a toy group judge and involved in a number of breeds in that group. A popular figure in the dog world as a whole, he was show manager of East of England, and a committee member of Bournemouth.

That remarkable character **Margaret Ferris**, over a long career, did much to raise standards in the pet trade, and edited *Pet Business World* for many years.

David Trowbridge served as the vet for a number of shows over several decades.

Allan Brooks was one of the greatest characters of the Afghan Hound scene, adding a touch of razzmatazz for 50 years. He produced a distinctive line of classic UK Afghans, including some of the greats of the '60s and '70s. He has involved in several other breeds too. **Frances Mallinson** was also an integral part of the Afghan world.

Helen Northrop-Searle had the Ioniok Afghans and Borzois, and **Joan van Schaick** the Vanathans in these and Beagles too. **Betty White**'s Rollinhills had a very distinguished record In Bassets. The Southcourt Beagles of **Glenda Young** were very influential in their day.

Mick and **Gwen Carpenter**, who died within two days of each other after 60 years of marriage, were involved with Beagles and other breeds but were best known for club administration; he was secretary of the Devon, Cornwall and South West Beagle Society for 33 years, of Dorset County and South West Hound and served on Paignton committee.

Ernie Tebbs bred some great Salukis including BIS winner Ch Almanza Kafiat and was just as successful on the coursing field. **Ken Allan**, with his wife Diana, had some excellent Salukis too including a Crufts group winner. He was also responsible, with his exceptional design skills, for some of the most beautiful breed magazines ever produced, and they wrote a book on the breed too.

Jan Banyard (Darquell) was involved in Whippets, Greyhounds and other sighthound breeds.

Helen Powell (Trailfinder) was a leading figure in the Bloodhound world, with husband David breeding working trial as well as show champions and known for their beautiful reds. **Joyce Smith** bred the Actaeons which were also successful in Otterhounds, including the breed's first champion of modern times.

In Dachshunds **Helen Parker** bred the Antway Smooths, **Joe Macaulay** the Timarus and **Len Mitchell** the Tocos, and in Miniatures Wires **Audrey Smith** had the Dunnspitts.

Chris Young had the Stiperden English Setters and in latter years did much to keep the Bleu de Gascogne breeds gong in the UK.

Margaret Rowe, who died aged 98, had a long and distinguished record as breeder of the Cairlie Gordon Setters, and wrote breed notes for DOG WORLD. **Brenda Partridge** founded the Clitters Gordons, famous for their field trial successes, as were the Assarts dogs of **Bob Truman**. The Yennadons of **Sylvia Ackerley** did well in both field and show ring.

Olwen Hunt of the Sowerhills had an exceptional record as a breeder of influential Irish Setters and **Liz Laughton-Moore** (Quilmark) was one of the senior figures of the breed, as were **Nan Treharne** (Redtops) and **Ray Armstead** (Mindenday) in the English.

Georgie Buchanan, who died aged 91, bred many significant Flatcoats under the Hallbent affix and was a considerable character. **John Simister** and his wife bred the Lacons Golden Retrievers. **Mary Beckett** was involved with Goldens but will be best remembered for her long association with South West Essex CA. Labradors in Scotland owed much to **John Steven** and the Rossbanks. **Margaret Hibbs**, with her late husband Ron, made a popular partnership in the gundog world with the Rockwin Golden Retrievers and Clumbers.

Patricia Shaw's Lochdene kennel of Cockers dated back nearly 60 years and enjoyed much success. **John Gillespie** will be remembered for handling so many of the Cockers and Americans from the great Lochranza kennel.

From the same breed, as well as Americans and Bichons, came an unforgettable personality in **Sue Pudney** (Cascadia), known to many as secretary of Crystal Palace and for her long and brave battle against ill health. **Alan Webster** played a significant part in the success of the Asquanne Cockers and his wife Anne's administrative roles, and himself made up a Vizsla.

Margaret Nicholls made a big impact in Fields Spaniels with the Lydemoors and also bred Welsh Springers with the Jonix affix.

The Dalati Welsh Springers bred by **Noel Hunton-Morgans** and his late wife Dodo were the breed's most influential kennel, with stars like Crufts group winner Sarian and top stud dog Sioni. His beautiful Welsh voice will be remembered by visitors to Welsh KC shows.

Tony Burgoin, with his wife Gillian, had the enormously influential Ragstone Weimaraners.

Keith McCallum supported his wife Beryl's interest in Airedales and other terriers and his own passion was for Siberian Huskies in which he owned the first group winner who became the first bitch champion.

Ian Phillips, along with wife Margaret, owned one of the most successful kennels of Bedlingtons, Rathsrigg. The first champion won a Crufts group as far back as 1965, and many of the later winners had an enormous impact on the breed. He served the National breed club well and also made up a field trial champion German Shorthaired Pointer.

Bruce Nicolls was involved in Staffords, Bedlingtons and Norwich and could not have worked harder for the breed clubs.

Judy Parker-Tucker had been an integral part of the Cairn Terrier world for the entire post-war period. The Uniquecottage kennel, founded jointly with the late Hazel Small (Avenelhouse) had produced over 40 UK champions and had a great impact around the world.

Gordon Knight (Sundalgo) made up several champion Border Terriers, and **Laura Brown** had the Padmacs. In the Dandie Dinmont world **Mavis Walkley** (Follycott) was one of the characters.

Vera Goold (Sidewater) was one of the senior figures of the Smooth Fox Terrier world and also played an important part in the early days of the Bichon in the UK through the Leijazulip dogs, importing dogs in both breeds. **Pam Robinson** also went back many years with her Pittlea Smooths and later also had German Shorthaired Pointers.

Jan Rabin (Kama) owned a number of breeds, also being involved with training clubs and breed rescue, and was perhaps best known for a famous Lakeland Terrier.

Friends throughout the dog world were sad at the death of one of its real gentlemen, **Peter Eva**, known with wife Ella for the

Sophyla Manchester Terriers but with much wider interests, serving as vice-chairman of Richmond. With his wife Gladys

Douglas Philp had the Muhlross Parson Russells, including the breed's first group winner, and wrote breed notes for DOG WORLD.

Julia Gibbons was one of the characters of the Skye Terrier world and bred a Crufts group winner among others. **Ian Southwick** bred the Clansmead Scottish Terriers in the UK and later Australia.

Dr Mike Wilson (Olton), with partner Robert Hill, did much for the West Highland White and in recent years had lived in France.

Countless dog people will miss **Mary Welch**, the first lady of Boston Terriers in which her Apposyte dogs, and especially her numerous top producing imports, made a lasting contribution. She was instrumental in the fight against eye disease in the breed. She also bred a champion Toy Poodle, wrote Boston notes in DOG WORLD until shortly before her death at 91, and her hospitality and support meant a great deal to friends in so many breeds.

John Beacock was one of the keenest Keeshond enthusiasts, not least through the magazine he produced. **Pat Parkes** (Vaderson) had a long involvement with the same breed and with her late husband Ron ran Gravesend and Medway Towns CS for over 40 years and worked for several other Kentish clubs.

Joe Neath and family bred many famous Buffrey Dalmatians and he was a stalwart of the North of England breed club. **Bob Wertheim** (Merithew) was a veteran of the Dalmatian world while **Marjory Walker** bred the Shoulao Chows.

Geoff Green (Kanchee) was best known in Bulldogs but was involved in a number of breeds.

A remarkable personality was **Margaret 'Mick' Watson** who with her late husband Les had the Petitburn and Bidabo Miniature and Toy Poodles, highly successful in their day, and later owned Japanese Spitz. She had a rare gift for writing amusingly about the world of dogs and its characters, in the two books with which she caused a stir in the '60s and later in her *Canine Follies* column in DOG WORLD.

Pat Salama (formerly Ashwell) was a colourful and sometimes controversial figure in Standards but no one could deny that she bred some exceptionally

influential dogs under the Torpaz affix over several decades including a BIS winner and the sire of Crufts BIS, RBIS and group winners. **Doris Poole**'s Glyndale Standards were famous in years gone by.

Elisabeth Cooke was a unique character in the Schnauzer world. With Pam McLaren she bred the often amusingly named Deansgates and they produced many champions including CC record holder Luke Lively.

Aileen Young (Balgay) had been involved with Tibetan Spaniels since the 1960s. **Eric Carter** had the Tricina Shih Tzu, remembered for a three-champion litter.

Joan MacLaren (Braxburn) was an intelligent, independent-minded breeder of Boxers over many decades, with a highly responsible attitude to health issues. **Chris Cray** (Klansted) was another strong personality who had been involved with Boxers, and Griffons too, for many years. **David Webb** (Cherryside) was yet another of the breed's keenest enthusiasts, who cared deeply on health questions.

Diana Cochrane had been a highly successful breeder of Rough Collies before becoming involved with the Bernese Mountain Dogs in which her Duntiblae imports and homebreds helped establish the breed on sound lines in the UK. She wrote a standard work on the breed, and also bred champion cats. Another great name in Rough Collies was **Vera Hickson** of the influential Bririchs. **Doris Mortiboy** bred the Silvermoors, **Nora Keeling** the Maivors and **Wynne Davies**, who was 101, the Franwyns.

Raymond Boatwright had the successful Glynpedr Mastiffs as well as a deep involvement with Poodles. **Fiona Karolus** (Starkenbichl) was the first to import a Leonberger to the UK and also had Wire Dachshunds. **Jean Whittaker**'s Esmeduna Newfoundlands had a big influence.

Jane Heath was a clever breeder of Rottweilers with the Vanhirsch affix, as was **Thelma Toole** (Chornytan) in Dobermanns.

South Wales shows won't be the same without **Gwen Mogford** (Baucottblues) who had a lifetime's involvement with Old English Sheepdogs and showed other breeds too. She judged the working and

pastoral groups, was founder secretary of the W/P Breeds of Wales and the Welsh OES breed club and served on South Wales committee too. Her husband Les survived her by just a few months.

Another Welsh personality was **Ivor Munday** of the Samovar Samoyeds. **Bill Chadwick** was known in various pastoral breeds including Briards and Old English Sheepdogs.

Bearded Collies lost one of its most senior figures, **Jenny Osborne**, whose Osmarts made an indelible mark on the breed's history.

Angela Gillespie (Detania) was one of the most enthusiastic Border Collie breeders. **Renee Millington**, who celebrated her century in 2011, was one of the best loved figures in the Irish dog scene, having been involved with Pyreneans for over 50 years with her Perenvay kennel. **Lin Hill** (Cluny) was another stalwart of this breed and contributed notes to DOG WORLD for many years; she died in a car accident while returning from Crufts.

Elizabeth Coleopy came from a four-generation 'doggy' family, her mother and daughter with the Bowerhinton affix and she with the Fullanis, involved with Norwegian Buhunds and Elkhounds.

Stuart Berry, with his wife, had the Simcourt Shelties, and worked for various canine societies including Darlington. Vet **Katherine Chapman** was a long-term supporter of the breed with the Exburys. **Richard** and **Joan Stanley** of the Tegwels died within weeks of each other; among others they bred Top Stud Dog Wild Ways.

Nicky Gascogne (Rosern) was one of the UK's earliest breeders of Swedish Vallhunds and wrote a detailed history of the breed. **Barbara Dowse** (Sunninglye) was a stalwart of the Belgian Shepherds.

An outstanding figure in the German Shepherd world was **Roy Allan**, breeder with his wife Clarissa of the Shootersways. They bred many good champions, gradually changing their type towards that of the country of origin, were both

qualified SV judges, wrote useful books and fascinating notes and articles in DOG WORLD. In latter years they were especially keen on the working side and did much to try to keep the breed and its people away from the extreme.

With his wife Mary **Colin Park** (Keyingham) bred the Cavalier CC record holder and won a BIS with an Old English Sheepdog. **Reg West** played a big part in the success of the family's Starvon Vallhunds.

Idris Jones, along with partner Allan Taylor, was Britain's most successful breeder of Pembroke Corgis. The Belroyd kennel produced 40 champions including legends like Lovebird and Nut Cracker. In later years Cardigans did equally well, including a 2012 RBIS winner.

Wendy Hall (Brynhall) worked in various capacities for the Cardigan Corgi. **Peggy Grogan** (Fanara) had supported the Pembroke for many decades.

Marjorie Ransom was unfailing support to her late sister-in-law Jackie with the pioneering Tresilva Bichons.

Eike Herold was one of the Pug world's most distinguished figures, with a deep interest in several other toy breeds. Born in Germany, he adopted England as his homeland and became involved in all aspects of the dog world, as chairman of several breed clubs, serving on the breed's council, helping breed welfare and as a judge. Many superb Pugs bore the Pugnus affix, and he had written breed notes in DOG WORLD. Griffons were another of his interests and a further great loss to than breed was **Betty Gorringe** whose Litahni kennel dated back to 1944 She served the breed club for over 50 years. **June Burke** had the Markaths in both Griffons and Lakelands.

Lesley Stanley bred the Elancie Bichons and was chairman of Birmingham Toy. **Joyce Wlliams** had the Huntsbank Cavaliers.

Eleanor Roberts (Chersya) bred several Smooth Chihuahua champions. **Jenny Langhorn** bred the Yorlang Yorkshire Terriers and wrote breed notes for DOG WORLD, while **Doreen Johnson** bred the Lyndoneys.

David Roe, along with wife Carolyn, had the successful Sunshoo Papillons (including some great Phalenes) and Maremmas and compiled two books on the Papillon. He served many dog show societies in various capacities and for many years was chief steward at East of England.

George Baxter had the Ikoura Pekingese and was involved with several toy breed clubs in Scotland and judged the group. He wrote regional news for DOG WORLD and often contributed show introductions, as well as serving on the Scottish KC council. An amusing character, he had an equally passionate interest in music. **Don Lee** (Frampton) was a true gentleman of the Peke world. **Sheila Gunn** of the Peteshes specialised in white Pekes and was the popular chairman of Worthing CS. **Lena Watters** (Yankui) had been a leading figure in the breed in Northern Ireland.

Margaret Journeaux from Jersey was known for her Navyvillas Japanese Chin and **Winnie Matches** (Fochai) was another personality from this breed in this and King Charles.

The 20 Year Club

As always, we would like to thank the Annual's advertisers for their continued support. Those on pages 143 to 221 and 223 are members of the 20 Year Club, having first advertised here in 1993 or earlier.

1963

ORMANDY

CH SOUPERLATIVE SILVERY MOON is the latest and perhaps the best of SUMMER QUEEN'S astonishing quiver of six champions. She is by Ch ROMANY ROMANTIC VISION, was bred by Miss WEATHERILL and is jointly owned by her breeder and by Mr OPPENHEIMER.

The consistency with which this kennel produces really first class sound Bull Terriers of the correct type is truly remarkable and I feel it needs no further comment from me.

LEO C WILSON

1993

MEADOWPARK

Services
Boarding
Cattery
Grooming

Breeds
Cavalier King
Charles Spaniels
Bernese Mountain Dogs

| Ch WAYS & MEANS AT MEADOWPARK | ROSS Ben's brother | The puppy MEADOWPARK PRIM 'N' PROPER | BEN with his David Hart orthosis walking frame | MEADOWPARK EARLY EXODUS |

This review is not intended to promote Meadowpark but a way to say a very sincere THANK YOU on behalf of **BEN HARTLEY**. Ben, now aged 5½, has cerebral palsy and is making steady progress. Your support has been simply outstanding and at times incredible.

BERNICE and JOHN MAIR and CAROLE HARTLEY
Meadowpark, Trows Lane, Castleton, Rochdale, Lancs

Telephone 0706 49900

1983

JOKYL Frensham Manor Frensham, Surrey GU10 3ED

Christmas and New Year Greetings from Olive Jackson and Mary Swash

Ch JOKYL BUTTONS N'BOWS

A fabulous year with three Jokyls gaining their title—Ch Jokyl Smart Enough, Ch Jokyl Buttons N'Bows and Vicky Irelan-Hill's Ch Jokyl Hot Gossip of Hillcross. The youngsters Jokyl Sunday Best and Jokyl Gallipants have both won Junior Warrant, one CC and several reserve CCs, and must surely be forces to be reckoned with in 1983.

We have stud dogs to suit most bloodlines and young stock often for sale from carefully planned matings. Many thanks to Chris and Dodo for their unflagging support and hard work.

Further details on request from Mary Swash, telephone Frensham (025 125) 4165

1973

Miss Ashton Cross **The Alderbourne Pekingese** The Wilderness Ascot, Tel 20029

ALDERBOURNE PRINCELY GIFT
AT JUST ONE YEAR OLD

These photographs are NOT touched up

THE ALDERBOURNE KENNEL HAS PRODUCED OVER 250 CHAMPIONS THIS DOG IS ITS CROWNING ACHIEVEMENT

1953

The Burydown Salukis

BURYDOWN ANOUK with Sandra

MRS Waters has had a busy and successful year. Shown is breed and variety classes, the Burydowns have collected an impressive list of awards. Salos include the export of Burydown Anouk to Italy, where she is the adored companion of Signor P. Bartoli and his family, as these attractive pictures show. Mrs Waters has taken up obedience work with her hounds. Burydown Inshallah and Burydown Aliya show particular promise. They will be competing in obedience tests in the new year.

Burydown Zomahli Fara is the mother of a fine litter of, the German imported dog, Uki. These puppies—one pale cream dog, one gold bitch, one black and tan dog, one black and white bitch (marked like a black and tan) and two black and fawn bitches—are ready for sale now.

The Burydowns live as members of the family, which accounts for their friendly temperaments. A visit to Jolyons is well worth while, and Mrs Waters has a warm welcome for all Saluki lovers.

—G. M. Angel.

Owned by Mrs. HOPE WATERS

Jolyons Bury nr. Pulborough West Sussex Telephone: BURY 87

BURYDOWN ANOUK with Marco

1943

The World-Famous **ARCTIC KENNEL OF SAMOYED**

(Owner) Miss M. KEYTE-PERRY (Chairman, British Samoyed Club), Oak Hall, HASLEMERE, Surrey.

This famous kennel was founded in 1924 and since then sixteen English champions have been bred, owned or in the home kennel. Look at the list:—

DOGS
1—Ch. Loga of the Arctic.
2—Ch. White Rover of the Arctic.
3—Ch. Surf of the Arctic.
4—Ch. Leader of the Arctic.
5—Ch. Snow Chief of the Arctic.
6—Ch. Spartan of the Arctic.
7—International Ch. Rex of the Arctic.

BITCHES
1—Ch. Kara Queen
2—Ch. Tchita.
3—Ch. Winter.
4—Ch. Arctic Dawn
5—Ch. Sleo of the Arctic.
6—Ch. Greta of the Arctic.
7—Ch. Rosca of the Arctic.
8—Ch. Silver Glow of the Arctic.
9—Ch. Joy of the Arctic.

IMPORTANT TO ALL

The Arctic strain is absolutely essential to the breed. Miss Keyte-Perry's devotion to the Samoyed is as widely known as her famous kennel.

MEADOWPARK

Boyde
**MEADOWPARK
SUGAR DADDY**

©Johnson

Breeze
**CH MEADOWPARK
WHISPER'S BREEZE**
Current Top Bernese Mountain Dog 2012

Thank you to all the judges who have thought so highly
of our dogs and made this year one to remember.

photo Whyte

Livvie
**CH MEADOWPARK
LIVING THE DREAM**

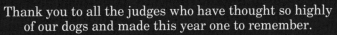

**BERNICE MAIR and CAROLE HARTLEY-MAIR
CURRENT TOP BERNESE MOUNTAIN DOG BREEDERS 2012**
Lawn Cottage Boarding Kennels and Cattery
Telephone 01706 649900

Life grants nothing to us without hard work.
Horace

VANITONIA

Edward

Graham

Ch Vanitonia
First N Foremost

Son of TOP DOG ALL BREEDS 2010
Ch Vanitonia Unwrapped
3 CCs & 3 BOB at 13 months
1 puppy 2012

Sh Ch Vanitonia
The Buck Stops Ere

The youngest male Sh Ch clumber
at 12 months 2 weeks

BIS Clumber Spaniel
Club CH show

BPIS National gundog

4 CCs & 4 BOB

Elliot

Ch Vanitonia You'll See
Runner up TOP DOG
ALL BREED 2012
1 Utility dog 2012

#1 Toy Poodle 2011 & 2012
8 All-Breed Bests In Show
3 All-Breed res Bests In Show
16 group firsts
CRUFTS BOB 2012
26 CCs & 25 BOB

healthy keen
balanced stamina
intelligent
agile alert animated **Dialynne**
happy
Aussies sound
loyal

Grumpy

Cookie

Tassel
Owned by
R & J Timperon

Elmo

ANTRIX

Boston Terriers

present their latest production, featuring ...

Peggy as
ANTRIX KISS ME KATE

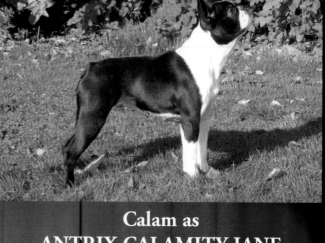

Calam as
ANTRIX CALAMITY JANE

Milo as
ANTRIX ON THE TOWN

Patsy, better known as
LISVARNA SUGAR BABE
AT ANTRIX
2 CCs, 1 RCC at 12 months

Produced by Joanne Kennedy
Directed by Anne Kennedy Clifton
Stage Directed by Daisy Kennedy Mitchell
Stagehand Peter Clifton

We hope the critics like our show and give rave reviews

Anne Kennedy Clifton and Peter Clifton
Beeches, Cuckoo Bridge, North Drove, Spalding, PE11 3JF
Tel 01775 713625 Email bostonuk1@antrix.co.uk

WINUWUK

WINUWUK THE OUTLAW,
1 RCC as a junior

Áine

WINUWUK RUMOUR HAS IT, 3 RCCs

The incomparable
CH/IR CH WINUWUK LUST AT FIRST SIGHT
71 CCs, Breed Record Holder

At the age of 8 Max is
now focused on his career
as a successful sire with
Champions at home
and abroad.

Two of his latest
homebred winning
progeny are pictured.

Frozen semen is available
internationally.

JULIE BROWN and TIM HUTCHINGS   e: winuwuk@btinternet.com   t: 01453 511303   w: winuwukboxers.com

Ingledene
est. 1967

Classic, Fit for Function, certified BVA/KC Health tested Collies since 1979
the Past .... Moving into the Future

CH. Ingledene All That Matters JW - BIS

CH. Ingledene Late Night Love -
Bitch Record Holder Top Rough 03,4,5

CH. Ingledene First Love JW - Top Rough '91

CH. Ingledene Cherish The Love

INT.UK.CH. Ingledene Power Of Love

Ingledene Love Is The Drug JW 5 RCC's

CH. Ingledene Penny Lover
BOB Crufts 1998 - Top Rough '97

Ingledene Slave To Love - BIS's

CH. Ingledene Blue Rain - BIS's

Valerie and John Geddes
Tel: 01938 811846   mobs 07429 437481 - 07429 429469 Email: ingledenecollies@btinternet.com
web: http://www.gamma.nic.fi/~geddes   http://www.collienet.com/breeders/Ingledene.htm

Yakee

THREE COUNTIES SHO[...]D

Ch Yakee
Ooh Aah Cantona

Top Pekingese
2012

Bred by ALBERT EASDON
and PHILIP MARTIN

Middlegill House,
Moffat, Dumfriesshire
DG10 9SW
www.yakee.org

Alan V Walker

153

Making the Headlines:
Top Pom Breeder (4th yr) Top Pom CC winner

LIREVA

THREE Lireva's at POTY

Top left; Lireva's Extreme Nobility
Owned; Julie Pike
Bred by; me
Qualified; East of England

Top right; Thelbern Valentino From Lireva
Owned; me
Bred by; Thelma Alsford (Jersey)
Qualified; WELKS

Bottom left; Lireva's To Hell An Black
Owned; Don Cawthera
Bred by; me
Handled; Fay Matthews
Qualified; SWKA

3 POTY Finalists—1 Final Cut

BIS Pom Club
Ch Lireva's The House Mouse
13 CCs 5 BOBs 2 x TG3

Overall Winner KC Breeders Competition

4 Lireva Doubles
UKTD, WELKS, Bournemouth & Birm City

Nikara Diamond Tiara for Lireva
Winner 3 Puppy Groups, BPIS WPBA Scot & 1 CC
POTY Qualifier

NEW CH - Lireva's Short Sir Kit
Now with 5 CC's 4 BOBs 3 Gp shortlists

Daddy's Boy Chayo Pulling Power at Lireva
BOB & Gp Shortlist Belfast, Twice RBD—only 18mths

Lireva's To Hell An Black
POTY Finalist JW Semi Finalist & 1st CC
Beautifully handled for us by Fay Matthews

Introducing the next generation:
Lireva's Dancing for Gold
RBPIS at 6mths SWPC Ch

In Poms winning our **204th** CC and making up our **19th** Champion
In Sams winning our **32nd** CC and starting off towards our **8th** Champion - Not A Bad Year!!!!

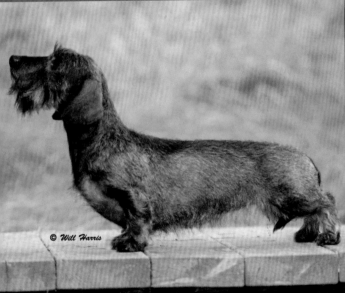

HERNWOOD

Home of Top Breeder,

photo Croft-Elliott

1 Litter sired by Hernwood Delaware Diamond JW
3 UK Show Champions
1 US Grand Champion
2 ProPlan/Dogworld Pup of the Year Qualifiers
2 Eukanuba Champion Stakes Qualifiers
3 Best in Show Winners

From left to right:
Sh Ch Hernwood Diamond Rock JW ShCM
Sh Ch Hernwood Indi Girl at Togipoto
Sh Ch Hernwood Talladega Racer JW ShCM

Gordon Setters
Top Brood Bitch and Top Puppy

photo K9 Photography

Hernwood Calypso Goddess JW
DoB 28.08.11

No 1 Gordon Setter Puppy
No 2 Gundog Puppy 2012*
Junior Warrant at eight months
RCC Welsh Kennel Club 2012
CC Gundog Society of Wales 2012

Pete and Chris Sandiford and Claire Lewis
Hazel Corner Dog Hotel, Windmill Road, Markyate, St Albans AL3 8LP
Tel 01582 842242   Email sandiford@btconnect.com

* at time of going to press

Bayard BEAGLES

20 Year Club

PRESENTS OUR SHOW TEAM

photo Denman

Ch Bayard Grafter

At his first outing in Veteran won Best Veteran in Show
under breed specialists Lynda Havard and Dianna Spavin

His daughter

photo Brace

Ch Bayard Make Amends

DOB 28.09.09
Sire Ch Bayard Grafter
Dam Bayard Daytrip
18 CCs, 3 RCCs, Group 1 and other Group Placings
Top Beagle 2011

JILL PEAK and SARAH JACKSON
Marcliff Kennels, Marsh Road, Banks, Southport, Lancs PR9 8DZ

Bayard BEAGLES

159

CH Pekehuis Applause

Tara

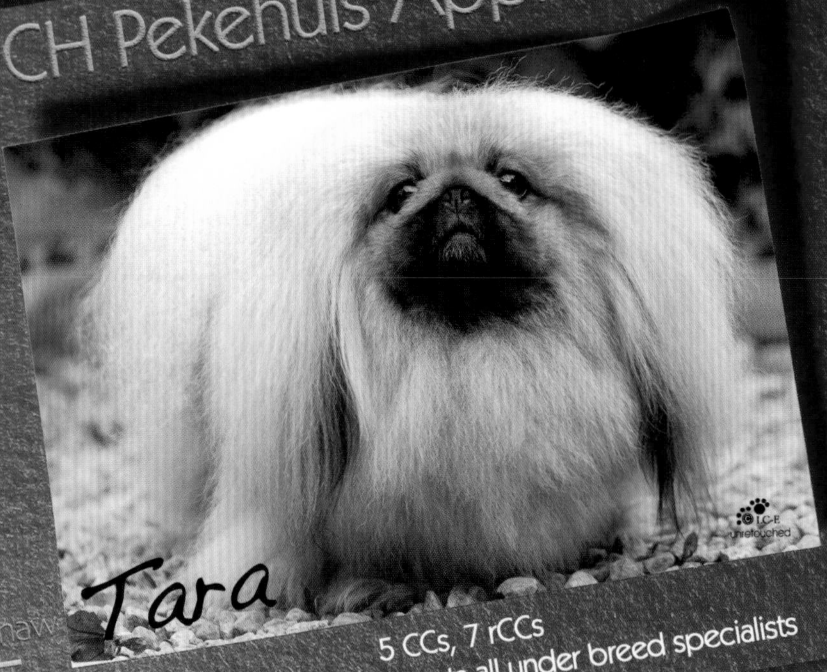

5 CCs, 7 rCCs

Multiple Group Placements all under breed specialists

Pekehuis Conquest

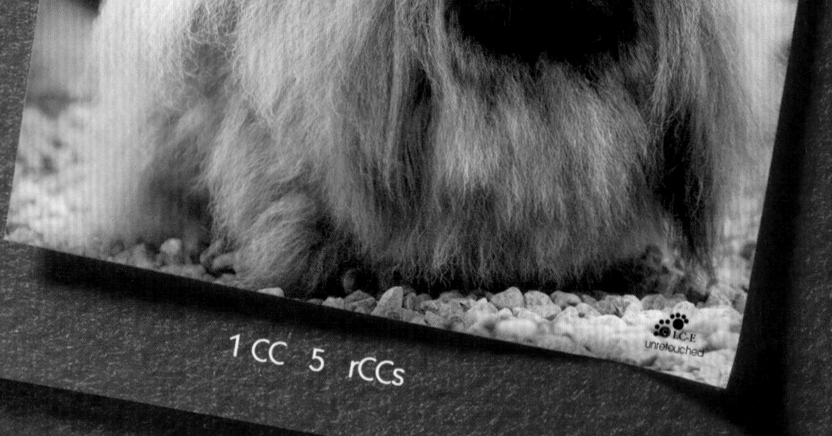

1 CC 5 rCCs

Pekehuis Midnight Magic

Scooby

pictured at just 9 months old

Fran Shaw
is Fran
Pekehuis

Pekehuis Black Orchid

Ebony

1 CC 1 rCC

Fran Shaw
is Fran
Pekehuis

Fran Shaw
is Fran
Pekehuis

John Shaw &
Maria Francis
Winifred Mee
mejowins64@btinternet.com 01594530848

Jet's

Greyhounds and Griffons

Jet's Moulin Rouge
Owners: Espen Engh and
Åge Gjetnes, Norway
and David Guy
espenjet@online.no

Anna Szabo

Pearl

3rd

unretouched

Dragon Quest

Eukanuba Plush Puppy

Maverick Sabre

This year we welcomed our first Shetland Sheepdog litter, from our USA import tricolour girl (above). We look forward to developing our own Sheltie breeding programme, utilising the best of North American bloodlines!

Familiar faces and new hopefuls for 2013.

After her stellar performance at the Eukanuba Ch Stakes final, it seemed clear that our dynamic young American Cocker bitch Pearl's A Singer [Top Bitch 2012] deserved another year of campaigning with co-owner and handler Susan Crummey. We anticipate great things from this duo who are just hitting their stride!

We have several exciting youngsters for the new year, including the Standard dog Maverick Sabre who has 2 CCs at press, and the sensational tricolour American Cocker pup Dragon Quest. Both are Top Puppy 2012, and both boys are POTY finalists! We are also pleased to introduce our lovely Irish-bred Pekingese bitch. Pearlstone Lady Jasmine who promises to be a wonderful addition to our growing Peke family.

Visit us online at our website www.afterglowdogs.com as well as our blog www.afterglow.blogspot.com

Mybeards

Top winning Polish Lowland Sheepdogs
since 1990
Breeder of 37 UK Champions

Ch Mybeards Dream

Breed Record Holder
25 CCs
2 Ch Show Pastoral
Group Wins

Ch Mybeards Wish

Top Puppy 2011
Top PLS 2012*
Pastoral Group
Winner
City of Birmingham
2012

Mybeards Havanese

Bomba z Domlina at Mybeards

Top Havanese 2010

Our Havanese will be campaigned in 2013

A special thank you
to all the judges for
our awards

DIANE MOTTRAM

mybeards.pon@btinternet.com

01246 205166

KC Assured Breeder
of Excellence

*at time of going to press

Kulawand In No One's Shadow JW

(1 CC & BIS, 3 res CCs)

Sh.Ch. Calzeat Causa Commotion
at Flatcharm   x   Ch. Almanza
Thank God It's Friday of Kulawand

All health tests &
pedigrees are
detailed on our
website.

www.kulawand.com

Kulawand

SH.CH. Bournehouse
Winter Sky of Kulawand

Kulawand Silver Shadow (2 res CCs)

SH.CH. Bournehouse Winter Sky of Kulawand

GUNILLA and **REBECCA AGRONIUS**
Sweden • www.kennelprefix.com

photo Rebecca Agronius

Introducing our latest
international champion
**Int/Swe/Dan/Norw Champion
PREFIX ROB ROY OF SCOTS**

By Ch/Int/Swe/Dan Ch Prefix Abraham Lincoln
    (By Angelwings Love Bug of Moonswift
     ex Ch/Int/Nordic Ch Prefix Swede Smell Of Success)

ex Int/Nord/Bel/Lux Ch Prefix Upstairs Maid
    (By Ch Moonswift Crazy Horse
     ex Ch/US/Int/Nordic Ch Prefix Really Something)

'Viggo' is 13 inches quality.

*Below we also introduce his half-sister
'Grace', our 8th UK CC winner!*

Top hairless
bitch in Sweden 2012

Crufts BOB 2011
Ch/Int/Swe/Dan Ch
Prefix Abraham Lincoln
Top Crested in Sweden 2011

**Crufts BOB 2008 group 4
Crufts BOB 2009 group 3**
Ch/US/Int/Nordic Ch VWW '11
Prefix Really Something
Top Crested in Sweden 2008

**PREFIX FAIR PLAY
ON BROADWAY**
Born January 2011
What a first year in the rings!
**1 CC, 3 RCCs, 8 CACs,
5 CACIBs & RBIS** at the
**Chinese Crested
Club of GB
ch show
May 2012**

photo Anna Carlsson

photo Sunstreaker

photos Kristy Bello
K Bello

See you at the GIA-Ceramic & Silhouettes stand in hall 4 at Crufts 2013!

★ NIKOLAEV ★

Continuing to produce HOMEBRED winning Bouviers

CH NIKOLAEV IDYLLA

Roxy is our 13th Nikolaev Champion

CRUFTS
BCC and BOB **Ch/Ned Ch Nikolaev Calla** (Hall)
RBCC **Orakei Elusive**
RDCC **Ch/Ir Ch Nikolaev Raffles** (Partner)

WINDSOR
RDCC **Nikolaev Tariq** (Pilsbury)
BCC **Nikolaev Tanzanite at Orakei**
RBCC **Nikolaev Idylla**

EAST OF ENGLAND
RBCC **Nikolaev Ursa ShCM** (Simmons)

NATIONAL WORKING AND PASTORAL BREEDS
BCC **Nikolaev Idylla**

WELSH KENNEL CLUB
BCC and BOB (her third!) **Ch Nikolaev Idylla**
RBCC **Ch/Ned Ch Nikolaev Calla** (litter sister)

CITY OF BIRMINGHAM
BCC **Nikolaev Amarande at Abbiville** (Jones)

BOUVIER DES FLANDRES CLUB OF GB CH SHOW
BCC **Ch/Ned Ch Nikolaev Calla**

BOUVIER DES FLANDRES CLUB OF GB OPEN SHOW
BOS and BV **Nikolaev Ursa ShCM**

Among the highs we had our low in saying goodbye to **Ch Nikolaev Amari** and **Orakei Dragonbank Sky Viking** (Bessie and Viking). Both are sorely missed.

Nikolaev are proud to own Top Sire **Ch Chepam Ojay at Nikolaev** and Top Brood **Ch Nikolaev Amari** (a repeat of 2011)*

NIKOLAEV
Lee Nichols
The Hollies, Aldham, Hadleigh, Suffolk IP7 6NS
Tel 01473 827620

ORAKEI
Frances Jonas
7 Chapel Street, Cromer NR27 9HJ
Tel 01263 514121

★ ORAKEI ★

* At time of going to press

FIND YOUR
LIMITS
AND
EXCEED
THEM

GUNALT

Top UK Weimaraner kennel in the history of the breed.
Proud holder of all records in the breed, including top brood,
top cc winner, and top breeder with over 72 UK champions.

In 2012 we celebrated 4 new UK show champions, 12 different CC
winners, current top-breeder all breeds, with 27 CCs between them,
as well as 6 different best puppy winners at championship shows.

Enquires about the breed, puppies or stud dogs
or for any of the breed books by Patsy please feel free to contact us.

Stephen & Patsy Hollings, Gunalt Weimaraners,
Carlton Hall Farm, Carlton, Yeadon, Nr. Leeds, Yorkshire LS19 7BG
Telephone 01132505113   Mobile 07968985582

stephenpatsy@gunaltweimaraners.co.uk
www.gunaltweimaraners.co.uk

www.facebook.com/GunaltWeimaraners

©advertising & photography Croft-Elliott

LC-E
unretouched

GLENIREN-SUNSHOO

TOP PAPILLON - TOP PUPPY - TOP BREEDER 2012

Ch Gleniren Tres Mannefico Sunshoo
Phalene History Made
Top Papillon 2012
Phalene Breed Record Holder
22 CCs – Groups 2/3/4

IRENE and GLENN ROBB and CAROLYN ROE
TEL: +44 (0) 1829 770909

Breeders of all time Papillon Breed
Record Holder Ch Gleniren Starlight Kisses

GLENIREN NIKOLIA MANIA SUNSHOO
2 CCs and 4 RCCs

GLENIREN BE BEDAZZLED SUNSHOO
4 BPIB, 2 RCCs - Top Puppy 2012

DONZEATA

Three Champions in two months!

Mother: Ch Donzeata Royal Thread

Son: Ch Donzeata Royal Tweed   Daughter Ch Donzeata Royal Silk

This year we are proud of our achievments, at the time of writing Top Breeder, Top Sire, Top Dam

DAVID GUY
david.donzeata@virgin.net

STUANE

©LLOVALLDesign

Ch Stuane Florette
22 CCs, 21 BOB, 9 Terrier Groups, Reserve BIS Blackpool and SWKA 2011
ProPlan/Dog World Pup of the Year Winner

Ch Stuane Burnt Oak

Bred in partnership with
David Guy, owned and
handled by Angela Corish

6 CCs and Group Winner
at WELKS 2011

Top Puppy sire 2012
(to date)

STUART PLANE
Vane Hall, Blandford Place, Seaham, Co Durham SR7 7RX
Tel 0191 5812200   stuart.plane@virgin.net

Ch Bohem Last Call

BOB from the Puppy class at 9 months at Santa Barbara Kennel Club, defeating six BIS or SBIS winners, owner-bred and handled under judge Mr Edd E Bivin

LOOKING BACK...

A high percentage of top Whippets in most parts of the world go back to Bohem dogs, close up or further back in their pedigrees.

Some homebreds of major importance in the past decade are Ch Bohem Adam's Rib and Ch Bohem Time Flies in Europe, Ch Bohem Circus Pony in Japan, and Ch Bohem Of Thee I Sing, Ch Bohem All About Eve, Ch Bohem C'est la Vie, Ch Bohem Just In Time and Ch Bohem Bon Vivant, all living in the US but with winning descendants in many other countries as well.

AND INTO THE FUTURE

The first homebred Bohem litter in eight years, born in late 2011, produced two puppies which many feel are among our best ever. Both completed their AKC titles by 10 months of age and both have a number of BOB wins over adult champions: Ch Bohem Last Call and Ch Bohem Swan Song, sired by GCh Counterpoint Painted by Bohem, SC ("Viggo" a Bon Vivant son), who is proving a successful young stud dog.

For something a little different, there is the 8-month old black, Shamasan Bohem Breezing Up, co-owned with breeder Phoebe Booth and also sired by Viggo. He was Best Puppy at his very first outing.

GCh Counterpoint Painted by Bohem, SC (left), winning the stud dog class at the American Whippet Club's specialty in California with his two young sons Ch Bohem Last Call and Bohem Final Act under judge Mrs Patricia Trotter. Viggo is owned by Scott Mazer and Bohem.

CH BOHEM SWAN SONG with owner/handler Barbara Wayne at 6 months

Bo Bengtson
PO Box 10, Ojai, CA 93024, USA
email bobengtson@impulse.net
www.bohemwhippets.com

The 350-page THE WHIPPET, by Bo Bengtson, won BEST NON-FICTION BOOK in the 2012 APDW competition. "Not only a stunning book to look at, but a very detailed and interesting one." (Joanna Russell, Dog World) Sorry, copies not available from author — please order from Amazon.com or as e-book via Amazon's Kindle store

Kanix

This was the year our dreams came true when
Sh Ch Kiswahili Martin at Kanix
went **BIS** at the **Scottish Kennel Club**

©Johnson

Martin has been the breed's most consistent winner during the last 4 years.
He has now won 25 CCs.
Kanix has made up 7 Pointer Champions and 57 UK Champions altogether.
We have won 48 groups and 13 BIS!

Kari & Sigurd Wilberg
Sigurd@kanix.cc

Heather & Joanne Blackburn-Bennett
Joanne@kanix.cc

Pointers

Sh Ch Afterglow Bare Face Lie at Kanix ShCM

Ledgands.co.uk

Sh Ch Kanix Chilli

Ransley Greyhounds

Ir Ch Ransley Simply Bewitched

(Int Ch/Ch/Ir Ch/DK Ch/Sw Ch/Jet's It's Been A Hard Day's Night With Ransley ex Ch/Ir Ch Mistweave Making Music With Ransley)

2 RCCs, 2 CACIBs, 7 Green Stars

Top Greyhound Puppy and Top Greyhound Club Puppy 2011

Ransley Majestic Style

(Int Ch/Ch/Ir Ch/DK Ch/Sw Ch/Jet's It's Been A Hard Day's Night With Ransley ex Ch/Ir Ch Mistweave Making Music With Ransley)

1 RCC

1 CACIB, 4 Green Stars

Owned by Rita and Paul Bartlett

Tel 01233 500067 ritabartlett@ransleygreyhounds.com

CH TRAVELLA STAR CRAFT

TOP WIRE 2012

20 Year Club

Alan V Walker

Travella

"...winning world-wide"

We would like to congratulate the owners of Multi Ch Travella Special Feature and his son Ch Travella Starlord for qualifying for the Eukanuba final in Florida and Ch Travella Skys The Limit who gained her World and European titles. We would also like to congratulate Franki Leung and Antonio Almeida on their success with Ch

IN 10 YEARS:
4 UK BIS WINNERS
7 UK GROUP WINNERS

www.travella.co.uk
wbc@travella.co.uk
+44 (0)117 965 5431

BILL BROWNE-COLE

Clynymona

Top winning UK Kennel

Breeding and showing Bolognese for 21 years

TOP BOLOGNESE
2008/09/10/11/12

CLYNYMONA HERCULES MORSE AT INGERDORM ShCM

Morse

Gib Ch and Jun Ch BOLOGNESE STAR DONALD AT HAVANESE STARS CW12

TOP BOLOGNESE PUPPY
2005/06/10/11/12

Donald

Top Puppy 2012
BIS Club Show Jan 2012 at 7 months
BIS3 Royal Manx Show
BPIS and BIS3 MKA show Jan 2012
Handled and owned by Virginia Dowty and breeder Margaret Seeberger

Top Bolognese 2012
1st British and youngest breed ShCM
14 Group places at Open Shows, shortlisted at Toy Group Ch Shows
Top Rare Breed (time of press)
Handled and owned by Andrew Stewart, Michael Boulcott and breeder Virginia Dowty

Gib / Ir Ch CLARCHIEN SAPPHIRE AT CLYNYMONA CW12

Top Bolognese Bitch 2012
BIS3 MKA OS
Top Puppy 2011
Handled and owned by Virginia Dowty and breeder Kathy Begg

Sapphire

Australian Silky Terrier MARFICK HIGH SOCIETY
Top Puppy in breed 2012

Not forgetting
CLEEVIEW POSH TOTTY
Top Puppy 2010 and BOBs 2012

Many thanks to all the 'co-owners' Kathy Begg, Andrew Stewart, Michael Boulcott and Margaret Seeberger and my daughter Tanya
VIRGINIA DOWTY, Clynymona, Marfick, Bombixmoren and Iberima affixes
Ballasalla Place, Ballasalla, Isle of Man IM9 2EH and Gibraltar
www.bolognese.biz   www.blognese.org   www.australiansilkyterriers.info   Email vdowty@yahoo.com

Sh Ch *Shannas* Daimler

'Bentley' with some of his pups bred by Steve and Carolyn Bennett in Australia using AI.

Bonnie & Ronnie Scougall
Shannas Kennels
Tel 01771 624327
email: Bonnie@shannas.co.uk
website: shannas.co.uk

LPS

Ferndel Top Story at *Shannas*

Sophie and her Pups
Ferndel News Flash
and
Ferndel Fashion News

Ballybroke

Due to our problems with Syringomyelia we had a quiet year in the ring in 2012,
we are unfortunately sure time will show we are not alone with this problem

Our New Youngsters For 2013

Margaret and Graham Foote

Hunters Moon, Old Brighton Road South, Pease Pottage RH11 9AG

Tel 01444 400384   Email Grahamfoote@aol.com   Fax 01444 401627

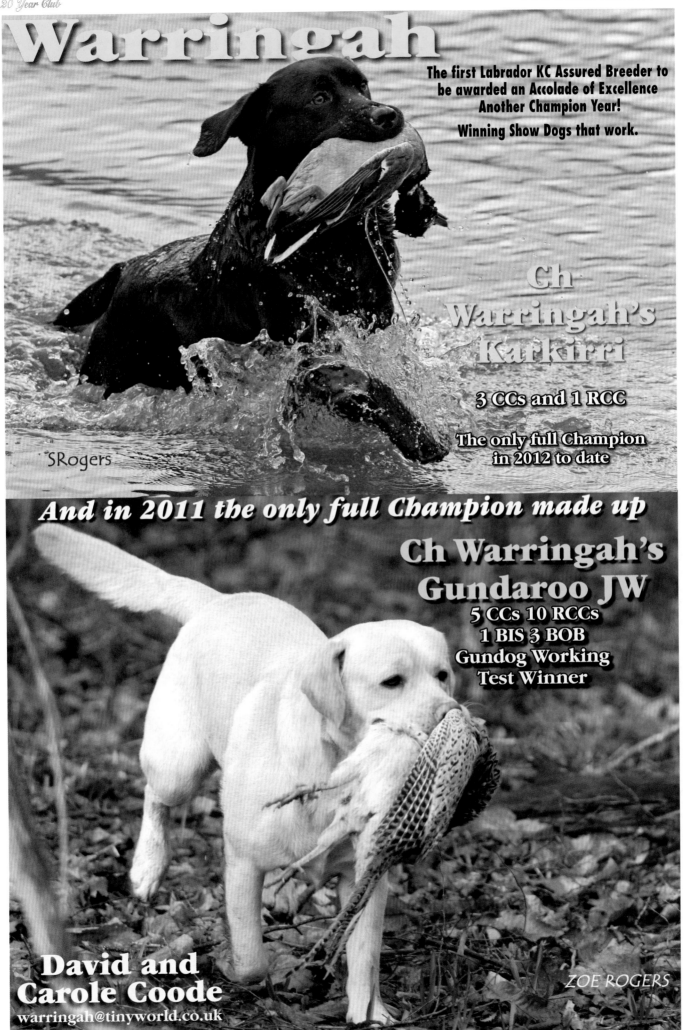

20 Year Club

Warringah

The first Labrador KC Assured Breeder to be awarded an Accolade of Excellence
Another Champion Year!

Winning Show Dogs that work.

SRogers

Ch Warringah's Karkirri

3 CCs and 1 RCC

The only full Champion in 2012 to date

And in 2011 the only full Champion made up

Ch Warringah's Gundaroo JW

5 CCs 10 RCCs
1 BIS 3 BOB
Gundog Working
Test Winner

ZOE ROGERS

David and Carole Coode

warringah@tinyworld.co.uk

*at time of going to press

Supreme Ch Statuesque Pumper Nickel
Multiple Best in Shows
2 times SBIS entry 96 and 100
judges Siv Jernhake and Professor Brian Corbitt

PURINA SYDNEY ROYAL DOG SHOW 2012

RUNNER UP IN GROUP

Proudly sponsored by
PURINA PROPLAN

Statuesque Griffons
Frank and Lee Pieterse
Australia

'Nickel' is owned and shown
on most other occasions by
Gemcourt Griffons

Risepark

Ch/Am/Ir/Int (FCI) Ch Hideki Who's That Guy with Risepark (Buster)
Ch Awesome's In The Mood with Risepark
ex Hideki Who's That Girl

Bandsman Aragon U Got A Friend at Risepark (Jay)
Am Ch Special & Luv Way's Designed Gift
ex Bandsman Uptown Girl

When **Ch Risepark Mark's Girl Libby** made her title this year she became the 59th Risepark bred or owned UK Miniature champion. When those made up abroad, and in the other 12 breeds here (across five groups), are also taken into consideration, they represent an impressive ongoing achievement and one to be proud of.

The attraction of the show ring no longer has the appeal that it once did but the challenge and desire to breed quality Miniatures continues as strongly as ever.

From the very first our imports have come from breeders whom we respect and who share our dedication to the breed. We are particularly proud that Risepark stud dogs have produced more Miniature champions for other kennels than anyone else's. Careful thought is always given to our own matings and we are able to confidently offer delightful puppies and a good choice of studs, each of outstanding and well proven breeding, delightful temperaments and an ability to enhance the breed.

Risepark Right Now (Tommy)
Ch Risepark Mister Right ex Ch Risepark Right Reasons

Ch/Am Ch Lonestar's Earmarked by Chattelane (Mark)
Am Ch Repitition's Cornerstone
ex Am Ch Chattelane's Roubi Slippers

Am Ch Repitition's Acclaim (Michael)
Am Ch Repitition's Cornerstone ex Am Ch Myla's Love Potion Number Nine.

Also at stud Risepark Sets The Mood (Carlos)
The Last Moodie Son ex Risepark Sets The Mood

Risepark Special Blend (Max)
Buster ex Starbound American Blend at Risepark

Peter Newman

+44 (0)1462 732007
www.risepark.com

Barry Day

+44 (0) 121 780 4030
barry.day@risepark.com

NERADMIK

Some of the lovely Neradmik puppies born in 2011
by Ch, Am, Can Ch Kemonts Skyline's Game Boy (Imp USA)

photo Ian Stubbings

Out of Ch Lady Godiva's Guilty Pleasures with Neradmik and from the litter of ten, born October 20, 2011:
(we hope to repeat this litter in December 2012)

NERADMIK HANDSOME HERO
'Digby'
One CC, three Reserve CCs, Best in Show and Best Puppy in Show at the North of England Keeshond Club Open Show 2012
Owned by Jean

CH NERADMIK STEPPIN' UP THE GAME AT NORKEES*
'Millie'
Three CCs, two with Best of Breed, one Reserve CC, Utility Puppy Group winner at Blackpool and South Wales Championship Shows 2012, Best Puppy in Show South Wales 2012, Best in Show North of England Keeshond Club 2012
Owned by Brian and Moira Curry
Tel 01207 271269   bcurry@tiscali.co.uk

Out of Ch Neradmik Chanel:
'Berry'
born December 14, 2011:

NERADMIK MISS HOLLY BERRY
Two CCs, one with Best of Breed, one Reserve CC, Reserve Best in Show, Best Puppy in Show North of England Keeshond Club Championship Show, Best Puppy in Show Keeshond Club Open Show 2012
Owned by Jean

NERADMIK GAME PLAN FOR LEKKERBEK
'Frisco'
One Reserve CC, Best Puppy Dog North of England Keeshond Club Championship Show
Owned by Joan Miles, Kristen Cullen and Susan Cullen
Tel 023 8026 1621   jad@barton.ac.uk

Also in the show ring: Neradmik Sunday Lovin'
Neradmik Meant To Be with Witchakees, Neradmik Kissing Game
Neradmik Late Night Love in Malta, Neradmik Help The Hero at Maldine
Neradmik Miss Mistletoe in Finland, Neradmik Beach Boy in Ireland

All bred by JEAN SHARP-BALE
Wiggs Cottage, Plumley, near Ringwood BH24 3QB
Tel 01202 824368   jsbneradmik@hotmail.co.uk

* subject to KC confirmation

If you think it's expensive to
hire a professional to do the job,
wait until you hire an amateur.
Red Adair

Mastering the Balance
Of Art, Light and Reality

Lisa
Croft-
Elliott

Multiple International Award Winning
Photography & Graphic Design
Lisa Croft-Elliott
& Carrie Russell-Smith

USA PHONE 1(203)542-0769
UK mobile +447908866522
www.eyefordogs.com
dogphotographer@mac.com

I.C-E
unretouched

MERRYBEAR NEWFOUNDLANDS

CH KENAMU BREAK THE MOULD MERRYBEAR
(subject to KC confirmation)

Ch Joy To The World For Shaddows Eternity
ex Ch/Ir Ch Merrybear Pattie Labelle of Kenamu

**3 CCs with BOB
4 RCCs
Group 2 Bournemouth 2012
BIS Southampton Open Show
BIS Newfoundland Club Open Show
All the above achieved by the
tender age of 18 months**
Photograph at 16 months

CH EVANPARK BEYONCE MERRYBEAR

FEARLESS BEARS KENDIS BOY

New Champion 2012

Merrybear Oscar
ex Evanpark Amie

Top Stud Dog 2012*
Merrybear Oscar

Top Brood Bitch 2012*
**Ch/Ir Ch Merrybear
Pattie Labelle of Kenamu**

**Current Top Puppy in Breed 2012
Puppy Group 2
Bournemouth 2012**

**6 shows all with
Best Puppy in Breed**

* at time of going to press

Gordon Cutts and Patrick Galvin
Tel 02380 570070 Email merrybear2000@hotmail.com

Varieties are the spice of life

Susan and Jason Hunt

www.carpacciodachshunds.co.uk

©advertising & photography Croft-Elliott

KINGROCK
est 1975

CH KINGROCK CAPTAIN COOK JW

Shown winning second in the group at Bournemouth under Peter Jolley.

Captain started the year in style by winning the **RCC and BPIS** at his first show of 2012 and his last in puppy. He was then shown at 9 championship shows through his junior career and won **7 CCs (all with BOB) and 2 RCCs.**

photo Higham Press

Captain's daughter

KINGROCK EASTER SURPRISE

made her debut at The Junior Bulldog Club's Centenary Championship Show and won a large Minor Puppy class at 6 months of age.

OUR FRENCH BULLDOGS WERE REPRESENTED THIS YEAR BY OUR NEW PUPPY

KINGROCK WILLO

photographed at her first show, Bournemouth, at just over 6 months of age, where she was 2nd from a class of 10. She followed this up a month later, at Richmond, where she was 2nd from an entry of 14. Willo is sired by one of our own stud dogs and out of a bitch who recently became our 11th French Bulldog champion.

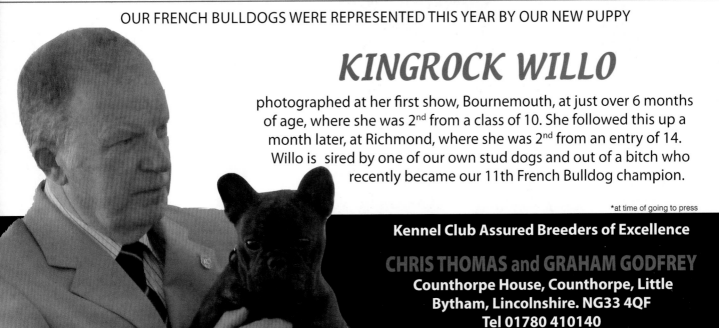

*at time of going to press

Kennel Club Assured Breeders of Excellence

CHRIS THOMAS and GRAHAM GODFREY
Counthorpe House, Counthorpe, Little Bytham, Lincolnshire. NG33 4QF
Tel 01780 410140
email kingrock@fsmail.net
website www.kingrock.co.uk

BIS (Stella) & Res BIS (Alex)

Lamlux Noma Brey at Waterley Imp DK

TTA Ch Show 2012

BPIS first time out TTA CH Show

The day after the show !

Breeder: Pat Tempest

America's
Number
ONE
Lakeland
Terrier

Multiple
BIS Winner

Westminster KC
BOB 2012

Owners: Tony Barker,
Maria M. Sacco and Susan Fraser

Breeders: Norman Kenney,
Lynda Kenney, Susan Fraser and
Maria M. Sacco

Handler: RC and Shari Boyd Carusi
Assisted by Catherine Pikul

We would like
to thank all of
the judges
for awarding
our Lakeland
The Best Spot
in the Ring

©advertising &
photography
Croft-Elliott

SPOT

America's
★Number★
TWO
Terrier

2

MBIS BISS AM GCH CAN CH
Larkspur Acadia Save Me A Spot

AM CAN CH Northcote No Doubt X
AM CH Larkspur Acadia October Sky, JE

OREGONIAN
BYMIL
+ BIMWICH
+ DEAVITTE

photo Andrew Taylor

His daughters

CH BYMIL GOLD SYLPH
and
CH BYMIL BLACK NYMPH
(born 1983)

... and today

photo Carol Ann Johnson

Sarah, Simon and Diana with

OREGONIAN SNOW QUEEN and
CH OREGONIAN RAISE AN EYEBROW

portrait by Deirdre Ashdown

CH FITZDOWN
DORIAN OF DEAVITTE
(born 1981)

photo David Dalton

His great-grandaughter

CH BIMWICH APHRODITE
(born 1990)

SARAH TAYLOR
bymil@btopenworld.com

DIANA KING
bimwich@btinternet.com

SIMON PARSONS
wortencottage@hotmail.co.uk

OREGONIAN

CH OREGONIAN RAISE AN EYEBROW
(Barwal Brave Beau, one CC, ex Oregonian Fay Wray, two CCs)

Three CCs,
each with BOB
Two RCCs
Best puppy in show,
Welsh Corgi League
Pet Plan junior stakes
finalist, fifth place

Litter sister
OREGONIAN RAISE A LAUGH
has **two reserve CCs**
Litter brother
OREGONIAN RAY BAN
has **one CC** for
Carrie Acors and
Matthew Thomas

© Will Harris

photos Will Harris

OREGONIAN SNOW QUEEN
(Ermyn Snow Knight, one CC
ex Ch Oregonian Lady Penelope)

photo Carol Ann Johnson

©Johnson

Four times **Best Puppy**, **Reserve CC**,
Puppy Group 2
Her dam won **her fourth CC** at National
Working and Pastoral, doing the double with
Raise An Eyebrow

BYMIL SMILE PLEASE
(Ch Belroyd Pemcader Cymro
ex Ch Bymil Picture This)

photo Andrew Taylor

Seven times **best puppy, three reserve CCs.**
Litter brother **BYMIL SCREEN TEST FOR CORBEN** has a **reserve CC** and many other
awards for Alison Benson
Their history-making dam won her **31st CC**
at Crufts, her only appearance of 2012.

Karmore Vallhunds

Vastgota True Topaz for Karmore (imp Canada)

Wenna continues her winning ways

2 CCs

3 RCCs

My thanks to all judges concerned

Chris Millard breednotes@btinternet.com

© Johnson

photo Johnson

2

TUSSALUD PAPILLONS

Ch Denemore Story's Echo at Tussalud   9 CCs and 7 BOB

Ch/Fin Ch Siljans Ragge JR Connection at Tussalud   11 CCs and 10 BOB

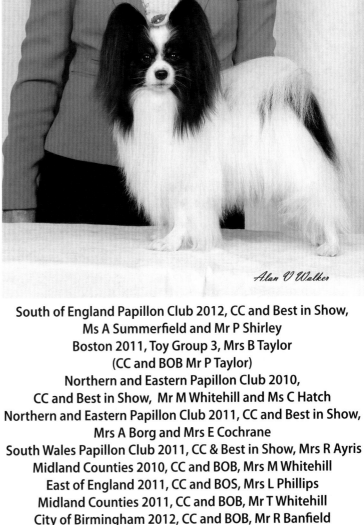

Alan V Walker

WELKS 2011, Toy Group 2,
Mrs Z Thorn-Andrews (CC and BOB Miss H Barr)
Darlington 2012, Toy Group 3, Mr S Bardwell
(CC and BOB Mr F Kane)
Three Counties 2012, Toy Group 4,
Mr W Browne-Cole (CC and BOB Mrs J Lilley)
Papillon Club 2012, CC and Best in Show
Mrs L Cartledge and Mrs J Banfield
Birmingham National 2012,
CC and BOB, Mr G Urquhart
City of Birmingham 2011, CC and BOB, Mrs C Roe
South of England Papillon Club 2011, CC and RBIS,
Mrs J Banfield (RBIS Mr R Banfield)
Border Union 2010, CC and BOB, Mr G Robb
LKA 2009, CC (at 7 months of age) Ms A Oliver

South of England Papillon Club 2012, CC and Best in Show,
Ms A Summerfield and Mr P Shirley
Boston 2011, Toy Group 3, Mrs B Taylor
(CC and BOB Mr P Taylor)
Northern and Eastern Papillon Club 2010,
CC and Best in Show, Mr M Whitehill and Ms C Hatch
Northern and Eastern Papillon Club 2011, CC and Best in Show,
Mrs A Borg and Mrs E Cochrane
South Wales Papillon Club 2011, CC & Best in Show, Mrs R Ayris
Midland Counties 2010, CC and BOB, Mrs M Whitehill
East of England 2011, CC and BOS, Mrs L Phillips
Midland Counties 2011, CC and BOB, Mr T Whitehill
City of Birmingham 2012, CC and BOB, Mr R Banfield
Richmond 2012, CC and BOB, Ms E Patrick
Midland Counties 2012, CC and BOB, Mrs S Morrell

Our grateful thanks to breeders Sean Carroll and James Newman (Denemore) and Ulla Hanis (Siljans)

Owned and handled by Kay Stewart and Kirsten Stewart-Knight
Grandmother and Granddaughter show team
01582 881223   tussalud@hotmail.com

SOLSTRAND HOUNDS

Mascotts Maserati

Solstrand Arthur Ardfhuil

Having scaled down on number of dogs over the past few years, we now only show occasionally the CC winner SOLSTRAND ARTHUR ARDFHUIL and hope to bring out his young daughter SOLSTRAND BILLIE JO.
Arthur has proved to be a really good stud dog, with two Champions and two further CC winning offspring.
He has won the Stud Dog Trophy for 2012 from both the Irish Wolfhound Club and the Irish Wolfhound Society.
Over the years 15 UK Greyhound Champions have been owned/bred at SOLSTRAND, as well as 11 UK Irish Wolfhound Champions, again owned or bred.
Numerous overseas and Continental champions also in both breeds

Nick Pordham and Dagmar Kenis Pordham

Peters Farm, Rusper, Horsham, West Sussex, RH12 4RN

dagmarkp@btinternet.com

Pendley
ROTTWEILERS AND CAIRN TERRIERS

PENDLEY PLAYAWAY JW
1 CC 1 RCC
(Ch/Sw Ch Raskens Romping Playboy
ex Birselaw Only Make Believe to Pendley 2 RCCs)

We are delighted to be back showing Cairns again, after making up twelve Rottweiler champions, as this is where it all started back in 1974. Pendley Playaway has won consistently through the year. She was joined by her half-sister Pendley Hester (Ch Larchlea Licence To Thrill at Stanedykes ex Birselaw Only Make Believe to Pendley) who attended 5 Championship Shows and won 4 firsts, 1 second and 3 Best Puppy awards. Hester is now growing a new coat and we hope to campaign both girls next year. The Rottweilers have taken a back seat this year with Pendley Goldie producing her first litter. From this Pandora, Phoenix, Parker and Patrick have all qualified for Crufts and we wish their owners continued success in 2013.
We hope to have quality litters in both breeds in 2013.

June Yates and Joanne Johnson
Newstead, Robins Folly, Thurleigh
Beds MK44 2EQ
01234 772542 07970 758291
www.pendleyrottweilers.co.uk

RiC

CH IR CH Blackdale Supreme

CH IR CH Blackdale The Diamond X
Blackdale Alma
DOB 16.11.2010

**Multiple All-Breed Best In Show
Winner from Puppy Class**
Dublin Dog Show Society
& Cloghran Dog Show

UK CH Title in 9 Days

Fox Terrier Expo Weekend:
BIS The Fox Terrier Club
RBIS Fox Terrier Club of Wales
Supreme BIS over both days
in a combined entry of over 300

BIS Wire Fox Terrier Association

BIS Fox Terrier Club of Scotland
50th Anniversary Show

**Blackdale Kennels, Ireland
Harry O'Donoghue**
blackdalekennels@eircom.net
00353 4293 35538

Handler Andrew Goodsell

©advertising & photography Croft-Elliott

OVER 30 YEARS WITHIN THE BREED

TOP BREEDER 2012 DOG WORLD

19 UK KENNEL CLUB CHAMPIONS & MANY OVERSEAS

HOME OF CH STARVON RUMOUR HAS IT

TOP VALLHUND 2010 2011 2012 DOG WORLD

THIS YEAR PAGE IS DEDICATED TO REG

TEL: 01672 540900

Top Vallhund Brood Bitch 2012 Top Pastoral
4th Overall (At Time of Press)

CH STARVON RUMOUR HAS IT
TOP SWEDISH VALLHUND
2010 2011 2012
DOG WORLD

2009 TOP PUPPY OUR DOGS

www.philgoughphotography.com

CH STARVON FANTASTIC LIGHT TOP STUD DOG 2010 2012 DOG WORLD

STARVON SWEDISH VALLHUNDS

STARVON VALLEY OF DREAMS

Tim & Ada West

www.freewebs.com/starvon/

STARVON VANQUISH

OWNED BY PENNY LEWIS

CH STARVON REACH FOR THE STARS

STARVON VENI VIDI VICI

OWNED BY DEBBIE HOWE & PHIL GOUGH

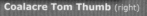

MELFIELD LOWCHEN and PORTUGUESE WATER DOGS

ROYAL GROWL LOUIS VUITTON VIA MELFIELD (IMP FIN)

BOB Scottish Kennel Club

Sincere thanks to ILPO OJALA for entrusting me with Louis, sired by the multi titled
Chic Choix Markey Lifar
ex Fin/Norw/Sw/Est Ch Melfield Sam's Angel, litter sister to my
Ch MELFIELD ANGEL IN BLACK, 10 CCs
(below)

©Johnson

MELFIELD CHASING DIAMONDS

Lucy has gained many
Best Puppy awards and
Best Puppy in Show
Sheringham and District
qualifing her for Top Puppy
of East Anglia competition

JOCELYN CREFFIELD

KC ASSURED BREEDER

email melfieldk9@btinternet.com

Tel 01449 744250

photo Walker

217

COPPERGOLD SIMPLY SURREAL AT TIGRATO

2 CCs, 2 RCCs won at:
Crufts 2012 –
judge Mrs Doreen Cram

Birmingham National 2012 –
judge Mr Andrew Brace

Boston Terrier Club 2012 –
judge Mr Frank Kane

Driffield 2011 –
Judge Mr William McKay

Also won RBIS, BB, BP Boston Terrier Club of Scotland
– Judge Mrs Maria Meredith

Many thanks to all the judges who have appreciated her many qualities
Dr and Mrs JACKSON, Haddington, East Lothian

ALLTOT OLIVIA

Miss Jenny Gorwill
Alltot Cottage
3 Grove Road
Llandow
near Cowbridge
CF71 7NY
01656 890249
email jengorwill777@
btinternet.com

COPPERGOLD BOSTON TERRIERS

Joss
COPPERGOLD SIMPLY A SWAGMAN

Phinn
TOPTUXEUDO ROCKET SUPREMO AT COPPERGOLD

Shown very little, but both our boys have done well in the show ring.
Coppergold Simply A Swagman would like to wish his sister Coppergold Simply Surreal well for the 2013 season, and we hope she does not have to wait too long before she gains her title.

Puppies due end of November

Mrs K M GLYNN, Ms J GLYNN and Miss J K WILLIAMS
Coppergoldbostons@ntlworld.com

ASTEREL Est 1977
Estrela Mountain Dogs
THE "A" TEAM STRIKE AGAIN IN 2012

TOP BITCH
TOP BROOD BITCH

TOP DOG
TOP STUD DOG*

LIBRIUM WHIPPETS
Top Whippet 2012

photo Morgan Slätt

Librium's Jazz Festival

We have had great fun in the rings this year including BIS and BOS at the Norwegian Whippet Show! **Norw Swed Dan Ch Librium's Incredible Love** (picture top left) is Top Whippet 2012 at time of writing. **Librium's Jazz Festival**, pictured above with Knut, is doing very well with several big wins in Norway and Denmark – all from junior and youth class. Our beautiful free moving baby, **Librium's Marmelade N Tea** made a stunning debut with BOB, group and BPIS! At her other show so far she won BOB and the group!

These lovely Whippets co-owned by Cecilie and Knut Fr Blütecher, Showline Greyhounds, are among our strong team at Librium Whippets.

Six different Librium Whippets won CCs in 2012.

Gerd Røssland
www.kennel-librium.com
Norway

NASAILLEEN

Dewerstone **TOP BREEDERS 2012**

WHAT A YEAR

PHOTO BY HILARY WHITE

roudi relaxing with debra

10 CC'S 6 BOB'S

GROUP 4 DRIFFIELD 2012

4 BOB'S WITHOUT CC'S

BPIS BELFAST & GSOW 2011

THANK YOU TO ALL THE JUDGES WHO HAVE THOUGHT SO HIGHLY OF OUR BOY

SHCH NASAILLEEN IN THE BUFF

TOP AMERICAN COCKER SPANIEL 2012*

ALSO HOME TO

Puppy

CAN CH & SH CH AFTERGLOW TANYA HIDE
TOP BROOD BITCH 2012

SH CH NASAILLEEN BEWITCHED   3 CC'S 3 RCC'S

BEST IN SHOW HOME COUNTIES AMERICAN COCKER SPANIEL CLUB

PHOTO BY HILARY WHITE

BREEDER OWNERS LISA BRYANT

& LEANNE BRYANT

CO OWNED BY MARK NELSON

LISA BRYANT@LIVE·CO·UK   07976007761

FYLDE PET PARLOUR   01772687396

* AT TIME OF GOING TO PRESS   ADVERT BY LEANNE BRYANT

Tirkane

Celebrates
Making
Toy Poodle
History

BESSIE

INT CH IR CH Tirkane Spiced Gold
CJW07 WW08

The First Apricot Toy Poodle
To Be Top Brood Bitch &
World Winner & Best of Breed

www.tirkane.com

CONSISTENT
Breeding
CONSISTENT
Results

Tirkane

Breeders
& Owners
Ann Ingram
& Kay Ryan

UK IR CH
Tirkane Deja Vue
CJW12

Bessie's
CH Kids

DE, INT, BEL, NL, LUX, IR CH
Tirkane Coeur De Lion
AW10, CWjnr10, 2 UK CCs

ESTAVA RAIN AMERICAN AKITAS

"PARIS"
Estava Rain Fashion Never Sleeps

Group winner at SKK
Triple Int. Show, Sweden

ESTAVA RAIN
AMERICAN AKITA

GBCH
Estava Rain Hold The News

Champion in 3
straight shows

First none UK/US breed
Akita to become GBCH

"DIAMOND"
Estava Rain Show Me a Rock

NewZealand – Kodo Akitas

Australian CH
Estava Rain Expand Your Horizon

Pictured winning BOB at
Brisbane Royal, Australia

www.estavarain.no

ESTAVA RAIN AMERICAN AKITAS

"AUDREY"
Estava Rain Carrying Stars

Nr.1 American Akita bitch
in Scandinavia 2012

Specialty BOB 2012

2 x Best in Show

GBCH INTCH NORDCH
Redwitch Adrenaline Junkie
Dog CC & BOS at Crufts 2012
World Winner 2012
Nordic Winner 2010 & 2011
No. 1 American Akita in Scandinavia 2012

Estava Rain Breeders Group
The World Dog Show 2012

No. 1 Breeder in FCI group 5
Norway 2011

ESTAVA RAIN
AMERICAN AKITA

www.estavarain.no

THE UK'S
TOP
DOG
OF ALL
BREEDS
2012

Lilly

© I.C-E
unretouched

CH Soletrader Peek A Boo

CH Soletrader Peek A Boo

Owned by
Sara Robertson
& Wendy Doherty

© LC-E
unretouched

© LC-E
unretouched

'VALENTISIMO' Spanish Water Dogs

'A tradition of quality' Presenting this rustic breed throughout the UK and Europe

Proud owners of

Sp & Sw Ch Curioso De la Ribera del Genil Del Valentisimo

During his short time in the UK with us Paco has racked up an astonishing...
14 BOBs (Including CRUFTS 2011/12), 2 Group 4s (Windsor 2011 and Richmond 2012)

His wins abroad include:

BIS Swedish Monografica 2011 BIS Spanish Monografica 2009, Andalucian Champion 2008/09/10 CACIBs,

9 CACs, 3 RCACIBs, 6 RCACs, Tvaaker National and International Shows Sweden 2011: Swe Ch, BOB, 1st Group 8, 3rd BIS... BOTH DAYS! Winner of the Champions Class at the Spanish Monografica 2011 and runner-up 2012

Our thanks go to those judges who saw Paco worthy of all of his wins and a huge thank you to Salvador Cabrera Garcia for letting Paco live with us!

Not to be outdone, our team of fantastic young bitches who have taken **multiple BB/ RBBs, BOB/BOS including BIS at the SWD Club Show 2012 Pona, Lizar and Tica** placed 2nd, 3rd and 5th in the Spanish Monografica 2012

We look forward to showing our new puppies:

Torres (Valentisimo's Torres) - 2nd Junior Dog GBAS 2012 (Crufts Qualified 2013!) Chica (Valentisimo's Chicita)- 4 Best Puppy in Breeds (3 Championship & 1 Open), Puppy Group 2 (Open Show) and Puppy Group 4 (Championship)

A special note of congratulations to all of those with Paco puppies and dogs bred by Valentisimo who have qualified for Crufts 2013, we look forward to seeing you all there next year as well throughout the year enjoying your dogs!

We would now like to take this time to thank all of our friends both here and around the world for the kindness and support you have shown in our journey to preserve the rustic and untainted qualities of this enchanting breed while still retaining its strong and unique working ability.

©Johnson

NIGEL, JENNY and BEN EGGINTON   Email nigel@spanishwaterdog.net   Telephone 01246 888081
www.spanishwaterdog.net or follow us on Facebook   www.facebook.com/spanishwaterdogs

KARAMYND

Introducing two new UK Champions in 2012 making a total of 14 UK, 10 International and 20 overseas Karamynd Champions

CH KARAMYND PLAY IT AGAIN
(Morgan)

Reserve Best in Show
Bath Championship Show 2012

5 CCs (4 x BOB), 5 RCCs

1 Group 1, 1 Group 3 and 2 Group 4

WHWT Club of England Pup of the Year 2009

Runner-up Pro Plan/Dog World
Pup of the Year 2009

UK/INT/DUTCH/BEL/GER KFT CH/GER VDH/DUTCH JNR CH/GER KFT JNR CH KARAMYND GUNS WITH ROSES
(Axel)

Top WHWT Male Netherlands 2011

Not forgetting **Ch Karamynd On Cue for Kingsview** CC Crufts 2012 and her litter sister **Ch Karamynd Drama Queen** who won 2 RCCs and **Karamynd Make A Splash** who won 3 RCCs in 2012

Thanks to all the judges who thought so highly of my dogs.

Owned and loved by Jennie Griffiths 01694 751326

CH ESQUIMAUX PRINCE OF FALLON JW ShCM

©Johnson

HOTdog mag

'Goose'
Handled by **ABBIE STOUTT**
UK Junior Handler of the Year 2012

CC - Richmond September 2011 - Keith Nathan
CC - Midland Counties October 2011 - Rodi Hübenthal
CC and BOB - East of England July 2012 - John Purnell
CC - Darlington September 2012 - Bob Cross

Bred by Peter and Nicky Shakeshaft
Owned by **SHELDON and CAROLINE STOUTT**
caroline.stoutt@tribune.co.uk Tel +44 7770 638536

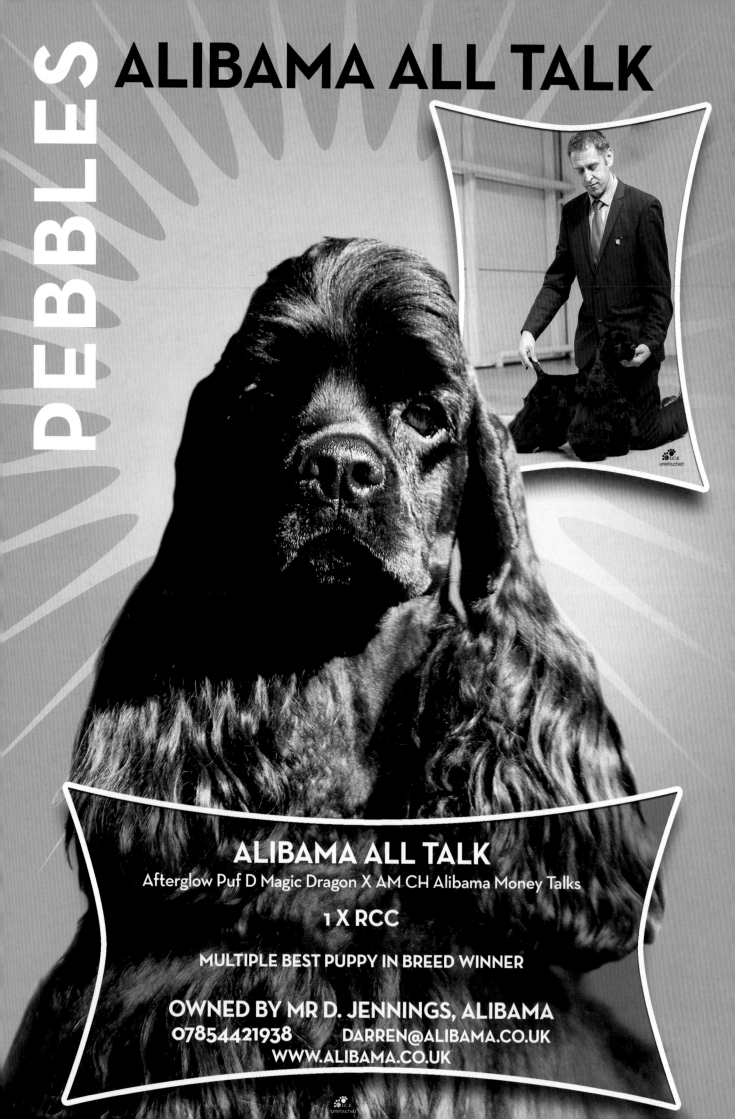

PEBBLES

ALIBAMA ALL TALK

ALIBAMA ALL TALK
Afterglow Puf D Magic Dragon X AM CH Alibama Money Talks

1 X RCC

MULTIPLE BEST PUPPY IN BREED WINNER

OWNED BY MR D. JENNINGS, ALIBAMA
07854421938   DARREN@ALIBAMA.CO.UK
WWW.ALIBAMA.CO.UK

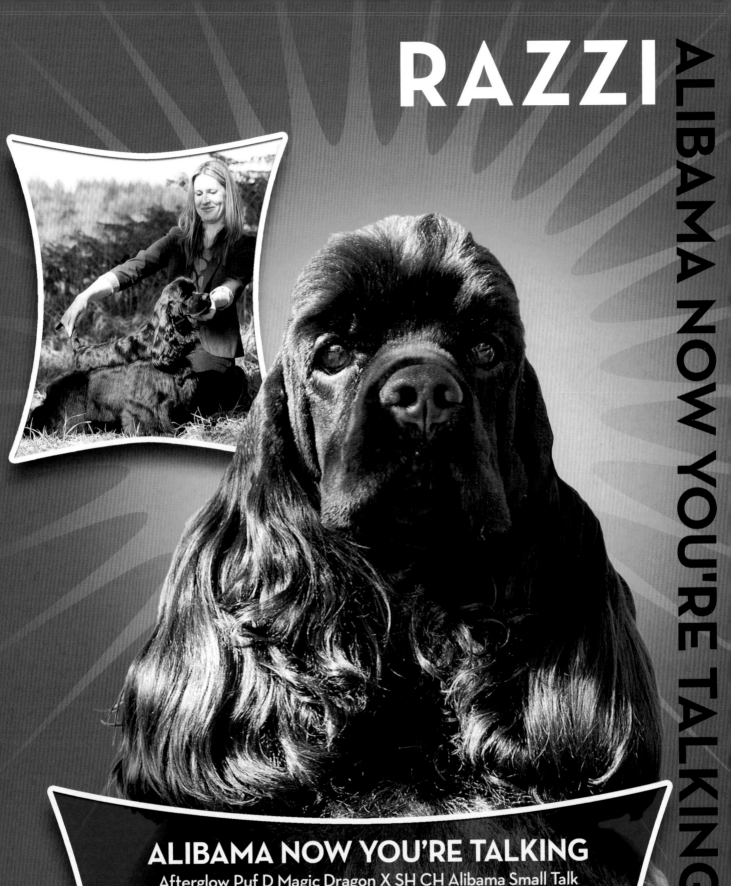

RAZZI

ALIBAMA NOW YOU'RE TALKING

ALIBAMA NOW YOU'RE TALKING
Afterglow Puf D Magic Dragon X SH CH Alibama Small Talk

BPIS Royal Cornwall, RBIS & BPIS Cornwall Gundog Show,
RBPIS Tavistock and district
MULTIPLE BEST PUPPY IN BREED WINNER

OWNED BY MR R. AND MISS N. WALKER

Bradley

Liskarn Forever Faithfull

Photo at 14 weeks

Frankie

Top Puppy 2012
Moyannbern Frankie
Goes To Bollywood

Liskarn

Lisa and Gordon Bridges
Lisabridges976@btinternet.com
07811498586

©advertising & photography Croft-Elliott

Every accomplishment starts with the decision to try

Smurf

Liskarn No Secret
We Love You

Top Puppy 2012
Best Puppy In Show
WPBOW 2012

photo Roberta Porter

Ch/Am Grand Ch Veldtkammer Assle Me Litely
RIO
2011 - the UK's joint TOP RHODESIAN RIDGEBACK
2010 - the USA's No. 4 Rhodesian Ridgeback Bitch (AKC Top Dogs All-Breed points)

photo J M Bates

photo Lena Piehl

Thank you to our 2012 Judges for another top-ranking year
Since returning to the UK in March 2011, Rio has been
awarded 15 CCs (11 with Best of Breed) 6 Reserve CCs
and 3 Group Placements.

Rio is owned, loved and handled by **Kim Hodge**,
Colkeririn Rhodesian Ridgebacks
www.colkeririnrhodesianridgebacks.com
Bred by Mr M J and Mrs L A Parke, Veldtkammer Ridgebacks

Ankors
Winners, champions and history makers

CH RARJO IT HAD TO BE YOU FOR ANKORS

Top Portuguese Water Dog 2011 halfway leader 2012. Teal has the honour of being the first Brown bitch champion and is looking forward to her litter in the new year – bookings are now being taken for well bred puppies.

LIDDYLEAZE LADY GODIVA FOR ANKORS
- Evie
(Left) 2 CCs, 7 RCCs

ANGELCREST DIZZY BLONDE AT ANKORS
-Vera
Owned with Mrs R Turley (right)

Our thanks to all those who have thought so highly of the girls and special thanks to Ruth Bussell, Rachael Reddin, Rose Turley, Louise Turley and Sarah McGill.

ANTONY BONGIOVANNI and JOHN HEARD
Portuguese Water Dog
ankorsph@aol.com

LINDA BISS and JIM SAWYER
Chinese Crested and Mexican Hairless
ankorsch@aol.com

In June we welcomed Pearly (pictured)
to Whittimere where she quickly
achieved her crown
(and Group 2 at Paignton) to become
Ch/Ir Ch Ennafort The One And Only
at 18 months of age –
our 14th Elkhound Champion

Robert Greaves,
Nicola and William Croxford
www.whittimere.co.uk

Ch Ragus Merry Gentleman

Top Terrier 2012

at press closing date

1 BIS

2 x RBIS

5 x Group 1

Numerous other Group Placings

Owned by

Lesley Crawley

and

Matthew Oddie

17160

PARIS

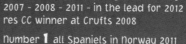

244

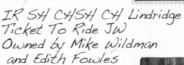

POST CARD

FOR ADDRESS ONLY

IR SH CH/SH CH Lindridge
Ticket To Ride JW
Owned by Mike Wildman
and Edith Fowles
20 CCs 9 BOB, 12 rCC
Best Veteran in Show
Cocker Spaniel Club
110th Anniversary
Champ Show 2012
& North Wales
Cocker Spaniel Club
Champ Show

..into the

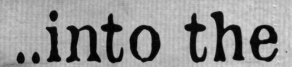

POST

FOR CORRESPONDENCE

SH CH Travellers Joy of
Malpas, Owned by Mike
Wildman and Mandy Edwards
4 CC, 2 RCC and 3 BOB
Made up to Show Champion
at Windsor Dog Show 2012

wild.

POST CARD

FOR CORRESPONDENCE   FOR ADDRESS ONLY

Charbonnel Ermine'n'Pearls JW,
Owned by Mike Wildman and
Sandy Platt

1 RCC - Our rising star
consistent class winner.

Enquires Mike Wildman
Classie Grooming
07793755905
Mandy Edwards
Marlinson Cocker Spaniels
07486550006

Series 321 A

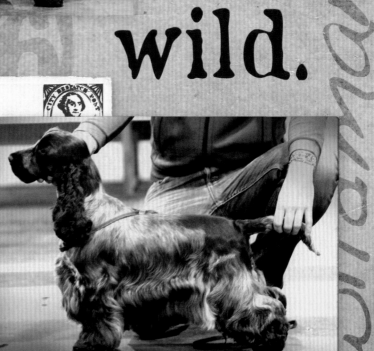

Glenchess

Alan V Walker

Glenchess Vaeltaja

Glenchess
Ilolas

Millermead
Quintessence
To Glenchess

Owned by ELAINE and STEVE SHORT Tel 01746 862323

TRAILFINDER BLOODHOUNDS

Ch Trailfinder Fortitude
Sadly missed
18 CC's ~ 9 BOB ~ 8 Res CC

FOLLOWING IN HIS FATHERS FOOTSTEPS
CH TRAILFINDER KITCHENER
8 CC'S ~ 4BOB'S ~ 4resCC'S
BEST IN SHOW
BLOODHOUND CLUB CHAMPIONSHIP 2011
BLOODHOUND CLUB CHAMPIONSHIP 2012
ASSOC. BLOODHOUND BREEDERS 2012

AT THE BEGINNING OF HER CAREER
TRAILFINDER MOONBEAM

INTRODUCING THE
NEXT GENERATION:
TRAILFINDER NIGHTHAWK & TRAILFINDER NICETY

Bred Owned & Adored
by David & Helen Powell
Tel 01647 24727
info@bloodhounds.co.uk

Lexi . . .

Tuwos Jackie 'O' JW
1 RCC
1 Green Star & B.O.B
Irish P.O.T.Y Qualifier

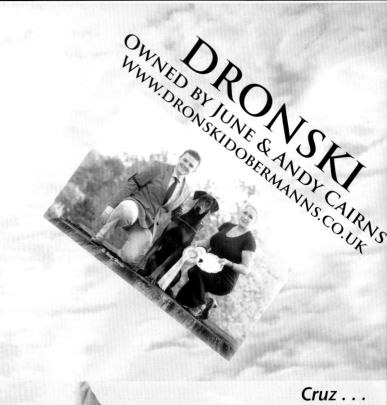

Cruz . . .

Uk Ch Supeta's Secret Wizard JW ShCM
6 CC'S 10 RCC'S
Group 1 W.E.L.K.S
Group 2 Three Counties
2 Green Star 2 B.O.B

Dronski's Amadeus
2 B.P.I.B
Pro Plan Dog World P.O.T.Y Qualifier

Boss . . .

Afilador show team

Afilador A Hint Of Jasmine
Jazmin

Along with her brother Bandit and mother Juno, she has been part of the winning breeders group again this year. We have exceeded the 25 points required to compete at Crufts 2013.

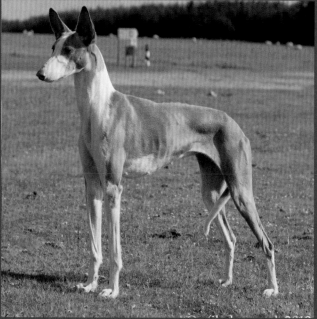

Diecisiete Mandarina at Afilador ShCM
Kalusha

After some time out of the ring Kally has returned as a veteran. On her début as a veteran, she won the Best Veteran in Hound Group at Torquay. She has won at both open and championship level again in 2012.

Afilador Moonlight Shadow ShCM
Bandit

Bandit has been a star again this year, competing in junior handling, handled by Maria Clark and Catlin Channon

© afilador.co.uk

Mansiya Witch's Familiar at Afilador ShCM
Raven

Raven gained his ShCM in July 2012, and again had a successful year in the ring in 2012 both at open and championship shows.

Thank you to all the judges who have made this all possible, and to my dear friends Chris and Di, aka the 'Beagle girls', for helping us out this year.

Thank you to all the other dog owners who have given me the opportunity to handle their beautiful dogs throughout 2012. Long may this continue.

Please visit us at www.afilador.co.uk and you can follow us on Facebook too.

**Amanda Carter (Afilador) and
Roberta Hozempa (Amahte) present our boy**

Amahte Runnin On Jamaican Time (imp Can) JW ShCM

Bolt

Winning Best in Show at SWHC at just 13 months old.

Has had a fabulous first year in the ring:

Gaining his Stud Book number by winning the RDCC The National Dog Show at just 8 months old.

Gaining his Show Certificate of Merit in just 11 shows winning his first Adult Hound Group at the tender age of 6 months old.

Gaining his Junior Warrant. The first Ibizan Hound for 6 years to gain this award.

Winning at open and championship show level.

All this before he was 12 months old.

© afilador.co.uk 2012

Thank you to all the judges who have made this possible, and to all Bolt's many fans for their messages and support.

Also to my co-owner, partner, and Bolt's breeder: Roberta Hozempa, for allowing Bolt to become a part of my family here in the UK

kennel
Larhjelm

Lars Hjelmtvedt
Odderudveien 20
NO-3089 Holmestrand
Norway
Tel: 00 47 416 60 485
www.larhjelm.net
lars@larhjelm.net

Design: westaway.no

Eukanuba

Yum Yum JW

Ziggy JW

Because I Am Yours
JW

Laura Wiltshire

Judith Gregory
www.tonkory.com

Fernlea, Yate Road, Iron Acton
Bristol, BS37 9XY
01454 228418
judith1gregory@gmail.com

Tonkory

Up And Coming

Alan V Walker

This year I pay tribute to my young dogs
that are doing so well:

Up and Coming - 1 cc & 2 Res cc's

Yum Yum - 1 cc & Best in Show BCCGB

Ziggy - 2 Res cc's

Because I Am Yours - qualified for the
Junior Warrant semi finals 2012

Thank you to all the fit young people who have run my dogs for me in the ring this
year & Congratulations to the many Tonkory Border Collie owners who are
doing so well in the ring and in other disciplines

Anita Gowing

255

ROMAINVILLE GLEN OF IMAAL TERRIERS

Romainville Billy Whizz
Joint Top Puppy 2012 (at time of going to press)
3 Res CCs, 2 Best Dog

Sire: Bailielands BB Ben
Dam: Romainville Rhian
Crd3/GPRA Clear

Romainville Lily
I CC, RBPIS

Sire: Gerrardstown Frederick of Knockroe
Dam: Co Co of Romainville
Crd3/GPRA Clear

We are proud of our show team results: Billie's sister Jean Genie has many wins to her credit, Romainville Inki (Top Puppy 2011) has four Best Bitch awards and Ellie has just gained Best of Breed under a breed specialist judge. We are pleased others have won well with our breeding as the photos below show, other exhibitors: Mr Whitehouse with R Tigan (Res CCs) and Kyla (I CC) Mr and Mrs Ashcroft with R Typhoon (Res CCs) and Ms Linda Smith with R Bodhran (2 CCs, 2 Green Stars, CACs). Puppies expected next year.

KATHY GEORGE

Tel 01432 880819   email kathy@romainvillegsd.freeserve.co.uk   www.glenofimaalterriers.co.uk

---

PAJANTICKS PRESENTS
Romainville Aoife
I CC, I Res CC

Sire: Feohanagh Bryan at Romainville
Dam: Romainville Ali Oop (RCC)
Crd3/GPRA Clear

Our new puppy Pajanticks Star Trouper makes his debut in December.
He is by Feohanagh Bryan ex Pajanticks Patsy Jane
Handling and hair by Lydia!
Puppies expected next year
JANE WITHERS 01635 201489
jwgranarykennels@aol.com

Ch Johnny Be Good at Romainville

Sire: Gerrardstown Frederick at Knockroe
Dam: Fizz of Romainville
Crd3/GPRA Clear

Handled by Simon Cockayne
'Woody's' CCs: Bath Eileen Foy; Darlington Paul Wilkinson; SWKA Harold Gay all with BOB

Proudly owned by CRESTA GARNER

TREVARGH THE ENTERTAINER
AT BRIZEWOOD
"WOODY"

62 BOB'S AT CH. SHOWS
BOB CRUFTS 2012
2 X GROUP 4
4 X BIS AT OPEN SHOWS

Proudly owned by

Babs Harding & Elaine Whitehill

email: uk.toller@btinternet.com

Tel: 01235 813749

© Brizewood

Ruddyduck

Finnish Lapphunds and Nova Scotia Duck Tolling Retrievers

Blairswolf Tulikki of Ruddyduck WW'12

(Fin Ch Chelville Tapio ex Thulens Jenni Beg Ex.)
Hips 6:5=11, Elbows 0, Hereditary Clear prcd-PRA, MDR-1 Clear, Current Clear Eye Certificate

Eeva has been lightly shown this year. She was BOB at Manchester (Stuart Band) and made her FCI debut winning World Winner, CACIB and CACA at the World Show in Salzburg (Jörgen Hindse, DK) and also World Club Winner, CACA and BOB at the World Club Show in Anif (Rodi Hübenthal, SE).

Camusmor Knockando at Ruddyduck Beg Ex.

(Narod The Impossible Dream ex Newfanova Jemima Bear at Camusmor)
Hips 4:4=8, Elbows 0, DNA Tested Clear for prcd-PRA, CEA/CH and DM, Current Clear Eye Certificate

Rupert returned to the obedience ring after a two year absence and promptly won out of Beginners at BAGSD Birmingham North Open Show (Gerard Paisley).

Rupert is consistently placed at Championship Shows in both Veteran and Open classes, he is planning to spend the winter training for Novice and attending the odd Open Show to keep an eye on the youngsters

He wishes all his offspring, current and future, continued health and success.

Both Eeva and Rupert are loved, trained and handled by Rachel Bradley

ruddyduck@duck-toller.co.uk   www.ruddyduck.org.uk

BITCON & FERNDEL

These two kennels have been responsible for 72 UK Champions

SH CH BITCON WIZARD OF OZ

4 CCs
3 Res CCs
2 BOB
Group 3
The youngest
UK Vizsla Show Champion
gaining his title at 15 months

MORAY ARMSTRONG
Bramdene, Cargo Beck,
Carlisle CA6 4BB
Tel 01228 674318

SH CH FERNDEL AERON MAGREGOR

Top Welsh Springer 2011
and 2012*
20 CCs
Group 1
and many group placings

JOHN THIRLWELL
Whickham Hill South,
Whickham Highway, Gateshead NE11 9QL
Tel 0191 4887168
Email ferndel@jthirlwell.fsnet.co.uk

*at time of going to press

Charibere Pyreneans

©Johnson

CHARIBERE SIMPLY SPECIAL AT CHEZANNA JW

'KODI'

Pyrenean Mountain Dog
Born 11.10.11
Ch Gillandant Rockafella ex
Ch Charibere Savannah
bred by Mrs Linda Marston

23 FIRSTS AT CHAMPIONSHIP SHOWS IN PUPPY, JUNIOR & POST GRADUATE COMBINED

1 BEST PUPPY IN SHOW AT A GENERAL OPEN SHOW

1 BEST PUPPY IN SHOW AT THE PYRENEAN MOUNTAIN DOG CLUB OF GB BREED OPEN SHOW

1 BEST PUPPY IN SHOW AT THE PYRENEAN MOUNTAIN DOG CLUB OF SCOTLAND BREED OPEN SHOW

14 BEST PUPPY DOG INCLUDING 7 BEST PUPPY IN BREED

PUPPY GROUP 4 THREE COUNTIES CHAMPIONSHIP SHOW

RDCC W/PB OF SCOTLAND

Many thanks to all the judges who have thought so highly of our special boy

Proudly owned and loved by **Christine Kenyon and Arthur Ward**
www.charibereandchezannapyreneans.com

262

Impressive Bull Lady Diana
(photo at 22 weeks of age)
Sire: Int Ch Be Ch Sebyan Wilson Ocobo
(Bulldog Of Year 2011 NL)
Dam: Snoopy Doggy Dog Sue
(daughter of Ch Iceglint I'm Harry
Bulldog Of Year 2008, 2009 and 2010)

Am & HK Ch Bee Serious Dream
No. 1 Top Gundog in Hong Kong 2010 and 2011
Best in Show at FCI Int Show 2011

Kingrock Easter Lily
(photo at 19 weeks of age)
Best Puppy in Group at FCI Int Show 2012
Sire: Ch Kingrock Captain Cook
Dam: Kingrock Charisma

Am & HK Ch Bee Serious Dawn
No. 1 Top Dog All Breed in Hong Kong 2005
Multi Best In Show Winner

www.traditionkennel.com

andler: Edmond Cheung   Owner: Alan Yi

Jansanleis

Ch Jansanleis Mayhem JW
5 CCs
2 RCCs
German Spitz Mittel

Ch Stormavon Sky Flyer to Jansanleis
3 CCs 3 RCCs
German Spitz Klein

Another great year in handling competitions for **Sinead Kerr-Moir, winning the JHA Utility 6-11years semi-final at Richmond with Purdi** (Ch Stormavon Sky Flyer to Jansanleis). Seen here with Mayhem

We are extremely proud that our homebred Mittel 'Mayhem' is the youngest champion in the breed, having won her **3rd CC** at only **13 months old**.

Owned by Jan, Sandi, Lisa and Sinead Moir
01968 672883

SCHERZANDO

Choices are the hinges of destiny

©advertising & photography Croft-Elliott

LC-E
unretouched

HAIR
IS
FAIR :)

CHINESE CRESTEDS
SHAMPOO

scherzandocrested.webs.com
chris@scherzando.co.uk
+44 (0)1962 793152

BALD
IS
BEAUTIFUL

CHINESE CRESTEDS
SHAMPOO

with   without

Scherzando Chinese Cresteds

THE BASSET GRIFFON VENDÉEN CLUB

The Officers and Committee of the BGV Club wish all BGV exhibitors and enthusiasts best wishes for 2013

Diary Dates:
BGV Club Open Show Sunday March 31
BGV Club AGM and Reunion Day Sunday April 21
BGV Club Championship Show Saturday November 9

Additional fun days, walks and events will be advised throughout the year.

For further information please check out the BGV Club website:
www.bgvclub.co.uk

CH DEBUCHER RIGOLE

7 CCs, all with BOB, 5 RCCs
His progeny constantly winning

Rigole's son

DEBUCHER GAUGUIN

RCC at his first show!
DOB 08/12/11

DEBUCHER XTRAVAGANT

2 RCCs, several BD and BOB awards
Co-owned with Dan and Danielle Baston
DOB 08/12/11

VIVIEN PHILLIPS
(00 44) 01442 851224
bassetsgriffonsvendeens.me.uk

DEBUCHER POMMES FRITES

DOB 30/06/12
I still breed lovely PBGVs and Dachshunds

DEBUCHER
strives to breed healthy hounds
with super temperaments and type

CH OVERBECKS CHEDDAR GEORGE

©*Dewerstone*

CCs from Mrs Jan Pain, Mr Rod Price and Miss Moa Persson

RCCs from Mrs E Bothwell, Mr A Rees and Mr J Pepper

Bred, owned and loved by

LYNNE SCOTT

Tel 01258 454613   email lynne.scott@overbeckspetits.co.uk

269

KEBULAK
Home of World Winning Terriers

- Top Kerry Blue Breeder 2011 and 2012
- Top Lakeland Terrier male 2012
- Top Kerry Blue Terrier Sire 2012*
- 40 UK and overseas champions
- 4 UK champions 2012
- 4 overseas champions 2012
- Top Lakeland Terrier and Top Breeder Ireland 2012
- Top Kerry and Kerry Blue Breeder Ireland 2012

Ch Kebulak Born To Tease 'Bruce'

Ch Kebulak Agent Provocateur
'Aleisha'

Ch Kebulak Man After Midnight
'Vegas'

Cara Davani
www.kebulak.com

cdavani@live.co.uk   01473 785411   07717 692854

at time of going to press

270

Musique German Spitz

Home to Klein and Mittel Champions
Introducing the German Spitz
Breed Record Holder Klein and Mittel

Photo by Nicky Garbutt

'Izzy'

Ch Nosregor Bewitched
for Musique
Breed Record Holder
with 32 CCs

Izzy's son
'Gibbs'
Musique Worth the Wait
Top Puppy 2012, one RCC
CC and BOB at South Wales
aged just 13 months

'Willow'
Ch Printzagems
Viva La Diva for Musique

Owned and adored by
Jan and Adi Chambers
musique@ntlworld.com
www.musiquegermanspitz.co.uk

Copyrights Karl DONVIL
www.123dog.net

ATILLA DU CLOS DE LA PRÈRE

Bitch   Born : 04.05.2005
Zeppo van het Kumtichshof ex Reine de la Sylve d'Or
Breeder : Mrs ROBERT Nicole (F)
Owner : Mrs Louis de Liedekerke-Ferraris
liedekerke.louis@wanadoo.fr

CSAUU – Temperament Test – Recommended Subject – French Schipperke Club
Junior European Champion and CAC – Helsinki 2006
Best Junior Bitch – *Princesse* – Belgian Schipperke Specialty 2006

Belgian, French, Gibraltar, Italian, Luxembourg, Monte Carlo, Portuguese and Spanish Champion
Greece 2 CAC/2 CACIB/2 BOB- Since 2012 no longer allowed to show docked tail dogs.
International Champion

Best Bitch– *Reine* - Belgian Schipperke Specialty 2008 and
in 2010
CAC – Hungarian Specialty club show 2008
Best champion bitch: Swedish Specialty 2008

Belgian Winner 2008 and 2010
Brussels Winner 2009
French Championship CACIB (2010) - BOB 2011
World Champion 2008 (BOS), 2011 (BOS) and 2012 (BOB)
Vice-WW Bratislava 2009
Vice European Champion 2008 and 2011
Bundessieger Tulln 2009
Spanish Centenary Championship 2011
CAC-CACIB Alliance Latine 2011

Mediterranean Winner 2012
BIS Bruxelles 2008
RBIS Athens 2008
5BIS Genk (B) 2009
RBIS Sintra 2012
Several times placed in the group 1 France, Belgium,
Greece, Italy, Portugal and Spain

**The best Schipperke palmares in the
2011 FCI Centenary year**
Int Bruxelles: CAC – CACIB
Dortmund: show not allowed to dogs with docked tail
Mond. Paris: CACIB
European Leeuwarden: RCAC-RCACIB

274

Atilla presents her new generation

Figaro des Grands Voyageurs

Born: 9.9.2010
Father: Gabber van de Moesdongen
Mother: Atilla du Clos de la Prère
Luxembourg Junior Champion 2011
CAC Monte Carlo (MC)
CAC – BOB Lommel (B)
WW Salzburg 2012

Gargantua des Grands Voyageurs

Born: 24.11.2012
Father: Zefke van het Kumtichshof
Mother: Atilla du Clos de la Prère
Nat Lommel (B): Best Puppy
Nat Sorges-en-Périgord (F): Best Young

To show is also to learn, to discover new bloodlines, to meet Schipperke owners and people, to discuss with them and to introduce the Schipperke"

Atilla, Figaro and Gargantua are shown by Costanza Ferraris

Breeders and Owners: **Mr and Mrs Louis de Liedekerke-Ferraris**
ferrarisnews@orange.fr
France

Claire Cooper 07855 255287

SuSu

Thank you to all judges for thinking so highly of my dogs'

Ch. Amcross A Proppa Parti
3 CC, 2 BOB, 5RCC

Amcross Pan-Tse For Eulyn
1 RCC

© 2012 Photos & Design By Will Harris

Susu Peak Into The Parti - 1 RCC

International CACIB shows in Denmark 2013

1. Fredericia, 9-10/2 2013

2. Roskilde, 4/5 2013
   Roskilde, 5/5 2013
   (Crufts qualification)

3. Vejen, 15-16/6 2013

4. Bornholm, 17/8 2013
   Bornholm, 18/8 2013

5. Ballerup 21-22/9 2013
   (Copenhagen Winner Show)

6. Herning, 2/11 2013
   Herning, 3/11 2013
   (Danish Winner Show Sunday)

Take your dog with you to Denmark

Denmark is a great place to go on holiday with your dog. All year round you are allowed to bring your (nice) dog unleashed in over 150 special "dog friendly woods". In the winter term you can also enjoy the beaches.

You can rent holiday houses through the Danish Kennel Club's partner NOVASOL-dansommer at www.novasol.dk or www.dansommer.dk.

Combine your holiday with one of the Danish Kennel Club's international CACIB shows, which have an international reputation of being very well organised. Read more at www.dkk.dk/en/Shows. It is possible to enter and pay on-line.

KIZZIT

Jayanel Royal Soverign (Darcy)

Phind Me A Valentine (Nella)

Christine and Clare would like to thank all judges who thought highly of Darcy and Nella in 2012

**Mhaybe A Disguise (Hero)
3 Best Puppy**

**Khing Of The Hill (Alvin)
1 CC, 3 RCCs**

Alvin will be campaigned extensively in 2013

Thank you to all judges for thinking so highly of them this year

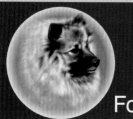

278

Group 2 Three Counties

Sh Ch Wilchrimane Ice Crystal

Sh Ch Chesterhope Watch my Step at Wilchrimane
(IMP NZ)

Clown

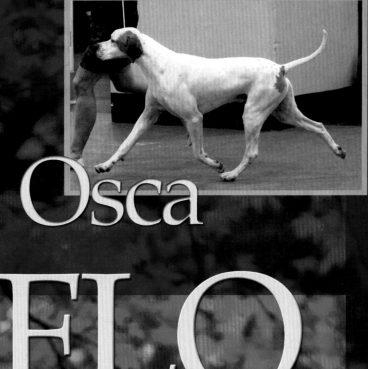

Osca

FLO

Sh Ch Wilchrimane Ice Maiden JW

TOP POINTER 2012*

IS Setter & Pointer

roup 1 Darlington

roup 1 South Wales

roup 2 East of England

x CC

x BOB

KC Stakes Final Winner Crufts 2012

ennel Gazette Junior Warrant Finalist

Debbie Fuller

* at time of going to press

Wilchrimane Pointers Annette & Amelia Siddle, Devon 01404 812624 sid.easthill@btconnect.com

COLLANSUES
Presenting our 2012 Champions

CH. Collansues Snowpatrol D.O.B. 7/3/10
Owned, loved and shown by Nicky and Dan Cotton
1 Kennel Cottage, Longfurlong, Findon, Worthing, West Sussex, BN14 0RJ Tel: 01903 872171

Photo by BW Photography

CH. Collansues Buildin Bridges at Bramikdel JW
D.O.B. 28/8/09.   5CCs (4 with BOB) 1RCC
Owned, shown and doted upon by Mark and Julie Wakeland
'Bramikdel', Annesley Woodhouse, Nottinghamshire.   Tel. 01623 758223

Bred By Mrs. Sue Flanagan - www.huntsmansdogandcathotel.co.uk

Cwsscwn

Cotton Fern Calico

Ferndel Butterkist Cwsscwn JW

IN THIS BRIGHT FUTURE

YOU CAN'T FORGET
THE PAST

Bob Marley

Chintz ShCM

Soul Sister Soul Mate

Sh Ch Cwsscwn Soul Mate JW ShCM

Christine morgan 01709 760124
Chris schofield 01246 418624

Davricard

DAVRICARD MARTINA

(Ch Dialynne Musketeer ex Ch Davricard Daydream)

Our puppy star, 'Tina' has made a great start to her career and had some memorable wins before her first birthday.

Pup of the Year qualifier at Birmingham National
2 CCs and BOB, Group 2 at Bournemouth
2 RCCs
BPIS at Windsor, Hound Association
and Bournemouth
Top Puppy in Breed 2012

The two new champions in 2012 are:

CH DAVRICARD
BUTTERCUP (above)
who gained her title at 14 months

CH BALDERSTONE
BUMBLE OF DAVRICARD
(opposite)

Not forgetting Ch Davricard Matilda who completes the quartet of our 2012 CC winning hounds

DAVID CRAIG
Paddock House, Hurworth Moor
Darlington DL2 1QG

Tel (01325) 285485
07815 312357
davbeagle@hotmail.com

Grafmax

Grafmax Louis Armstrong Sh CM

(Lux Ch Aritaur Histabraq SchH3 x Cosajoro Nina Simone at Grafmax)

BD Darlington 2012

BOB Darlington 2011

'Wow, what a boy' 'has everything going for him, he has the presence and cockiness I like in a dog' 'Beautiful with sharpest of outlines'

Thanks to all the judges who have recognised Satchmo's quality.

Sue Thorn
Grafmax Dobermanns
www.grafmax.org

07545 330851
suejthorn@yahoo.co.uk

© Photos & Design By Will Harris

GLADSTYLE

'The Dude'

Jim & Dawn Coates
www.Gladstyle.com

TOKAJI

BASENJIS & HUNGARIAN VIZSLAS

THE TOKAJI BASENJI TEAM
TRISH HALLAM & DEE HARDY

CH. TOKAJI CALIFORNIA DREAMING (PRISCILLA) 02.12.10
4 CC'S - PUPPY STAKES FINALIST 2011

CH./AMCH. KLASSICS MILLION DOLLAR BABY AT TOKAJI (MILLIE) 27.11.04
43 CC'S - BIS WINNER - 10 GROUP WINS IN BRITAIN – GROUP WINNER USA – CH. STAKES FINALIST – UK
BREED RECORD HOLDER – 5 CONSECUTIVE BOB CRUFTS 2006-2010 – TOP HOUND 2007 – TOP BROOD
ALL BREEDS 2011 – CURRENTLY TOP BROOD 2012 (DOG WORLD) – DAM OF 5 UK CHAMPIONS, 2 IRISH
CHAMPIONS AND 1 MALTESE JUNIOR CHAMPION.

CH. TOKAJI AMERICAN BEAUTY (COCO) 05.12.08
3 CC'S – CAC–CACIB–WORLD WINNER 2010 – PUPPY STAKES FINALIST 2009

CH. TOKAJI KENTUCKY BLUE (ELVIS) 02.12.10
6 CC'S – PUPPY STAKES FINALIST 2011

CH./AMCH. KAZORS MAKE WAY FOR RILEY (RILEY) 03.01.06
17 CC'S – BIS WINNER – GROUP WINNER – CH STAKES FINALIST – 3RD TOP SIRE ALL BREEDS 2011
FROM ONLY 4 UK LITTERS – SIRE OF 7 UK CHAMPIONS, 2 IRISH CHAMPIONS AND 1 MALTESE JUNIOR
CHAMPION, NUMEROUS AMERICAN CHAMPIONS.

DEE AND TRISH CAN BE CONTACTED AT TRISH.HALLAM@YARA.COM OR DEE.HARDY1@NTLWORLD.COM

A MY

INT. DUTCH. LUX. ENG. CH
PENLIATH FATAL ATTRACTION

Top Brood Bitch 2012
Top Brood Bitch 2011
Top Dog 2005
Multiple Group Winner

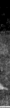

Winflash

2RCC
2xCH BestPuppies
BISEastMidlands2012
WinflashBornToBeWildJW

www.winflash.co.uk

WinflashEllesBellesJW
ICC&RBIS
2RCC
2xPuppyGroup1
2xPuppyGroup3
9xCH BestPuppies

TopDalmatianPuppy2012

Eardley Beagles
go to AMERICA

After competing in the Pup of the Year final early 2012 in the UK
'Barbi' finishes the year by going to
The National Beagle Club of America 125th Anniversary Show
Best of Winners 15inch

...to taken when 'Barbi' won her other Major in the States at Warrenton
under Keke Kahn just one day after flying in – what a star!

EARDLEY BARB DWYER JW
(...n Eardley Duncan Disorderly JW ex Ch Eardley Early Opening JW)

TIM JONES and STEVE JEPSON
www.eardleybeagles.com
Eardleyhall@aol.com

Bregantia and Rarjo Portuguese Water Dogs

TOP BREEDERS 2009, 2011, 2012*

©Johnson

CH RARJO SHE'S THE ONE (Jodie)
9 CCs, 3 RCCs, 1 CAC, 1 CACIB, 1 G3, 1 G4, BOS Crufts 2012,
BIS PWD Club of GB Ch Show 2008, Top PWD 2008 and 2012*,
Breed CC Record Holder

Owned and bred by RACHAEL REDDIN and RUTH BUSSELL
Tel 01945 440431
Email rachael-reddin@supanet.com

Bregantia and Rarjo Portuguese Water Dogs

**CH RARJO SCOUTING
FOR GIRLS (Fin)**
4 CCs, all with BOB, 3 RCCs,
1 CAC, 1 CACIB, 1 G3, BOB
Crufts 2012, Top PWD 2009

**RARJO FOR YOUR EYES
ONLY (Jimmy)**
1 CC, 6 RCCs, 2 RCAC,
1 RCACIB, BPIS PWD
ch show 2010

**BREGANTIA FUNKY DIVA
(Amy)**
5 RCCs, Top Brood 2011,
2012 Working Group Leader*

**CH BREGANTIA THE X-FACTOR
AT WINTERKLOUD (Alfie)**
Owned by Sarah McGill
3 CCs, 3 RCCs, 2 G4,
BOB Crufts 2007,
Top Stud 2011 and 2012*

**CH RARJO REVOLUTION
AT WINTERKLOUD (Rico)**
Owned by Sarah McGill
3 CCs, 2 RCCs, 1 G4

**BREGANTIA DON'T STOP
ME NOW AT WINTERKLOUD
(Mabel)**
Owned by Sarah McGill
Lightly shown in 2012

**RARJO HE'S THE KING
AT MOONSTYLE (Tux)**
Owned by Emily Hammond
BIS Newmarket
open show 2012

**BREGANTIA
THE GLORY FOREVER (Una)**
Owned by Emily Hammond
Successful puppy career 2012

**RARJO HERE SHE COMES
TO MAJESIXS (Diva)**
Owned by Heather Killilea-Gibson
RCC Leeds 2012

**CH RARJO IT HAD TO BE YOU
FOR ANKORS (Teal)**
Owned by Antony Bongiovanni
6 CCs, 7 RCCs, 1 G3, BOB
Crufts 2011, BIS PWD Ch Show
2011, Top PWD 2011

TWEEDSMUIR

All our dogs are fully health checked, puppies sometimes available

Proudly owned and loved by **HILDA and PAUL MONAGHAN**

Ivydene, The Marsh, Walpole Marsh, Wisbech, Cambs PE14 7JG

Tel 01945 780293 Mobile 07981 593319 email hilda.monaghan@btinternet.com Web www.tweedsmuir.org

Top Breeders for the last 12 years, Top Stud Dog 2012,

Top Brood Bitch 2012, Top Puppy 2012, Top Clumber 2011/2012 (Konnie owned by Dave and Sue Boden)

TWEEDSMUIR MIKADO
'Jensen'
TOP PUPPY 2012
13 Puppy wins at Championship shows, 8 BP
Sh Ch Tweedsmuir Dambuster JW
ex Dockwray Snapdragon
To Tweedsmuir

SH CH TWEEDSMUIR DAMBUSTER JW
'Miller'
Best Dog Crufts 2012
6 CCs, 4 BOB,
1 Group 4
Numerous RCCs

Waiting to make her debut in 2013
TWEEDSMUIR KRUSHED ICE
'Ice'
Tweedsmuir Klassic Edition
among Suelynda
ex Tweedsmuir Duchesse

SUELYNDA

Proudly owned and loved by **SUE and DAVE BODEN**

16 Rowallan Avenue, Gosport, Hampshire PO13 9RE   Tel 0239 26066   Email susan_boden@sky.com

Konnie is Top Clumber for the second year 2011/2012

All our dogs are fully health tested

SH CH TWEEDSMUIR BEAUTIFUL DREAM AMONG SUELYNDA
JW ShCM
27 CCs, 25 BOB, 9 RCCs
1 x Group 1, 3 x Group 2,
3 x Group 3, 2 x Group 4

Waiting to make their debut in 2013
Monica and Ralph
Sh Ch Tweedsmuir Dambuster JW
ex Sh Ch Tweedsmuir Beautiful Dream
among Suelynda

TWEEDSMUIR KLASSIC EDITION AMONG SUELYNDA
'Kameron'
8 RCCs
Numerous other wins to his credit
At stud to approved bitches

Awards at time of going to press

SH CH/IR SH CH FLYNGALEE NORTHERN LIGHTS JW ShCM

(Sh Ch Stanroph So It Had To Be JW ex Flyngalee The Sun Shines)

34 CCs, 17 RCCs
and 28 BOB,
3 Group 1,
1 Group 3,
1 Group 4
Top Golden Retriever
2009, 2011, 2012*

Owned by MRS JENNIFER MACDONALD

Reynolds

*, at time of going to press

SERENAKER AND HALLAM

New Champions 2012

photo Croft-Elliot

CH/ AM CH HALLAM'S GYSAI KACEY AT SERENAKER

RBIS Pharaoh Hound Club 2012

photo Croft-Elliot

CH SERENAKER HEY JUDE

Crufts BOB 2011

photo Harris

CH SERENAKER FOXTROT

Crufts BOB 2012

photo S&S Productions

BIRKHALL HALLAM'S BRODIE AT SERENAKER

(Ch/Am Grand Ch Hallam's Busiris Ra Qena ex Ir Ch Antefa's Renenet at Birkhall)

Brodie is maturing into a handsome, well constructed hound; he has 2 CCs and multiple RCCs to his credit.

Co-owned with Dominic Carota and Stephen Sipperly

Belle has matured into a beautiful bitch with sound free flowing movement; she is getting more like her illustrious dam every day!

STOP PRESS: Belle wins the CC and RBIS at West Mercia Beagle Club under breed expert Dianna Spavin.

photo S&S Productions

SERENAKER MEMPHIS BELLE
(Ch/Am Ch Barristers Yankee Doodle Dandy at Fallowfield ex Ch/Ir Ch Serenaker Devil Woman)

Serena Parker and Graham Stevens

Dominic Carota and Stephen Sipperly

Tel 07792 570307   www.serenaker.co.uk   email serena@serenaker.co.uk

www.hallamhounds.org   email hallamhounds@aol.com

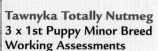
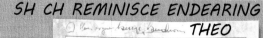

Cloverwood Dandie Dinmont Terriers

Ch Cloverwood Royal George

(BIS AM Can Ch Gateway Sparks of Glahms ex Cloverwood Absolute Angel)
In his brief show career George has already attained: Top Dandie Dinmont 2012
5 Group placings from 6 BOBs 8 CCs
Winner, National Terrier Best Open Show Dog Competition
BOB and World Winner at The World Dog Show, Salzburg, Austria 2012
4th in Group, Crufts 2012

Our Beautiful *Ch Cloverwood Lemon Drizzle* (number 3 Terrier, number 10 All Breeds 2011 and the first Dandie to win BIS at National Terrier) will be bred to George in 2013

JOAN-GLEN TINSLEY (Owner/breeder – Top Dandie Breeder 2012)
Blackboy Farm, Wellington, Somerset TA21 9QD
Tel 01823 663436   email joantinsley@aol.com   www.wellingtonboarding@co.uk

Laurelhach

Gordon Setters With Personality Plus

Home & Abroad

www.laurelhach.co.uk

PHARAOH HOUND BREED HISTORY MAKERS

CH NAQADA SHAKEN NOT STIRRED

NAQADA FOR YOUR EYES ONLY AT TYYSGOL

The first siblings awarded BOB and BOS from the puppy classes at the tender age of 10 months
at the 'National' and the breed's youngest champion at just 13 months.
Ch Naqada Shaken Not Stirred bred and owned by Marie Richmond
Naqada For You Eyes Only at Tyysgol owned and loved by Jayne Barrett-Williams
*We'd like to thank all judges concerned for the multiple Best Puppy in Breed, Puppy Group Placings
and Best Puppy in Shows that they were awarded.*

Tidemill Pugs

Established 1978

CHAMPION TIDEMILL CHERRY COLA
(Champion Yorlander Ronaldo at Tidemill JW
ex Tidemill Bizzie Lizzie)
8 CCs and 6 RCCs, Top Pug 2011
**Best in Show Wales and West of England Pug Dog Club
Ch Show 2011**
Best Opposite Sex Northern Pug Dog Club Ch Show 2011
**Reserve Best in Show, West Pennine Pug Dog Club
Ch Show 2012**

CHAMPION YORLANDER RONALDO AT TIDEMILL JW
(Champion Murbren Adam Son Of Eve
at Yorlander ex Yorlanders Montoya)
Bred by Mrs Kath Hindley
**22 CCs, 15 RCCs, 19 BOB at Championship Shows
CC and Best of Breed at dfs Crufts 2010,
RCC at dfs Crufts 2011**
Top Pug 2009, Top Stud Dog 2011, Top Stud Dog 2012

DELWIN'S BLACK REBEL AT SALDAWN
(Jessygaff Tasmanian ex Delwin's Little Black Number)
Bred by Mrs Grace Godwin
Jointly owned with Joyce Grant, Rebel is making his mark and is a
Championship Show First Prize Winner.

Starting their show career in 2012 were **Tidemill Be Bop Bessie &
Claripugs Celtic Star Over Tidemill** (Best Bitch Puppy in Show, Wales
& West of England Pug Dog Club Ch Show 2012), both of whom were
first prize winners at Championship Shows and Crufts qualified.

CHAMPION YORLANDERS MAX AT TIDEMILL
(Champion Briditch Jerry Lewis JW ShCM
ex Briditch Katrina at Yorlander)
Bred by Mrs Kath Hindley
**Winner of 8 CCs in 2012, making him the top CC winner in
Pugs 2012. 6 Best of Breed, 6 RCCs**
**Reserve Best in Show, West Pennine Pug Dog Club
Ch Show 2011.**
Reserve Best in Show, Northern Pug Dog Club Ch Show 2011
**Best in Show, Wales & West of England Pug Dog Club Ch
Show 2012**

TERRY PURSE and NIGEL MARSH
Tel 023 8086 4963
Email nigel@tidemillpugs.co.uk   www.tidemillpugs.co.uk

TEAM ALOPEX SMOOTH COLLIES

The team do it again ■ ■

■ ■ ■ *IONA becomes our latest homebred Blue Merle Champion*

Ch Alopex Out Of The Blue

Iona's daughters

Katy Coates'
Alopex Blue Moon
1 C C & 1 Res C C

Marianne Benton's
Alopex Marionette Of Oakestelle
4 Collie Club B I S
2 Reserve C Cs
EACA Pup Of The Year
Romford C.S. Dog Of The Year

Isobel & Tony Griffiths   Alopex@btinternet.com

Ch Vandreem Imperial Hermioni by Berezniki JW ShCM

photo Alan Walker

(Vandreem Imperial Jazz
ex Ch Vandreem Imperial Capri for Berezniki JW)
BVA hip score 3/5 total 8

**BIS World Sam Meeting 2012
(NSS 50th Anniversary Show)
Top Winning Sam UK 2008, '09, '10 and runner-up '11
Top Pastoral 2008, RBIS Crufts 2008
34 CCs (Bitch breed record holder)
(Multi BOB) and 9 RCCs
12 x Group 1, 5 x Group 2, 3 x Group 3, 3 x Group 4
4 BIS, 7 RBIS (Ch Shows including Richmond 2012)
Sam of the Year contest winner '08 and '09 NSS
Also Bitch CC Crufts '07 and Champion Stakes finalist 2011**

Sincere thanks to all judges for 'Mioni's fabulous awards, also to breeder, Andrea, and to all who have supported her. Mioni is shown infrequently due to coat drop times and repeat judges. She is leading Sam 2012* (DW/AG)
*at time of press.

Loved and owned by Lisa Bobrowski
lisabobrowski@yahoo.co.uk

Lovetrac

Cavalier King Charles Spaniels

Thank you for another wonderful year

CH MAIBEE ROSELYN AT LOVETRAC

(Maibee Montrose ex Maibee Moonbeam)

3 CCs and 3 RCCs

Gained her Crown in 2012

LOVETRAC MARKOFDISTINCTION JW

(Ch Maibee Make Believe JW ex Phrenchy Am A Boverred Lovetrac)

1 CC, BOB and 2 RCCs

Youngsters:
Phenomena (left) Multiple
1sts including BPB at SKC and BPB at NICKCSS

Picasso (right)
Multiple 1sts despite being sparingly shown

Philip Lovel
01482 862636

Haley and Sarah Dog Handlers and Trainers

We are two ex-junior handlers who now show dogs for other people in breed, handling and stakes classes. We handle a number of dogs from a number of different breeds regularly, some of whom are shown below. These are just a few of our main handling dogs and their best results.

Above (left to right) Maud (Golmas Gaudy Maud at Bearhard) owned by J Bearman, George (Indizak Hot Or Not) owned by D Carey, Sarah Gibbons, Louie (Lynton Le Praz Darbello Lad) owned by S Gent, Storm (Kitado Born A Warrior) owned by Mr and Mrs Rayner, Breeze (Lindgreave Summer Breeze) owned by J Lindley, Haley Jones, Angel (Truejoy Angel Delight) owned by C Grist and Casper (Allmark Spirit Of St Louis ShCM) owned by Mr and Mrs Longhurst and Mr Routledge.

Haley and Jasper (Abbiville Avitus), 2 RCCs, 1st YKC Working Stakes Crufts 2012 making the second year Haley has won this out of the past three years winning it initially with Elli (Nikolaev Albany at Abbiville).
Sarah and Libby (Tobamorrey Sitting Pretty at Silkcroft JW ShCM) won BCC and BOB at Paignton on the first time of ever handling her.
Sarah also handled Casper (Allmark Spirit Of St Louis ShCM) to 1st Limit Dog at just 19 months gaining his Stud Book Number and he now has 1 CC, 2 RCCs and Group 4 at Working/Pastoral Breeds of Wales, all were won under the age of 2.

Handling wins: 1st in 7 classes with 7 different dogs, qualifying for Crufts handling finals 6 times with 5 breeds across 4 groups and all in one year.

We would like to thank all the judges who have thought so highly of our dogs and our handling and have given us such a special year. We would also like to thank all the owners who have allowed us to handle such special dogs and everyone who has supported us over the years.

CH SNOWMEADOW NUMINOUS
NIILO ShCM (Neo)
3 CCs, 2 BOB, 1 BD, 8 RCCs
(5 this year)
Owned by Mr and Mrs Lawrence

NIKOLAEV AMARANDE AT ABBIVILLE
(Bess)
1 CC, 2 RCCs, 1 BB, 2 BOS,
1st YKC Working Stakes at SKC
Owned by Mrs and Miss Jones

ROHANTIA NIKOLAI AT FERNWOOD
(Zube)
8 BP, 2 BPD, 1 BOB, 3 RBD, Working Puppy
Group 2, 1st Working Puppy Stakes W/P
Breeds of Scotland and Current Top Puppy
Owned by Mr A M Smith
All won under 12 months

We also like to give something back to the junior handling community and hold regular individual handling training with up and coming young handlers who have had some fantastic results.

If you wish to have some handling training or wish to contact us about showing a dog please feel free to contact us on the following or for further information look on our website.

HALEY JONES 07930 485 587
Email: haleymariejones@hotmail.co.uk

SARAH GIBBONS 0751 765 6006
sarahjgibbons@hotmail.co.uk

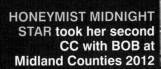

CHANDHALLY DALMATIANS AND ITALIAN SPINONE

We have had Dalmatians since 1989 and have only bred 6 litters. We bred UK and Ireland's first multi-country International Champion - **Ir/Int Ch Chandhally Chantilly Lace, CCs and RCCs.** We have bred/owned 6 champions.

The Italian Spinone is a new challenge and we have only had that since early 2011. We are a small kennel, well known for our dogs' outstanding temperaments, and we only breed occasionally so that we can continue our line. I go abroad for stud dogs to ensure (hopefully) healthier offspring and wider gene pool.

We have had some outstanding years showing here in the UK and abroad. We travel extensively across Scandinavia and Europe and are doing extremely well, where the dogs are winning on their merits - conformation and movement - not by who or what we are.

A most fantastic achievement was the Mediterranian circuit at the end of April 2012. The only British dogs to do so well, we took home **3 CACs, 3 CACIBs, 1 Group 7 (gundog group)** with Lola (at only 15 months old) and **CAC, 2 RCACIBs, 1 CACIB and a 3rd in group 6** with Pia. In Norway, summer 2012. Lola also took home **3 certificates, 1 RCACIB, winner of group 7 and a BIS3 (17 months old).**

All have outstanding temperaments. All dogs are hip scored. Dalmatians BAER tested. Hall is retired from the show ring but has proved to be a super stud dog. Available to approved bitches.

We are hoping for a litter from Lola late in 2013. Puppy and stud enquires welcome.

Breeder, exhibitor, judge and very proud owner
NINA R FLEMING
supported by **NORMAN G FLEMING**
Cae Bach Hose, Cae Bach, Machen, Caerphilly
CF83 8NG, South Wales, UK
01633 440371
n.fleming27@btinternet.com
www.chandhally.co.uk

CHANDHALLY CUVEE DU PRESIDENT (Hall), his mum **NORW CH CHANDHALLY SNOW QUEEN** (Pia) and **REDRUE CHERRIECOLA TO CHANDHALLY** (Lola)

JAEGEROT ROTTWEILERS

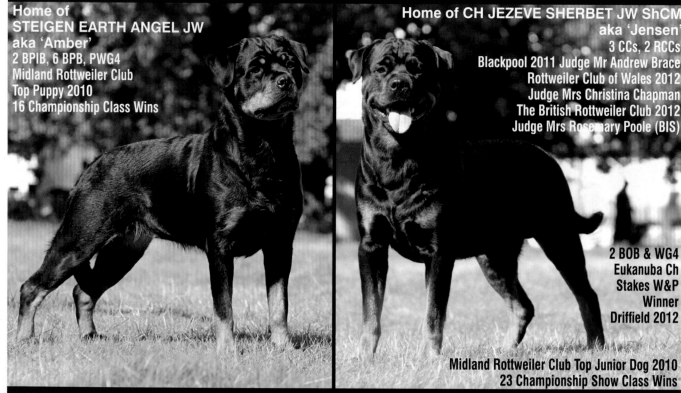

Home of
STEIGEN EARTH ANGEL JW
aka 'Amber'
2 BPIB, 6 BPB, PWG4
Midland Rottweiler Club
Top Puppy 2010
16 Championship Class Wins

Home of CH JEZEVE SHERBET JW ShCM
aka 'Jensen'
3 CCs, 2 RCCs
Blackpool 2011 Judge Mr Andrew Brace
Rottweiler Club of Wales 2012
Judge Mrs Christina Chapman
The British Rottweiler Club 2012
Judge Mrs Rosemary Poole (BIS)

2 BOB & WG4
Eukanuba Ch
Stakes W&P
Winner
Driffield 2012

Midland Rottweiler Club Top Junior Dog 2010
23 Championship Show Class Wins

Huge thank you to all the Judges who have thought so highly of our dogs. Special thanks to both Jezeve Rottweilers and Steigen Rottweilers for your continued support and encouragement.
IAN TRUEMAN & CAROL BROWNRIDGE, Jaegerot Rottweilers
www.jaegerot.co.uk   email jaegerot@sky.com   Tel (0) 7795 436 364

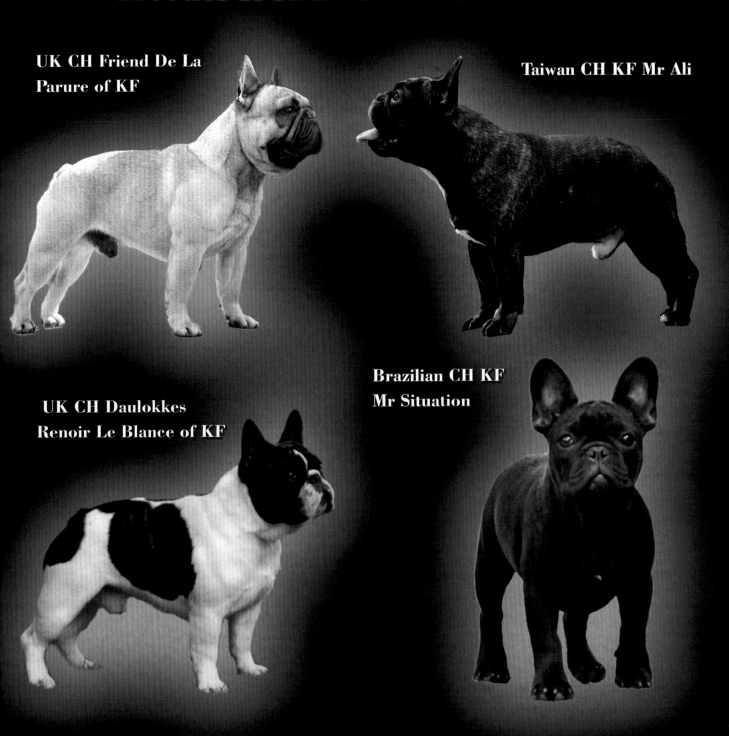

310

Avigdor Tibetan Spaniels

photo Walker

GB & Ir Ch Avigdor Jarko
11 CCs, 9 BOB, 5 RCCs, 1 Group 4
Adding 2 Club show CCs and a BIS,
Crufts RCC, a Group win
and Group 3 on the Irish Circuit and
Midland Counties Champion Stakes,
runner-up to his tally in 2012

Celebrating <u>two new champions</u> in 2012

GB & Ir Ch Avigdor Elvira 5 CCs, 1 RCC	GB Ch Sommerlyst's Zi-Mi Piu 3 CCs, 2 BOB, 1 RCC

photo Johnson

Res BIS TSA 2011, TSC of Scotland and Northern TSC 2012	Group 2 – Manchester '12 Group 4 – Bath '11

www.avigdor.eu

LAZEYBEARS ST BERNARDS

©Johnson

CH LAZEYBEARS BACK TO BLACK
Owned in partnership with Carol Schofield
2 BIS, 6 BOB, Working Puppy Group 1 and 4, Top St Bernard Puppy 2012
Passing every vet check required

LAZEYBEARS BAD INFLUENCE
co-owned with Alan Mease
Twice in the ring and
already gained a RCC

ZAFIRA NA KAZDA POGODE
LAZEYBEARS (imp Pol) lightly shown but
has already gained 3 BPIB and 1 Reserve
Best Bitch

Proudly owned and adored by SARAH FARRELL and HAZEL LAMB
www.lazeybears.co.uk
lazeybears@btinternet.com
Tel: 01733 222295

314

OFFORDALE
Top Breeder 2011 and 2012

CH OFFORDALE CHEVALIER
Top Dalmatian 2012

Following his Best Puppy Dog at Crufts 2011 Mr Darcy has had a wonderful 2012 and has now had the following wins at Championship Shows.

18 CCs, 4 RCCs, 15 BOB

4 Group wins, 3 Group 2 and 2 Group 4

Plus

2 BIS at Club Championship Shows

Many thanks to all the judges who have thought so highly of Mr Darcy and Holly.

A special thank you to Helle Hoie for letting me use
Multi Ch Bell-A-Mir's Elegant Envoy on my
Ch Offordale White Lady to produce this wonderful litter.

Top Brood Bitch for 2011 and 2012*

All proudly bred, owned and loved by

JENNY ALEXANDER

Tel 01480 810259

email jemalexander101@btinternet.com

CH OFFORDALE SAPPHIRE JW

Following Holly's Best Puppy at Crufts 2011 she has now achieved the following at Championship Shows.

9 CCs, 5 RCCs, 4 BOB

1 Group win, 1 Group 2 and 1 Group 3

Runner up - Contest of Champions 2012

*at time of going to press

Another great year for...

DAVENHEATH LEONBERGERS

Ch Davenheath Court Jester JW ShCM
remains Top Leonberger 2011/2012*

Chester relaxing with our puppy 'Ben' who has had 3 BPIB at Championship Shows

Mum Zoe (Ch Davenheath Almost an Angel) with two of her sons Chester and Boris

Our young lady 'Lilly' 19 months, Davenheath Dark Secret, 1 CC and BIS at Kent County

We would also like to acknowledge the wonderful results of Lilly's sister 'Annie' Davenheath Dream of Olwyn at Clyrocko at Irish Championship Shows - Junior Champion, 1 BB, 2 RBB, 3 GS, 8 RGS, CJW12 – Junior Diploma, 2 BBP in Breed, and at Belfast Championship BOB, BP and BOS. Owned and loved by Richard and Denise Maeer.

*at time of going to press

Heather and David Niall
davenheathleos@btinternet.com   Tel: 07768 505572

Glenda and Joe Rothery
grothery@btinternet.com   Tel: 07538 434985

16 CCs, 16 RCCs, 13 BOB
2 x Group 1 and 3 x Group 2
Winner of the East Anglian Supermatch 2012

FOXTHYME

Carefully breeding for quality since 1982, owned 1957! 1st UK CHAMPION

CH FOXTHYME ELIZA   CH FOXTHYME OLIVER CROMWELL ShCM

photo Lehtinen

Nemo

photo Walker

Their Sire Foxthyme Orinoco
Their Dam Foxthyme Ellie - Top Brood Bitch Lancashire Heeler Dog World/Lintbells 2008/9/10/11 and leading 2012

10 CCs, 3 RCCs
Best Of Breed Crufts 2006 2008 2012
BCC Crufts 2009, RBCC Crufts 2010 2011
3 x BIS Lancashire Heeler Club Ch Show

This from her two outings a year!

Foxthyme dogs have been BOB at Crufts 7 times.

Foxthyme has numerous LH European Champions.

Many thanks to all the judges over the years who have thought so highly of them, a big dog in a small package.

18 CCs, 16 RCCs, 1 x Group 3
Joint Top Heeler 2009
Reserve Top Heeler 2008 2010 2011
Top Veteran 2011
2 x BIS Lancashire Heeler Club Show
Reserve BIS Open Show

Group 3 Bournemouth Ch Show with many thanks to judge Andrew Brace and to all the judges who have thought so highly of him.

He is the sire of **Foxthyme James Bond**, European Jnr Ch & Dutch Jnr Ch 2011

Available at stud to approved bitches
DNA hereditary PLL tested clear

Bred, owned and loved by **Enid Lord**
Tel 01772 322064 (Lancs) KC Assured Breeder
Lancashire Heeler Club Breed Rescue for 25 years

Much loved, owned and shown by **Mrs Jackie Cartledge**
Tel 07904 586253

Selmalda
GREAT DANES

ELEGANCE, MAJESTY — DIGNITY & TYPE

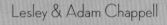

www.selmalda.com

Bred, Loved, Owned.   Conditioned & Presented by   Lesley & Adam Chappell

Georgia
Selmalda In The Name Of Love
1 RCC 1 CAC 1 CACIB

LC-E
unretouched

Ola
BEL UK CH Selmalda Rock Ola Baby JW
3 CCs 4 rCCs 6 CACs 3 CACIBs

Rocco
BEL, UK CH Selmalda I Am Rock JW
4 CCs 10 rCCs 4 CACs 3 CACIBs

LC-E
unretouched

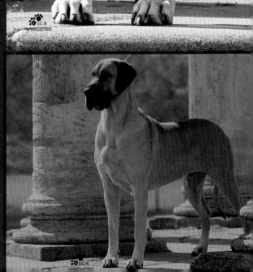

photo Roberts

Glynderys Gwennol JW

'Iola'
DOB 16.09.11

PRA rcd4 clear, BVA/KC HD 8/5

(Drumdaroch The Xpat to Liric (imp Aus)
ex Graylacier Amber Destiny at Glynderys)

Best Puppy in Show
British Gordon Setter Club Open Show

3 Best Puppy and
5 1st Junior at Championship Shows

Thanks to all judges who thought so highly
of 'Iola'. We are pleased that she
is maturing into a lovely young lady

DR MARIAN THOMAS
Email glynderys@yahoo.co.uk
Tel 01763 272968

Colin N Waddell

©Johnson

RANGALI

RANGALI LITTLE TED
PBGV

3 BPIS, 4 Puppy Groups
9 BPIB at Championship Shows
Best Dog at Border Union and Leeds
Puppy Group 4 at Windsor
Owned, loved and bred by Heidi and
Richard Allenby and Louise
and Adrian Walder

Our English rose between two French imports. HIRONDELLE RANGALI
(imp France) at 4½ months, our new girl to the team. RANGALI MAGIC
MOMENT, top Fauve puppy 2012, BPIS and RCC at club show, 3 RCCs and
just a year old. GIGOLO DU RALLYE SAINT PAUL FOR RANGALI (imp
France) at 17 months and his second show CC at Houndshow. Winner of
junior class at the French Elevage, BOB at Driffield and shortlisted in the
group. Thank you to Colin Makey for helping to handle at the club show.
And a big thank you to Marc Augin for letting me have my two lovely
French dogs. They are a pleasure to own.

Owned by Richard and Heidi Allenby
email heidi.allenby@googlemail.com
07886 454587 / 01327 857886

JAY AND MARTIN HORGAN
www.aritaur.co.uk
www.germanpinschers.co.uk
01538 703072

THIS IS
ARITAUR
DOBERMANNS, GERMAN PINSCHERS & POINTER

© Photos &
Design
By Will Harris

CESKY
Terrier Club

www.cesky-terrier-club.co.uk

OPEN SHOW

Best in Show
Janski Celtic Ceska

Reserve Best in Show and Reserve Best Bitch
Darling du Champ d'Eole

Judge: Jane Withers

OPEN SHOW

Best Dog
Lastarean Dufek ShCM

Reserve Best Dog
Polede Lforluka

LIMITED SHOW
Best in Show
Komidion Jacara
Reserve Best in Show
Lastarean Kral of Zidout
Best Puppy in Show
Lastarean Knezna of Kessima

Forthcoming events in 2013:

Seminar – Saturday February 23 at Mappleborough Green

Annual General Meeting and Limited Show – Sunday April 21 at Shipston-on-Stour

Open Show – Sunday August 4 at Shipston-on-Stour

GRIFFON BRUXELLOIS
HUVIKUMMUN
DATE OF BIRTH 24/09/2006
RED JACKET

VICE WORLD CH. 2012
EUROPEAN WINNER 2011, 2010
ASIA & THE PACIFIC SECTION WINNER 2011
CH. OF KOREA
CH. INTERNATIONAL DE BEAUTE
MEDITERRANEAN CH., CH. DE FRANCE,
CH. DE BEAUTE DE MONACO
FINNISH WINNER 2010
NORDIC CH., DANISH CH.
FINNISH CH., SWEDISH CH.
RUSSIAN CH., CH. OF POLAND
POLAND WINNER, POLAND CLUB WINNER
CH. OF CZECH REPUBLIC,
CH. OF MONTENEGRO
CH. OF REPUBLIC MACEDONIA
CH. OF HUNGARY, HUNGARY CLUB WINNER
CH. OF BULGARIA,
CH. OF ITALY, BIG INTERNATIONAL DOG SHOW
LATINA (Italy) 22/09/2012
CH. & GRAND CH. OF UKRAINE
LITHUANIAN CH., CH. OF SLOVENIA
AUSTRIAN CH., BIS DE LA NATIONAL
D'ELEVAGE PONTOISE – 11/09/2010, BIS
FRANCE PONTOISE INTERNATIONAL DOG
SHOW – 12/09/2010
RESERVE BIS PARIS DOG SHOW 2011
INTERNATIONAL DOG SHOW – 09/01/2011

*I WOULD LIKE TO SAY
THANKS ALL JUDGES
WHO EVALUATED MY
DOG AT ALL THE SHOWS
AND CONTRIBUTED TO
ITS TRIUMPH.
SPECIAL THANKS TO
LEVINA ELENA AND
FIRSOV VICTOR.*

Kazval and Feldkirk

CC Winning and Group Placed Dogs, Owned, Bred or Handled in 2012

We would like to say a big thank you to all the judges who have thought so highly of our dogs.
We would like to give a special thank you to Mr and Mrs Armstrong and Ms K Anderson
for their support and allowing us to use their bloodlines.

Two of the Top Flatcoats 2012
(Brother and Sister)

SH CH FELDKIRK FASHION

Top Flatcoat 2012
20 CCs, 13 BOB, 4 Res CC, 2 G2, G4

SH CH BALLYRIVER BLAKE

Best in Show United Retriever 2012
8 CCs, 4 BOB, 5 Res CCs, G2

Sh Ch KAZVAL HUGO BOSS
4 CCs, 2 BOB, 3 Res CCs

We hope to have a new Vizsla puppy entering the ring in 2013
and hope to have Flatcoat puppies next year.

Our dogs are health checked and available at stud to approved bitches.

Tom H Johnston
Tel (0044) 01461 800372
email tomstjohn17@yahoo.com

Frank H Whyte
Tel 07775 701057
email Fhwkazval@aol.com

Mariglen and **Christter**
proudly present

SH CH MARIGLEN
BLUE FLAME FOR CHRISTTER

'Delta'

**Winner of 22 CCs,
5 RCCs and 13 BOB**

Shortlisted in the Group at
Crufts 2012

Winning the Group at
Border Union 2012

'DELTA' is the **UK's top winning
English Setter for 2012**, bred by co-owner Jane Dennis, by **Sh Ch Mariglen
Pengtsson's Legacy
9 CCs, 6 RCCs, 8 BOB,
DW/Royal Canin Top Stud Dog
2012*** ex **Sh Ch Mariglen Flaming
Colours**, winner of **24 CCs, BOB
Crufts 2006.**

He lives with and is always handled by
co-owner Chris Sayers. He has won this
year, **Group 1 Border Union, Group 3
Paignton, Group 4 National Gundog,
Group 4 Three Counties**. He has also
won **13 CCs bringing his total to 22**.
His other achievements have included
**BIS at the English Setter Association
2012 Championship Show.**

Jane Dennis (Mariglen)
www.mariglen.com
janemariglen@yahoo.com

Chris Sayers (Christter)
Tel 01892 740170
chris.sayers@caravan-club.co.uk

*at time of going to press

RATTUSTRAP

Where elegance, quality & excellence count

ONNI

RATTUSTRAP ENGLANDS OWN
Back in the UK & causing a storm.

© LC-E
unretouched

Making Breed History
1st September - 25th October 2012
7 Championship Shows
6 BP B, 2 RCC's, 1 BOB, 1 PG3, 1 BPiS
The first Manchester Terrier to qualify for
The POTY final in the competition's 41 year history

Proudly owned by Paivi Hituri & Timo Virta (Finland).
Proudly bred by Phil Dale & Estella Saxton

©advertising & photography Croft-Elliott

www.rattustrap-manchester-terriers.com
rattustrap@live.co.uk Tel: 01623 439105

Gayteckels

Adrian, Chris and Russell Marett

LASTAREAN GRACE AND FAVOUR FOR GAYTECKELS

Best of Breed
Three Counties and Paignton
Best Opposite Sex
Welsh Kennel Club
Reserve Best Bitch
National Terrier, Blackpool **and Windsor**
Best in Show Jersey
Reserve Best in Show Guernsey
Jersey CC

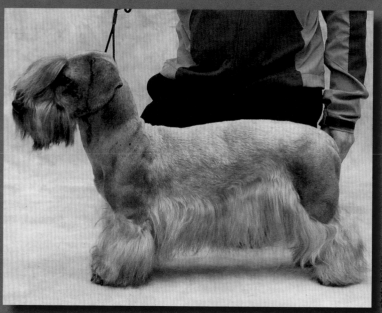

photo Jackson

LASTAREAN KRAL OF ZIDOUT

Best Dog Three Counties
Reserve Best Dog National Terrier

Still successful in the agility ring
at nine years old

LIMIER DIDIER AT GAYTECKELS P'DH

Won his **Prix d'Honneur** award
in Guernsey after taking **3rd BIS**

JSY CH GAYTECKLS HIGHFLYER PD'H

took **BVIS** at Chertsey CS

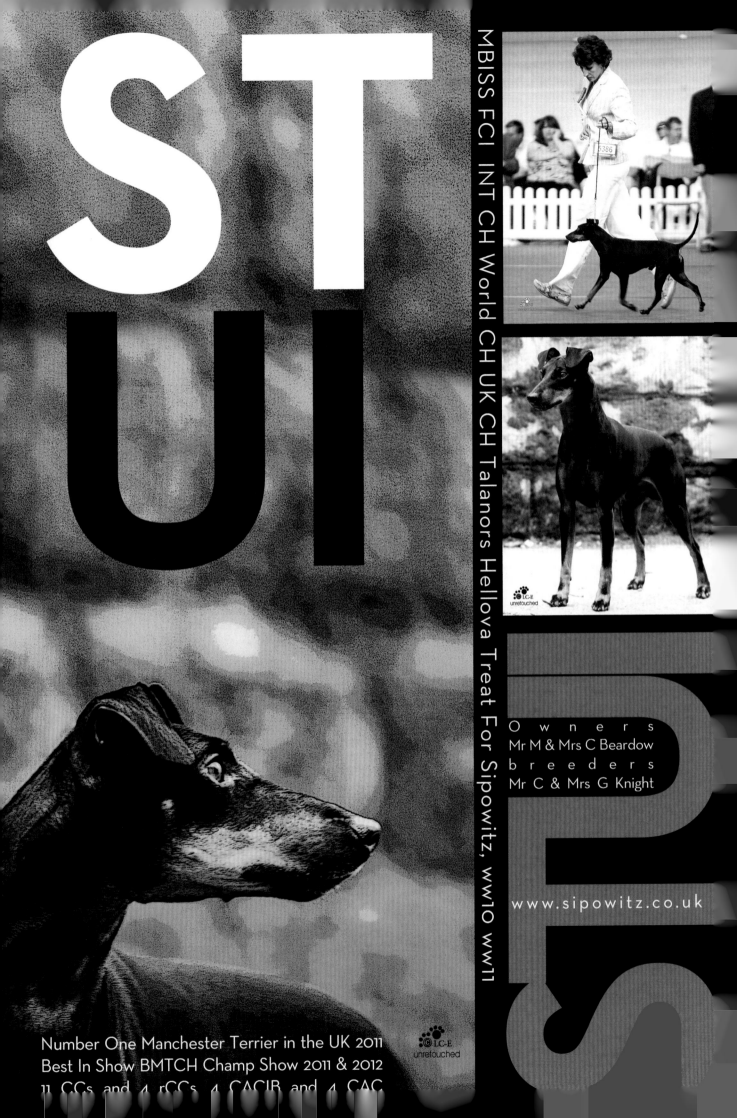

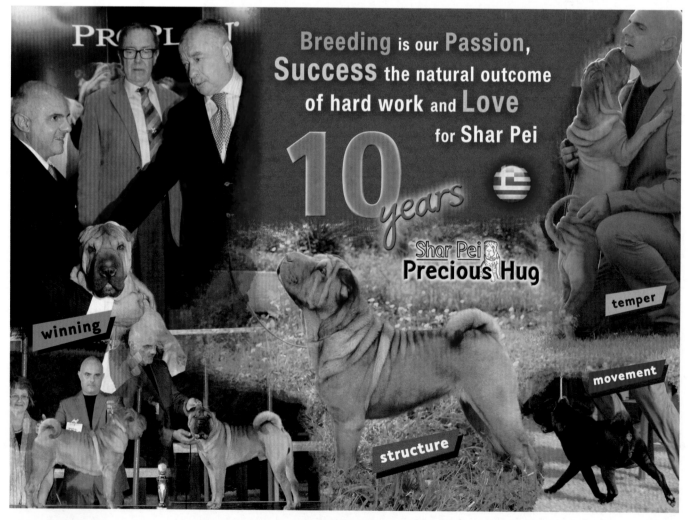

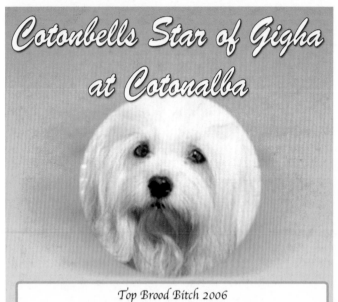

Uireda

Miniature Schnauzers

CH UIREDA EVERYONE'S AT IT WITH JENNAYR

An amazing year for 'Mr' Riley

Bred by Gareth and Tracy Hards (Uireda) Owned, prepared, handled and very much loved by Lisa Gudgin and Elaine Campbell (Jennayr)

Riley has enjoyed the following success in the show ring:

BPIS SCGB 2011 – F Somerfield
CC, BOB and **BP** East of England 2011 – T Fletcher
CC and **BOB** Paignton 2011 – G Wise
RCC BUBA 2011 – C Wareham
CC and **BOB** Crufts 2012 – C Clay
CC Border Union 2012 – K Durso
RCC Blackpool 2012 – L Anness
RCC City of Birmingham 2012 – A Arch
BOB (no CCs) Windsor 2012 – D Webb
BIS Miniature Schnauzer Club April 2012 – B Brown
Schnauzer of the Year 2012 – M Gadsby

Riley gained his all-important crowning CC at Crufts 2012 at the tender age of 19 months

A huge thank you to judges, family and friends who have thought so highly of 'Mr' Riley

Alan V Walker

UIREDA FIX YOU

©Johnson

Owned, bred and loved by Gareth and Tracy Hards

Lucy made a promising start to her show career and has enjoyed the following results:

SCGB Open Show – Minor Puppy Bitch **1st**,
Best Miniature Bitch, Reserve Best of Breed
Windsor – Puppy Bitch **2nd**,
Reserve Best Bitch
Blackpool – Minor Puppy Bitch **1st**
Three Counties – Minor Puppy Bitch **1st**

We are looking forward to 2013 and the opportunity to show off this girl throughout the year. Many thanks to all who have thought so highly of her.

WWW.UIREDA.CO.UK

331

BROBRUICK

Gordon Setters
EST 1979

Home of only Ten Gordon Setters since 1979,
5 Show Champions
4 Junior Warrants

Shehallion Peacemaker
by Brobruick
'Uncle'

Sh Ch Abelard Scotch
Poacher by Brobruick JW
'Grandfather'
TOP SIRE 2008
Our Dogs
Sire of Best of Breed
Crufts 2009

Ecameadow Black Cavendish
by Brobruick JW
2 CCs 2 RCCs
'Son'
Pets As Therapy
Show Dog Of The Year Finalist
Crufts 2013
Joint Runner up
Top Gundog Puppy 2010
Our Dogs

Spingor Pride Of Orkney
By Brobruick JW
'Father'

All stock health tested
Proud to be owned by them
and handled by Sue Mitchell
Eyres Cottage, The Rye,
Eaton Bray, Bedfordshire.
LU6 2BQ Tel/fax 01525 221128
email brobruick@yahoo.co.uk

www.wattswhere.co.uk

Sponsored by
FISH4DOGS
www.fish4dogs.com

333

KILNRAE *Gordon Setters*

... the future
KILNRAE SCOTCH THE RUMOUR JW

Born 12.01.11
Sh Ch Lochfain
Not To Be Denied
For Bareve
ex Kilnrae Lil
Black Number

Also home
to Kilnrae
Lil Black
Number and
my German
Shorthaired
Pointer,
Koolwaters
Pacific at
Kilnrae

KAREN MARSH
Kilnrae
24 Pantheon Rd
Chandlers Ford
Eastleigh
Hampshire
SO53 2NS
Tel 02380 263604
Mobile 07887 622032
Email kmarsh393@btinternet.com
Website www.kilnrae.moonfruit.com

photo Timmermann

CH MARKSBURY SCRUMPTIOUS
4 CCs   1 RCC
Top Bitch 2012*

©Johnson

1 BOB and shortlisted in the group at Windsor Ch Show
RBIS Bloodhound Club Ch Show
RBIS Association of Bloodhound Breeders Ch Show

CH Marksbury Scrumptious joins her brother
CH Marksbury Scribble and her sister
CH Marksbury Serious at Maplemead
as the **third Champion in this litter**

Bred by Mrs S M Emrys-Jones
Owned by Julie Hudson
email graceminster@btinternet.com
01937 831333   *at time of going to press

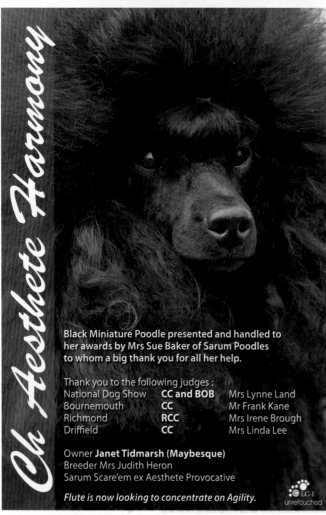

Ch Aesthete Harmony

Black Miniature Poodle presented and handled to
her awards by Mrs Sue Baker of Sarum Poodles
to whom a big thank you for all her help.

Thank you to the following judges :

National Dog Show	**CC and BOB**	Mrs Lynne Land
Bournemouth	**CC**	Mr Frank Kane
Richmond	**RCC**	Mrs Irene Brough
Driffield	**CC**	Mrs Linda Lee

Owner **Janet Tidmarsh (Maybesque)**
Breeder Mrs Judith Heron
Sarum Scare'em ex Aesthete Provocative

Flute is now looking to concentrate on Agility.

LC·E
unretouched

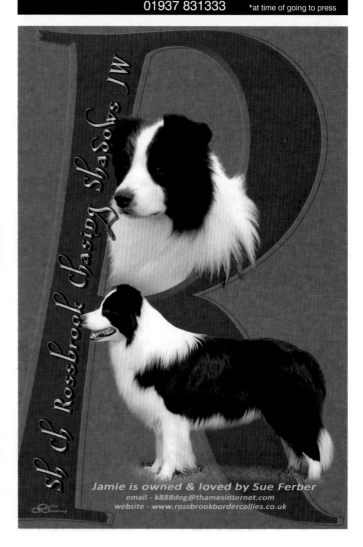

Sh Ch Rossbrook Chasing Shadows JW

Jamie is owned & loved by Sue Ferber
email - k888dog@thamesinternet.com
website - www.rossbrookbordercollies.co.uk

Shanshal
Chinese Crested & Mexican Hairless/Xoloitzcuintle

Sharon & Shannon Roberts
01245 360320
www.shanshal.co.uk
contact@shanshal.co.uk

Owned by Roberts & Cawley
DOB: 04/02/2011

1st MEXICAN HAIRLESS IN THE UK TO QUALIFY FOR CRUFTS 2013
1st and only Mexican Hairless to win a Young Kennel Club Handling Class In the UK Qualifying for Crufts 2013 YKC Handling Finals

❖ Joint Top Mexican Hairless Puppy 2011/2012*
❖ BPIS & RBIS Mexican Hairless Club UK (Provisional) 2011
❖ 3x BOB Import at Championship Shows
❖ 2x BOB Puppy Import at Championship Shows
❖ 5x RBB at Championship Shows
❖ 10x BOB Import at Open Shows
❖ 3x BOB Puppy Import at Open Shows
❖ Holds her Good Citizens Bronze Award

All under the age of 2!

"Ima Little Miss Sunshine"
Making Breed History . . .

All of the dogs here at Shanshal are handled by Shannon Roberts. With experience of handling over 35 different breeds over the groups to BPIB, BOB, Group Placements, Puppy Group Placements, Crufts qualifications, CC's and to RCC's here in the UK and in Europe. Shannon is also the writer of the Mexican Hairless/Xoloitzcuintle Breed-Notes for Dogworld.

"Shanshal Major Look ShCM"

Owned by Roberts
DOB: 18/10/2010

❖ RBIS, BOSIS, BPIS Winner
❖ BOB, RBOB, BPIB Winner
❖ Toy Group Winner/ Toy Puppy Group Placed
❖ Young Kennel Club Handling Winner

Holmchappell

photo Victoria Moon

CH / DUTCH CH HOLMCHAPPELL BIEN EN VIE
(Joie de Vie du Greffier du Roi ex Holmchappell April Fool)

A champion in the UK in three shows; a champion in Holland in three shows, including the Amsterdam Winner Show 2011, where she was also second in the group to Gavin and Sara's Jilly. Numerous group and BIS wins on the Continent.

I am proud to work in close co-operation with dear friends Jolanda Huisman (du Greffier du Roi, in Holland) and Gill and Paul Clark (Plainville ,up in Cumbria). Together we exchange bloodlines and strive to produce REAL GBGVs of beautiful type, conformation and temperament. Take a look at our most recent imports, the third and fourth new bloodlines we have brought to the UK in the last twelve months.

Plainville

CAILLETTE DU GREFFIER DU ROI
(Ch Sauce Solferino du Greffier du Roi ex Alpha du Hamel de la Renaudie)

GILL and PAUL CLARK
Tel 07971 315515
www.plainvillehounds@aol.co.uk

Holmchappell

GRUYERE DE L'EMPYREE
(Delf des Hautes Clauzes ex Quelle Quine du Greffier du Roi)

Dr Jessica Holm
jessica.holm@btinternet.com
www.jessicaholm.co.uk
07876 482398

PEASBLOSSOM
ENGLISH SPRINGERS

Sh Ch Norduch Barecho
Hold Your Horses at Peasblossom JW
21 CCs 11 RCCs

Sh Ch Peasblossom Butterfly at Beresford
3 CCs 3 RCCs

WW12 EUJW11
Peasblossom Heaven Sent

Peasblossom Aria
2 CCs 1 RCC

Peasblossom Escape
to Beresford JW
2 CCs 3 RCCs

DAVE and JACKY MITCHELL
www.peasblossom.eu

MAINTAINING THE STANDARD

Cz/Dk Ch Ridley Pamatka ShCM IS the Standard

www.ridleyceskyterriers.co.uk

Bonario Bracchi Italiani

Bocia Del Bonario

Polcevera's Romeo At Bonario

photos Jan Anderson

Int Ft Ch King ex Int Sh Ch Aida Del Angelo Del Summano   Int Sh Ch Int FT Ch Xeres Delle Terre Alliane ex It Ch Polcevera's Megan

Two exciting males joined the Bonario kennel from Italy this year, both combining the best of Italian working and show lines. Romeo has already sired a stunning litter (dam Bonario Aude Sapere), they will be seen in the field and the ring in 2013.

Alan and Sue Parr's Bonario Chatelaine was awarded second place at the Bristol and West Field Trial '12, only the second time a Bracco has won an award at a UK Field Trial.

Although we only attended five shows this year the team achieved 2 x BOB 1 x BD, 1 x RBD, 1 x BP,

Braccanza Benedizione at Bonario twice winning BVIS at the Bracco Italiano Society shows (Feb & Sept).

The Aldermoor Shoot Team

Bonario Burlesque

Jean Powell had an amazing start to the year at Crufts: Bonario Burlesque (Sienna) made breed history in the Gamekeepers Classes winning the AV Pointer, Setter, HPR class. Abbi Goree handled Sienna to first place in the Junior Handling and then the Aldermoor team consisting of Bonario Burlesque, Madreliath's Renata and Bonario Baroque took second place in the Regional Gamekeeper Team Competition, again a first for the breed. Jean and Sienna also took BIS at the Bracco Italiano Society show in September.

Madreliath's Renata (Weim), not to be left out, was third in the Open Class at the World Show in Paris from the largest breed class of group 7.

Kim Parris 01425 471104 — Jean Powell 01747 841126

www.bonario.co.uk

British Sieger VA1 2011
VA Ch. Elmo vom Hühnegrab

SchH3 Kkl1 LBZ 'a' normal hips and elbows
Sire: VA Zamp vom Thermodos, SchH3
Dam: Ofi vom Hühnegrab, SchH1
British Sieger 2011 British Vice Sieger 2009
Crufts 2012 CC BOB & Pastoral Group 3
Crufts 2011 CC BOB & Pastoral Group 1
SWGSDC CC & BIS 2012

Elmo winning progeny Group British Sieger 2011 and 2012
and his winning daughters

VA Veneze Gucci
VA2 British Sieger 2012

SchH1 Kkl1 'a' normal hips and elbows
Sire: VA Ch Elmo vom Hühnegrab Sch
Dam: Vicky vom Grafenbrunn SchH2
German Sieger Show SG9 2011
Swiss Siegerin 2011
British Siegerin 2011
SG2 Heinz Scheerer 2012,
SG1 M Ossmann 2012
V1 Herr Nitschke 2012
V1 Dr. Lauber 2012
V4 Herr Setzer 2012
V7 Herr Setzer 2012
GSD Club of Wales BOB D O'Neil 2011
West Yorks GSDC BPB Res CC Herr Tuborg 2011

Veneze Immy
SG1 British Sieger 2012

'a' normal hips and elbows
Sire: VA Ch Elmo vom Hühnegrab SchH3
Dam: VA Ch Veneze Chaos SchH2
British Sieger VP1 Herr Gabriel 2011
SG2 Herr H. Scheerer 2012
SG2 Herr C. Ludwig 2012
SG5 Herr P. Knaul 2012
WPB Wales CC S. Hall 2012
SATS Res CC S. Binden 2012
SKC PB, BPIB Gill Gray 2011
CRUFTS Best Puppy Bitch Mr J Parody 2012
North Wales GSD show CC Gary Gray 2012
Richmond Ch Show RCC Carol Marsden 2012

BANNONBRIG SPINONI
Top Breeders 2010, 2011 & 2012
~ Carole, Mike & Nicola Spencer ~

Bannonbrig Ruben Rude

Nicola & Bannonbrig Bona Marta

Bannonbrig Rubie Rude

AKC Champion
'h Bannonbrig Basil Rathbone TD CA

Top Male 2012

Show Champion Bannonbrig Al Fresco Sh CM

Sh Ch Bannonbrig Love in a Mist at Diggm

Celebrating 30 years of Beauty & Brains
www.bannonbrig.co.uk

Winner of 13 CC's
& 16 res CC's

Taranza Jack of Diamonds at Belsmard JW

SIMBA

Owned by Marina and Kriss Scott

RCC at 16 months
JW at 11 months
BPIS breed club winner
Border Collie & BC pup of the year qualifier 2012/13
Kennel Gazette JW semi-finalist

Advert by Amelia Siddle   Main image Dan Kyprianou

TARANZA
Border Collies

PHOTO COURTESY OF HAYLEY EMERY

TONKORY YARLEY AT TARANZA JW
EDDIE is siring beautiful puppies who are inheriting his wonderful temperament –
they will be landing in the show ring in the New Year

Also the home of
**SH CH LOCHEIL ECLIPSE OF THE MOON ShCM JW
LYNTROM FASINATION WITH TARANZA
TONKORY PHOENIX AT TARANZA**

Congratulations to Marina Scott and Simba
TARANZA JACK OF DIAMONDS AT BELSMARD JW
RCC at 16 months, JW at 11 months, JW semi-finalist

All of my dogs are genetically clear for TNS/CL/CEA, hip scored
and gonioscopy tested normal

ALI CHAINEY - www.taranza.com - Tel 07710 695692

Covenstead My Cup Of Tea JW

(Imp Nor)

Bred by Nina Skjelbred
Owned and loved by
Netty and James Morrissey